BEVER-LEIGH BANFIELD

YOU CAN CHANGE THE WORLD

Be a change wizard and get it like you like it

Copyright © 2017 by Bever-leigh Banfield
All rights reserved.

No part of this publication may be reproduced, distributed or transmitted in any form or by any means, including photocopying, recording, or other electronic or mechanical methods, without the prior written permission of the publisher, except in the case of brief quotations embodied in critical reviews and certain other noncommercial uses permitted by copyright law. For permissions and requests, write to the publisher, addressed "Attention: Permissions Coordinator" at:
Twinkle Entertainment, 3727 W. Magnolia Blvd. Ste. 103, Burbank, CA 91505

Cover Design by Clarissa Yeo of Yocla Designs
Interior Design by JT Formatting

Publisher's Cataloging-In-Publication Data
Names: Banfield, Bever-leigh
www.youcanchangetheworldbook.com

Title: You Can Change the World: Be a Change Wizard and Get It Like You Like It / by Bever-leigh Banfield

Description: First edition. | ISBN 978-0-9986348-8-3 (paperback)
ISBN 978-0-9986348-0-7 (ebook) | ISBN 978-0-9986348-2-1 (audiobook)

*To my cherished parents
Leo and Theresa Banfield
one my angel in heaven, the other my angel on earth
who love me unconditionally
and believe that I can change the world*

TABLE OF CONTENTS

	FOREWORD	i
ONE	THE ALCHEMY OF CHANGE IS THE SOURCE OF JOY	1
TWO	BECOMING A CHANGE WIZARD	11
	Recognize That Your Life Matters	11
	Understanding How You Impact Others	17
	Embrace Your Uniqueness	20
	Share Your Gifts Generously	24
	Commit to Being A Beneficent Spirit and Highly Beneficial Force	28
THREE	HOW CHANGE REARRANGES	34
	Your Thoughts Create Reality	34
	Protecting A Positive Thought Zone By Transforming The Nature of Negative Thoughts	38
	Your Words Have Power	42
	It's Important That You Do What's Right	45
	Act On Your Meant-To-Do	48
	Know You Can Have Whatever You Want And Help Others Do The Same	55

	Decide To Be Happy And Healthy	57
FOUR	THE COAST IS CLEAR	60
	Your Passion Is Your Purpose	60
	Give Yourself Permission To Do What You Love	67
	Feeling, Embracing and Living Your Bliss	72
	Examine Your Possibilities	76
FIVE	FOCUS POCUS	83
	Love Yourself And Love Others	83
	Stand Up For What You Believe In	88
	Believe That You Can Do Anything . . . Because You Can	96
	Decide To Do Only Good	101
	Live An Authentic Life	104
	Connect Through Integrity	109
SIX	SPECIFIC IS TERRIFIC	112
	The Lengths of Your Strengths and Weaknesses	112
	Your Skill Set	116
	Learn And Grow From Every Experience	119
	Visualize Your Future	123
	Visualization	129
SEVEN	PREPARE FOR THE JOURNEY	134
	Keep An Open Heart And Mind	134

	Meditate To Hear The Voice Within	137
	Purify Your Body	140
	Your Past Is Not Your Future	142
	Free Yourself From Fear	146
	The Twelve Universal Laws	148
	Embrace Change	157
	Unclutter Your Environment	160
	Try New Things	163
	Welcome A New Chapter of Your Life	165
EIGHT	TRUE YOU	168
	Who Are You?	168
	Know What You Want To Be And Be It	170
	Accept Who You Are And Be Willing To Grow	173
	Listen To Your Inner Voice	175
	Stand Firm And Know What You Stand For	177
	What Is Your Meant-To-Do?	178
NINE	YOUR BIG DREAM SCHEME	181
	Your Dream Is Meant To Change The World	181
	Be The Solution, Not The Problem	185
	Be Willing To Do Any Good Thing To Achieve Your Great Dream	191

	Engage and Indulge Your Imagination	192
	Your Memory Memo Pad	194
	Create A Dream Board	198
	Ask The Universe For What You Want	200
TEN	THE ROLE OF YOUR GOALS	203
	Plan The Steps To Realizing Your Dream	203
	Choose Your Path Or A Path Will Choose You	205
	Be Prepared To Change Your Course	207
	Set Priorities	209
	Short-Term Goals And Long-Term Goals	212
	Plan The Steps You Will Take To Achieve Your Goals	214
ELEVEN	BUILD YOUR TEAM TO PICK UP STEAM	218
	Network Online And One-On-One	218
	Form A Core Group With Whom You Work Well	224
	Mentor Mojo	225
	Be A Mentor	227
	Pioneer As A Volunteer	228
	Be A Great Communicator	230
	Believe You Can Change The World For The Better	233
	Be Open To Constant Miracles	236
	Believe You'll Receive What You Ask For	237

	Receive And Remain Unattached To Outcome	240
TWELVE	**CHANGE YOUR RANGE**	242
	Learn To Live And Live To Learn	242
	A "Problem" Is Only A Question That Hasn't Been Adequately Answered Yet	246
	We Cannot Be The Solution To Any Problem If We Are A Problem Ourselves	247
	Spread Peace Everywhere You Go	249
	Let No One And Nothing Steal Your Peace	250
	The Magic Of Rebooting	252
	Birds Of A Feather Change Together	255
	Gratitude	257
	Give To live and Live To Give	260
	No Resistance + No Judgment = No Pain	262
	Be Thankful For Something You Once Resisted	266
	Proceed Like You Can Only Succeed	269
THIRTEEN	**YE SHALL OVERCOME**	272
	A 'Mistake' Is Just A Stumble On The Road To Success	272
	How Beliefs Come Into Being	274
	Inner Peace Creates Outer Peace	278
	Calm The Qualms	281
	If It's Looming, Just Un-Loom It!	283

	The Sun Never Sets On Your Dream	286
	Ask For Your Meant-To-Be And Do What You're Meant To Do	288
FOURTEEN	OBSTACLE COURSE	293
	Persevere Past The Severe	293
	#LetItBe	295
	Suffering Is A Choice	298
	Merry-Go-Round Or Rollercoaster	303
	Schedule Time For Your Self	304
	Guided Self-Discovery Tour	308
	Your Ship Is Coming In	324
	Messages Come In Many Voices	325
FIFTEEN	STAR POWER	331
	The Age of Change	331
	The Universe Is On Your Side	339
	One Schlep At A Time	343
	Giving Is A Privilege	347
	Love You, Baby	348
	Keep Dreaming Until Your Dream Comes True	350
ABOUT THE AUTHOR		353

YOU CAN CHANGE THE WORLD

Be a change wizard and get it like you like it

FOREWORD

You hold in your hands a beautiful invitation to remember that you are nothing short of a unique, individualized expression of Spirit, who has taken a human incarnation to continue your spiritual evolutionary journey, all the while leaving your heaven-sent footprint on our precious planet.

In *You Can Change the World*, Bever-leigh Banfield graciously places before you this profound truth: "You are The Changer, and you are The Change." Each chapter in this book invites you to enter the *experience behind these words*, and for that reason I encourage you to read and re-read them, mindfully pausing to let their meaning sink in your heart, fill your mind, nurture your body, open you to the joyous dancing spirit that accompanies you in every step of your journey. In that hushed pause, you will give Spirit enough space to whisper how you, as an emanation of itself, are perfect, whole, and complete, and that your journey is to consciously arrive at that self-realization as you deliver your gifts, talents and skills as a beneficiary presence on the planet.

What deeply moved me as I read the pages of this book is how readers are not only inspired to expand in consciousness, but also are provided the spiritual principles and practices to rise to high levels of awakening according to their own soul's evolutionary path. But she doesn't stop with the individual change! Rather, in great detail, Bever-leigh reveals how collectively—as one world family—we are empowered to create tremendous social change, honoring and assuring that the needs of all beings are met, that all beings are treated with dignity. During these unpredictable times in which we live, she leads us in the direction of unconditionally claiming our divine birthright of happiness, freedom, peace, wisdom, compassion, creativity and enlightenment.

May *You Can Change the World* be a blessing on your path.

Michael Bernard Beckwith
Founder, Agape International Spiritual Center
and author of *Spiritual Liberation* and *Life Visioning*

THE ALCHEMY OF CHANGE IS THE SOURCE OF JOY

Welcome. I'm so glad you're here. You are my brothers and sisters, and I'm excited to get into this. Okay, first let's claim your ideal life—because it is ready to bring you joy. Your ideal life is the one the world is waiting to experience, watching to see it reveal and unfold.

When you envision the life you most want to lead, what do you see? Great health, of course. Maybe the perfect body, at the weight and shape that makes you feel invincible, relatable, and up for anything at any time. A high-paying, cool job, with health benefits—or maybe self-employment you can't wait to get to every day. Let's toss in some work that fulfills you, stretches your talents and abilities, and challenges your mind. Perhaps you desire Prince Charming too, riding up on his mighty steed to take your hand, or a Sleeping Beauty awaiting your sexy kiss to awaken her love. You might only long for a roof above your head that doesn't leak, or that new car that doesn't break down, puff smoke from the tailpipe, or embarrass you when you pull up to valet park. You may simply desire security, whatever your concept of that is. Maybe you crave a weekly mani-pedi or massage, relaxing vacays in exotic ports, a closet full of designer clothes, the latest tech, some diamond bling, a pair of name-brand athletic or red-soled shoes and cozy creature comforts. You could be aiming to play a sport, or pursue a hobby you adore. And who doesn't want some excitement, adventure and fun to liven up their days? If you've chosen to have children, you will want them to grow up happy, healthy, prosperous, kind, educated and free. You will want all that's good for them, and resolve to help that happen.

Though you might not want any of these, it might also be true you want all of them. And yet, there is something you must want most. Are you in touch with what that is? If not, then this is the time to seek it out and have it come to you. When you're alone—or not alone—in the dark at night with your active mind, or when you wake up in the morning and realize the universe has gifted you with another day of living your life, what do you want to do with it? Do you want your life to shine, or are you content to just get through it, putting one foot in front of the other, surviving as the clock ticks and the years fly by like soaring jets.

When someone discovers an abnormality in some vital body part, or loses a parent, a child, a marriage, their business or a job, or is presented with some other ginormous hill to climb to reclaim their life, things tend to zoom into focus. Disparate ideas seem to coalesce into helpful realizations. They're given to epiphany, become open to insights they've never received before. They often drop all pretense, and become able to skirt trivialities that might have irked them earlier. Other people in their life come closer or fall away. Those remaining are held cherished, and communication blossoms. Long-repressed yearnings surface that may cause them to rethink their choices and mull over past mistakes or missteps they may feel have brought them to that point. People look for the meaning of their lives, and seek to address and fulfill it when the rubber is meeting the road, the chips are down, and their back is to the wall.

Why wait for such a cataclysm? Life is occurring with every breath. Every *now* gives way to another now that presents great opportunity. Every instant is calling you to rise up and reach your highest consciousness, and nothing is standing in your way. On the contrary, even the beat of your heart is designed to uplift and support you.

You are the answer to all of your questions.

You are the change you've been waiting to see.

Are you asking, who do I want to be that I'm not yet being here and now? What is my next transformation? What are those angel wings fluttering inside me, catching a headwind and longing to fly? I know I can do, and be, more than I'm giving *me* credit for in the way I'm living. I am a giant with shoes that fit way too tight at present. I am meant to change the world.

What do you inwardly seek while you're sitting in church, synagogue, or a mosque, or a temple, feeling the breath of those around you, knowing we all are One? Renewed with the strength of your Higher Power, do you compare your spirit's reality with what we experience in the world of contradiction and illusion? What is it that you wish for then? What is most priceless and precious?

I know what I want is love. I want to feel love, give love, be loved, *be* love in its purest form. I want my life to mean something to someone, lots of someone's, to the world. I want a spot in the scheme of things, such that others' lives are better for having met, and known, me, experienced my essence, shared what I give, laughed till they cried with me, held my hand. I want to help people smile. I want to be beneficial, and beneficent and bold. I want to be a sparkling light. I want to leave this world much better than I found it in some way. My way is creativity. I want to create more beauty, joy, entertainment and enlightenment. I want to be an angel here on earth, a treasure trove of goodness happening perpetually.

Okay, so I haven't gotten there, but I'm working on it all the time. Not in an airy-fairy way, although I'm not saying that isn't fine—fairies, nymphs and genies are charming—but it's work that gets it done out here in the land of Making-It-Happen. Angels are constantly on their grind. One has to do more than just flap one's wings (or gums) to make an idea fly. One has to put boot in it. Regularly. Angels don't sleep in, get discouraged, flake, or miss opportunities. An angel shines up her halo, gets out with the early bird catching its worm, and scoots through every opening. She makes the best of what she has. She uses what she's got to get what she wants. And what she wants is good for all—not just the angel, the whole wide world. That's why she spreads her wings.

Now, if we turn on the news to the latest mass shooting, report from the front lines of one of the multifarious wars that span the globe, political foolishness, megalomania, or consequences of unchecked greed corrupting institutions we once revered, we might feel it's impossible, a tall order way beyond our reach, to affect anything beyond ourselves. We see details of the latest heinous crime, or the bone-crushing stats about those of us who have no home or food to eat, or those who are suffering pestilence, ill health and unspeakable cruelty, and we can feel powerless.

But big things happen through small steps. Big dreams require big people. I'm not talking about physical stature here, but spirits so open, accommodating, and spacious a conduit for good that only the best can manifest. A big life has little to do with the circumstances and situations with which we're presented from day to day, but rather with what we bring to our environments as a result of who we are, and the frequency of the energy vibrations we emanate. In other words, who we are creates reality for more than just ourselves. We're changing the world just by flashing a smile or wearing a frown that's not turned upside down. Thus, where we place our attention makes a difference. How we focus, where we focus, and what we decide to focus upon increases, manifests, and continues to thrive. Our actions, when they're accountable, widen the scope and effectiveness of our existence in the world.

We see what we believe, not the other way around.

What people perceive of us, and are able to gather from our interactions, arises from where we're centered at the innermost core of our being. No matter what face we plaster on, we are who we are, and in the end, we materialize our consciousness. Our beliefs are making things happen, whether we buy into that or not. Whether or not we accept the responsibility of our power to shape our environment, what we think, do, and feel is a cause that has an effect. Who we are makes an impact on how we make people feel, and on what they think and do, and thus, on the rhythm and flow of everything around us.

Think about those who have inspired you, and those who tried to block your path, and you'll see that, though ultimately what you thought, felt, and did was all on you, other people have an had an effect on your life, for the better, and for the not-so-good, depending on how you handled things. We are all interwoven into a fabric. We are divine, and we are One. Each of us plays a title role in the human drama that's unfolding.

We are the storytellers, writing our story and acting it out. Whether a comedy, tragedy, morality play or action yarn, what is your story going to say, and who will be your audience? Are you the heroine of a romance, or a vengeance thriller? It's your choice. Are you a victim, or are you the champion, challenger or adventurer?

Whoever you are at present, you can change, because you are built to transform. Your ability to transform yourself transforms the world you're living in. Transformation is not just within your reach, it is actually your destiny. And when that is paired with your genuine desire, you can become anyone you want, and accomplish beyond your fantasies.

Change is your very birthright as a spiritual being incarnated into a human existence on this plane that we've agreed to see as our reality. You can define your reality for yourself, in any way you choose. Reality is perception. What you perceive is real to you, and you are not meant to play small ball, confined to react to what's pitched to you in the sphere of the material. You're meant for a chameleon life of constant transmutation. You are like flowers that change and grow. You are a Change Wizard. You're born to be able to turn on a dime in a noble journey toward the truth. You're called to, like Jack, be nimble and quick on the twisting, turning paths of life. You are not here to stagnate, bask in recalcitrance, clutch mediocrity, or amble along at the pace of a slug. You are meant to explore opportunity, and believe in vast possibilities. You're built to shift, and switch, and soar.

We cannot settle for merely enduring this marvelous, magical incarnation. It is our nature to evolve. We are evolving all the time, changing our surroundings in the process of becoming more. We must overcome any urge to limit our concept of what is doable to only that which has already occurred. The next big thing is waiting to happen—through us—so that we will all grow through it. Thinking small only serves to reject that imperative, stop us in forward-thinking tracks, and smother potential and promise in their infancy. We're more than that. We move at the speed of a supernova. We have perennial potential constantly working with, for and as, us, making us better than we were. We are possibilities convinced we can be greater still.

We can employ our "conception capacity" for the benefit of all, and in so doing, change the world. Our thoughts and ideas promote all change. As change is the only constant, we have a value increasingly meaningful to the extent we can embrace and facilitate change, and nurture change in others. Change for the better. Change that works for everyone. Change that makes a big check mark on the list of ever-expanding good.

We live organically in change mode by radiating love.

Love is the very substance of the universe, the source of change, its substance.

Positive changes come from loving everybody, all the time. From thinking, and speaking, and doing from the eternal energy that is love unlimited and uncompromised by the pull of lower vibrations. There is no greater power than the almighty force of lasting love.

Love is the beginning. Love is the middle. Love is the end.

Change without begins within.

Living from love is the primary step, the hub from which you'll change the world.

Acting from love works every time. It always has, it always will. No matter how things may appear, love can turn anything into good. Whatever the question, the answer is love.

We create what we see in the world with each thought we think, each word we speak or write, and every deed we set in motion. Even our "vibration"—that being the level, intensity and quality of the frequency of energy we emit—is as a pebble tossed in the ocean, flowing out into the cosmic seas, creating ripples, shifting tides that therefore change the world. Every thought, word and deed causes shifts in the cosmos, often subtle, sometimes stark. Whether consciously or unconsciously, we usher things into being that only we can create, because we are unique. What each of us actualizes from our given purpose in the world is entrusted to us for us to share, and we share it whether we know it or not, whether or not we have taken responsibility for it yet. Whether we strive to improve its innate quality or quantity, or even care what we produce.

It is when we commit individually to upleveling what our presence means, that the world is changed for the better, because *we* are changed for the better when this is our goal.

We *are* the world. There's no outside force acting upon us in unseemly ways. We humans, and everything in the world, are one and interdependent. This is the nexus between world change and our personal growth—they are one in the same.

World change begins, and is centered, in YOU.

We all have a gift. We all are a gift. Our gifts are meant to be given.

In the joy of the world, you will find true joy. As you bring the world joy, you become it. You become more of your genuine self—the person you were created to be—as you live in the realization we all are One, and that you *are* the change. What you are and strive to be pops up in your life as experience, and spills over in the world.

You are the change you've wanted to see. Decide now what that's going to be. Stop waiting. Make it happen. What you don't choose will be chosen for you by what's being fed into your mind by bottom-feeding energies that troll around for empty minds to fill with doubt and worry. If you aren't controlling what you think, the random world of ups and downs is glad to make your mind its home. Avoid letting low energies think for you. Think from the good on your inside, out—rather than from the outside in. Think for yourself, and elevate. Align with the truth of the universal mind speaking as your inner voice, and let it design your experiences. Allow it to radiate your light. Will your light to shine.

You have an effect on the world. Choose what it's going to be. Make that your goal, find your way to a plan, and shift your new world into overdrive—not neutral, certainly not reverse, but turbo. Get it moving. Avoid spending another second farting around in self-pity, victimization, I-Don't-Have-A-Clue Land, How-Am-I-Going-To-Get-Over-This Ville, or If-I-Only-Had-X-I'd-Be-Happy Town. Those aren't paved with gold. I'm not saying you're on a dead-end street, but if you are, turn off of it. If you're sensing you can do better, this is your moment. You're telling yourself to change. If you've been coasting, turn on your engine. If you feel like you're down in a hole, climb out. No hole is as deep as you might think, and there might not be a hole at all. If there is, you will escape it. Holes only open to teach you something, not to take you off your course. Holes can be deep, but they're never, ever bottomless. That's an illusion. If you're truly working at your best, but things aren't shaking out the way you planned, then make another plan. Keep at it. Your dream is designed to come true.

You have what it takes to do anything you can conceive of. You can make it work—not only for you, but for so many others out here turning pages, turning over new leaves in their lives. Nothing is outside your realm of attainability. Anything's plausible, workable, doable, once you're doing it. The fact that you're doing it has a long-lasting effect, because you are the seed of change. What you plant is bound to grow.

Stand for something, fall for anything, lie down with dogs and get up with fleas, or fly the skies with angels—it's your choice, and I urge you to make it now. The world is counting on you. How are you going to keep your promise, the promise of your potential?

There are those who will improve discourse in medicine and technology. Those who are gifted to lift up through arts—with dance, via drama and comedy, graphics and visual artwork, music, various forms of literature. There are those who will teach, or inspire through speaking. Those who will care for nature, and the priceless gifts our planet holds. There are scientists exploring space. Anthropologists. Fashionistas. Mothers and fathers. Chefs and architects. Mathematicians. Religious leaders. Gurus of every ilk and stripe. Psychics and clairvoyants.

Whatever your thing is, roll with it. Do it, and let it bring you bliss. It can change the world. We each are prepared to change the world in different ways, at different times. If you're reading this book, your time is now. I truly believe this is why we're connecting in this space, and at this moment. We're coming together to make a change, a change that is momentous.

Whether you change the college you attend, your place of worship, workplace, town, community, or profession—or maybe every one of these—by choosing to make a contribution, you will lift up every place you go. You will be choosing to uplift self, and that energy will be transformative to the collective, as you dream your dreams and explode them into reality with goals and tasks that move things forward through your inspiration. Commit to uplift a city, state, country, village, or the whole wide world and the billions of galaxies out in space, and your pledge will begin to implement incrementally or all at once, making magic happen. Commitment builds momentum, so be increasingly open to reaching your highest potential in your inner space, beginning your work with agape love and the strength you develop through inner peace. You are the pipe that delivers the water, a channel for heat, electricity, sound. Your influence is dynamic, filled with aptitude and amplitude, and an attitude coming straight from the loving source that lights the sun and moon, and twinkles all the stars.

You have a message to bring to the world. You are the diligent messenger spreading good tidings. You are hope and change. This is your mission, and this is your quest—to fulfill your ordained destiny. To be more the beneficent entity. To do what the world is watching for. To give the gift sublimely yours. To explore other-orientation, oneness, wondrous self-realization.

Intend to do work for the common good, approaching it uncommonly.

The great Chinese philosopher Lao Tzu said, "The journey of a thousand miles begins with a single step". Step out now. Accept the challenge. Everyone's waiting with open arms.

I am beginning this book as a movement, connecting with you on my birthday, as my gift to you, to light your path, and mine, as we seek to change the world to a place that works for all. A world animated by peace and love. My wish is that we change together, acknowledging what is best in us, and spreading it around the globe. You motivate me, and I'm praying you feel the pure intent infusing the content of these pages.

I see your beauty. I want it to shine even brighter than it's shining now. I see the eternal within you, and I'm excited to help you tap into it. I want to see into your life, and be open to you seeing into mine. I invite you to embark on a journey now—our voyage into inner space.

TWO

BECOMING A CHANGE WIZARD

RECOGNIZE THAT YOUR LIFE MATTERS

You are the only YOU that is, and will ever be, or ever could. Your specialness lasts for eternity. Imagine that. The only you. No one looks exactly like you. No one feels exactly like you. No one thinks exactly like you. No one *is* exactly like you. The more you evolve, the more special you get, because you were created to be unique, and as you grow through your own will, you become even more of your essence. You become more of a treasure. You come closer to the Source of Things, and your light shines even brighter. You are not your experiences, your past, or any circumstance. You are a spiritual entity living a human life in a physical body. You are artwork from a universe that is love and pure creativity, an expression of the ultimate. You are unparalleled, more than rare.

Your presence is significant. When people experience you, they behold an energy never seen before. They are treated to the divine in you. You are ear-marked for a specialty. As your life progresses, it becomes more suited to the enterprise afforded you amid the grand design. You are here for an assignment only you can do. You're designated, meant to be all that you can be in an aspirational universe, which is expanding all the time and intends for you to do the same.

At your core, you are the winds of change. You are changing all the time. Every thought you think, every word you say, every act you take upon yourself is causing a change to occur in you, for the better or for the not-so-good, depending upon your concept of yourself, and of the world. When you see greatness in yourself, you take on the character of the change that's always for the better. You commit to change that benefits the greater good. You *are* the change.

As you change for the better, so goes the world. Commit to self-transformation for the better, and you cause a seismic shift in the global composition.

Nothing stays the same when *you* change. Everything moves when each of us moves.

You are change, and I am change. And together we can, and do, change the world.

All that remains is to have the will to change for the better with constancy—to change as individuals, and to also join hands to change the world to the loftiest vision we perceive.

The first step toward becoming a Change Wizard is to take responsibility for your one-of-a-kind-ness in the world, and for how it affects the scheme of things. You have a profound effect.

Your life matters. You're important. You are as potent as raging fire. You are as elemental to this world as metal, water, wood or air. You are needed, wanted, loved. You contribute to the well-being of every creature on the planet. You matter to humans, animals, vegetables, minerals, every grain of sand, and each snowflake that gently falls. You're an important aspect of the way the world is functioning. With, and through you, others thrive. You have a distinct place in the world. There is only one you, and without you, the world is missing something vital. Without you, the world is incomplete. Devoid of you, the world is wanting.

You are not a lonely being confined to operate in distant outposts, disconnected, set adrift. You have a context all your own, connected to all you sense around you. Regardless of how alone or lonely you may feel at certain times, it is a trick of the mind, an illusion.

We are all One.

You are always connected.

There is a power greater than us, a power in which we all belong—in which *you* belong—in which we live, and which is alive in all of us. Whether or not you actively worship a Higher Power, as I do, it is inescapable that you are part of every life. Who you are, and what you do, improves or has a consequence. Realizing and taking responsibility for this fundamental fact is key to unveiling your highest self.

The presence of your consciousness is a linchpin in the universe.

You are called to greatness.

Exploring your greatness, summoning it, is a function of perceiving it, believing in the magnitude of what you have to offer, of seeing yourself as purposeful and vital to a huge degree. Of realizing the enormity of what your life can mean.

Do you see yourself as meaningful? Do you imagine improving the human condition? Do you feel forceful, potent, strong, persistent, perseverant, brave, abundant, clear-eyed, smart and calm? Do you see yourself as others see you, swayed by the way you are perceived—or do you remain self-confident and self-possessed, no matter what? Do you compare yourself to others, favorably or unfavorably? Or do you perceive yourself through your own lens, using your personal value system, following your moral compass, setting your standards, following your instincts? Do you hear a parent's voice that praises, scolds or criticizes? Do you imagine your spouse or lover judging what you're worth? Does what your boss is thinking of you constitute your own opinion? I'm not saying any particular view is good or bad to contemplate, in and of itself. I'm just saying you need to determine how you're thinking, and what you wish to think, and bring the two into alignment.

What is important is whether your viewpoint works for you. Examine that. Is your world view manifesting goodness? Are your beliefs and inner thoughts creating a wonderful world?

How you see yourself is of the utmost. Your self-image comes to pass, affecting your reality. You are becoming your instant thought. That bleeds over to the world, transferring onto others. Think about actually being the thought you're thinking at this moment, and imagine you might freeze right there, for now and forever. How does it feel? What will your life be like if the thought you think right now is your character, your face, your health, your bank account, the results of your creativity, and every person in your life? For the rest of your life. Huh? Try that on. Because, if you don't change the thought, well, guess what. That's how it is! You think your life. What if the last thought roaming your mind—entering it and filtering through—is all that you could *ever* think. Would you be thinking differently? If a genie popped out of a bottle you found on the beach and gave you just three wishes, would you be happy to go with the first three thoughts you had when you woke this morning? The last three thoughts you thought last night?

You are the thinker and changer of thoughts. Thoughts that create your reality.

You have the power to change everything about you for the better.

Change your perspective, change your life. It's as simple as that. It's as easy as thought.

Close your eyes for a moment and ask yourself: When I look inward, what do I see? Do I like me? Is what I see when I look at ME, everything I wish to see? Who do I want to be, and why? Am I improving, growing, morphing, becoming the person I dream about? Do I need to rethink my self-concept, so the results I generate in my life align with my potential? Am I putting my best foot forward? I want to transform, to live in the now, to be loving, to model joy and peace, and to live every day in gratitude. *Is this person I am who I'm meant to be?*

Whatever your answer, it is important. Regardless as to what conclusion you might reach this second, in this now, you can change at any moment. Right now. You can re-invent. You can alter your life's course just by intending to do so. Your intending can actually change the world. Repeat: You can change your world. Right now. By intending right now to change *yourself.*

Commit to evolving, because you matter.

Once you recognize you truly matter, inward change takes place immediately with this single revelation. You're liberated, gratified, excited to take on the mantle of "Champion For A Better World". Suddenly, things you once thought were beyond your influence seem within your reach. Things you thought you could do nothing with, or about, become quite changeable. You will accept nothing short of improvement of the things you feel unjust, inequitable, or just plain wrong. It is enlivening and revitalizing to take responsibility for making the world a better place through concrete actions you can take because you believe in a better world, and you're willing to sacrifice for it.

Even if you are beginning your process, this is your goal—to become a Change Wizard.

Where to begin? Begin right now. Turn just one thought around to facilitate joy and increasing empowerment. Your power and joy will translate into power and joy others draw upon. You will become an electrical outlet able to charge up human devices. You'll be a people surge protector, wireless router, battery backup and portable power pack—all in one.

Begin in the quiet recess of your mind, by going within to determine who, and what, you are in your current state, and where you want to go from there. You're never stuck. You're always free. Shed the dim light of complacency, and take a good look at your present state of mind, out in the sun. What is your state of mind producing? Is what it's producing desirable? If it is, you might want to set out to produce a lot more of it, spreading the good around. If it isn't, set out to make a change.

Your dreams are your dreams because they can come true.

Choose. The choice is always yours. You can know who you are, or become the thoughts that trickle in over the Internet or come at you through your TV set. You can be easily swayed, or you can determine to master what you think, and why, and be a mastermind. You can check where you fit—or don't fit—in, and bring change where change is needed. You're a change whisperer. You're a Change Wizard. You can change. You can conjure change. You can even change a change. You don't have to just go on auto-pilot. No circumstance is your lot in life, it's only a situation. You don't have to give up, or give in. You can launch an entire self-revolution.

Forget about whether you're going to fit in. You don't want to fit in, you want to stand out. Not for your sake, for the sake of the change that's the reason you're alive. Besides, you'll never not fit in. Everyone fits in somewhere. You're an integral part of all that lives, and all that will ever live. You're woven into the great mosaic. You can go where you want to go. Are you occupying the space you need? Are you situated properly, or are you just in with a herd, content to head off where it's roaming with blinders on. Are you happy where you are right now? If not, go get it like you like it. Where you like it, is your spot. That is why you like it there.

Appreciate what you have, and what you want to give. You have plenty to give, if you think of it—physically, mentally, spiritually.

You'll surprise yourself with the *you* that you are, if you give yourself a chance. Go on, take a moment to check yourself out. Providing yourself with a greater self-knowledge lends a refreshing starting point from which to evolve and transform. It also instructs you by helping you see the extent to which your life impacts the rhythm and flow of your family and friends, your home, workplace, community, and a cosmos in constant motion.

Take a look inside yourself. Love what you see, and who you can be. You're as much of a force in the atmosphere as weather, and change is your middle name.

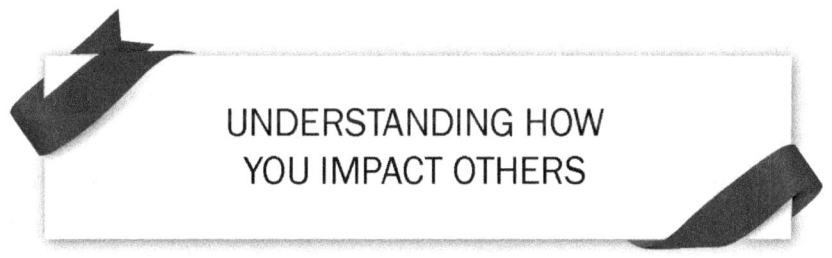

UNDERSTANDING HOW YOU IMPACT OTHERS

When you believe your life impacts others more than superficially, you not only see that you impact others, you begin to see how you impact them.

Like the lead character in the film *It's a Wonderful Life*—who is visited by an angel that allows him to see what life would be like for others had he not been born and touched their lives—we all need to recognize what we contribute. This way, we see what we can contribute, and how prominently we play a part in the fabric of life and the way others live.

There may be people in your life whose literal survival has depended on the way you've taken care of them—children, seniors, neighbors, friends. People you've fed, or clothed, or saved from themselves in one way or another. People you've helped to get over addictions, people who didn't die alone, because you stood by them until the end. People to whom you've lent money, or lent a hand when they've needed a helping hand—to move, or grieve, or start over again. People you may have nursed back to health. People who've followed your lead when you didn't know you were leading, but nevertheless, you led by your example, an example that led them to better lives. People you've given that great idea that helped them get back on their feet, catapulting them into a new career. People you've cheered, encouraged, lent your hope to, patted on the back. People you've complimented when others did nothing but put them down. People you've been there for when no one else would gather around. Just your companionship means so much in places you've inhabited in a way that no one else could.

Think about people who lose a dog, and can't ever ponder replacing it. No other dog, or cat, or horse, or any other pet or non-human companion, or creature could ever take its place. You're human. You're irreplaceable. Whether or not you feel you're appreciated or valued, or you'd be missed if you weren't around, you are loved and relied on more than you know. Your positivity catches on.

On the other hand, negativity takes a toll we often don't expect. Ever notice how you and your co-workers might, for instance, be laughing it up over lunch, and just one Debbie Downer enters the group dynamic and crashes the fun. The "up" the group was experiencing is tested to its limits. Folks may scatter, slip into silence, or worse, into gossip, complaint or depressive chat. The downer has no more personal power than any other in the group, yet can suck the air out of the room without trying, by giving off toxic energy. And yeah, it's on each person to respond to the negative input from a store of positivity, but there is impact either way. The microcosmic world has shifted. Everyone has to deal with that, or not deal, as the case may be, being positive or negative, narcissistic, caring, tolerant, resentful, kind or understanding. So it goes with the macrocosmic world. We either contribute or detract. There is no in between.

Now, let's flip the script. Ever walk in a break room when everyone's eyes are riveted to their cell phones? Despite having physical company, they've opted to flee the inherent challenge the gathering may present—a group, by the way, whose configuration might never recur the same way again. And yet they would rather play Warcraft, text someone in the room next door, or try their hand at online gambling, solitaire or pornography. But suppose you walk in, with your dazzling smile, open mind, and hilarious sense of humor. Your compassion enters. *Bam!* Woo-hoo. Everybody's face lights up, tongues loosen and begin to wag, and you start hearing exhales. The once-alienated group engages due to the fact that you entered the room. Newly engaged, they engage with each other—others whom they may enliven, enlighten, entertain or energize. The Ripple Effect. Exponential change. All because you wear a smile.

You might never know how your positive or negative input magnifies and changes all it touches, but you know what you bring to the world has distinct repercussions and aftershocks.

One-on-one, a warm smile, or a hug, or kind word can change someone else's entire day, or year, or maybe entire life, belief system and behavior. Even the smallest gesture of kindness or act of generosity can bring about substantial change. Just listening can soothe or revive someone, and a complement, whether large or small, can change another person's outlook, boost self-confidence, spur some hope, and encourage somebody so much that they run out and change the world.

Changing the world for the better or worse is a matter of choice. We always choose.

We can choose to criticize or encourage, recoil or engage, ignore, pay attention, demean or uplift. We can cultivate a thirst for knowledge, passing it on at every turn, or revel and bask in ignorance. We can choose to show up or spew excuses, be there or be irresponsible, phone it in or do our very best. We can excel and help others excel, or take pride in mediocrity. We can walk with our head up, or let our head hang. We can develop healthy habits, encouraging others to do the same, or we can decide to languish. We can keep, or break, a promise, quickly forgive or hold a lasting grudge. We can be grateful for all we have, or concentrate on what we don't have rather than on our blessings. We can worry, sweat the small stuff, making others sweat along with us, or we can believe that everything works together for our good. We can do what is good, then decide to do better.

It's up to us, how we impact others. Impact is determined choice by choice. Each choice is a link in the chain of life. Each has an exponential effect, like a tremor roiling through a body, affecting those with whom we interact, those with whom they interact, and so on, and so on, up the chain. We are strands woven into life's tapestry with the fibers of our being.

As changing the world is a matter of choice, what are you choosing? Do you know? Are you taking responsibility for what your choices bring about? Is what you claim to be choosing reflected in your thoughts, speech, and actions? If it is, this state will bring you peace.

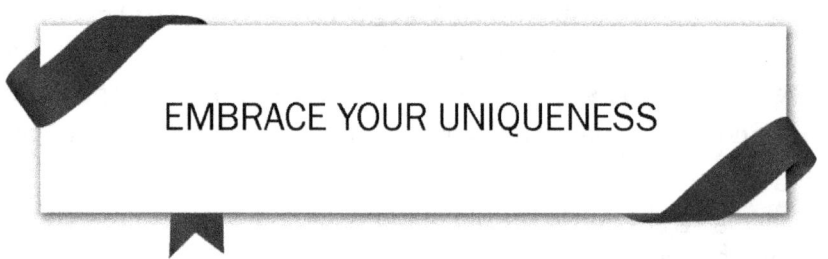

EMBRACE YOUR UNIQUENESS

Each of us is incomparable. No one can compare with you, and no one should be trying. Nor should you try to compare yourself to anyone else who has ever lived, because you will not ever be the same as anyone else. You're special. Often, we're able to see the special in others, and not in ourselves. Extraordinary features others display can tend to appear as benefits, even as we overlook our own. But when we compare ourselves to others, we compare apples to oranges. Both are sweet and juicy, and the difference between them makes them more so. So it is with each of us. We have a singular personality, function, awareness, individuality and way about us. We each represent a new joy, a fresh face, an eye-opening perspective.

People in media—particularly actors, writers, athletes, politicians, newspeople, CEO's and reality show personalities—can be lauded for doing exceptional things that others who get less attention are doing day in and day out without much praise. Celebrities just get more press. We may compare our accomplishments to theirs, and find ours wanting. We are none of us the same, and that's exhilarating, isn't it? We all have more in common than could ever separate us, yet we each are so exceptional. I might not have met you yet, and I know you're exceptional. Others know it, but do you?

Take a moment—and of course, now is best!—to list your exceptional qualities. Divide a clean sheet of paper into three (3) columns, and then begin like this: In the first column, list your positive traits, things about you, you think are pluses—character traits or learned responses. Go ahead, do it train-of-thought, jotting the first things that come to your mind without ruminating much. Be objective. You're not bragging, you're just evaluating what you have to give, and being grateful for it. If you have to undertake this like you're describing maybe someone else, okay, that's a little problematic in regard to self-esteem, but take that approach if it's all that works. Make no harsh judgments of yourself. Be kind. Be open to your gifts. Your self-description may include whatever attributes you like—adjectives such as patient, kind, intelligent, brave, understanding, bold, optimistic, fair-minded, spiritual, charismatic, sensitive, affectionate, generous, imaginative, creative, thoughtful, organized—anything you see as a plus. And yeah, go ahead, pat yourself on the back as you go. Your list is admirable.

In the middle column, keep it going. Innumerate the many things you can do, your known abilities, whether innate or learned. Your talents and skills are assets you can call upon to make a difference anywhere you go.

These can include collaborating, management, leadership, organizing, typing, filing, fundraising or other expertise. List proficiency at Excel spreadsheet, Microsoft Word or other computer software, writing, producing, painting, singing, dancing, golfing, tennis, bowling, soccer or other sports you play. You may also want to tout good habits—excellent posture, healthy eating, exercising, learning fast. Are you talented at carpentry, or cycling, or recycling? If you're a pianist, drummer, violinist, cook or baker, add that too. You can note housework, childcare, knowing how to fix a car, repair a lamp, or make a necklace, knitting, plumbing, sewing, cleaning, being adept at interior design. If you know how to rap, pen poetry or invent new gadgets, put that down along with anything else that's laudable.

Then, in the third column, list your accomplishments. Maybe you've earned advanced degrees, or won Employee of the Month, or some other awards. Include them all. Maybe you've raised four children, or run a ranch with lots of animals. Maybe you've started a business, run a non-profit organization, or volunteered at local schools, Big Brother, the Girl Scouts, homeless shelters, hospitals or the PTA. Maybe you've sung in a church choir, built a home with Habitat for Humanity, or been awarded a military medal for your bravery. Maybe you've won a Nobel Prize, an Oscar or a Pulitzer. Maybe you've been a recovering addict, lost weight, kicked cancer, run marathons. Whatever you've done successfully, be proud of what you've done, and claim it. No one has lived the life you've lived. Your story is inspirational. Not that you're telling your story now, except to tell it to yourself. This is for your eyes only. You can afford to stick your chest out some.

Now look at your list.

Wow, you're awesome! Aren't you incredible?

If you saw these things in someone else's bio, wouldn't you be impressed? If you would, congratulations! You are starting to see yourself and your power to bring about change in a whole new way—employing the many gifts you have, and standing on the platform of the good you've already allowed to happen just by living your life. That's cool. You can build on this foundation, make it bigger and better.

If, by some chance, you're not impressed, think about why. Are you being shy? Well, consider being impressed. Are you disappointed in yourself? Consider that it isn't over. You're still breathing. You're still going. You can make up for lost time. And the time isn't really lost at all. You've been preparing for what you can do right now, and going forward. You've been becoming the person you are, and she is incredibly wondrous. This is the perfect time for the changes you can make, within and without, to remake your life into what you've always wished it'd be. If you'd done it before, you could not do it now. And now is the time it is needed. Now is the time *you* are needed. You are right on time. Your time is now.

Resist the urge to fill your plate with the worst experiences of your past to feast on them in your future. The past is gone. When you live in the now, in no time at all, you're filled with all new self-respect. You're a Change Wizard. You see change in you, and the change you see can change the world.

You are the only person in the world that can bring about the change set out for you to effectuate according to your mission. You've been assigned a magnificent quest. Only you can do what you're meant to do. Your soul is evolving uniquely prepared for the task that is before you now. You are the ideal doer of good deeds the world is looking for. Never mind that you may look different, speak with an accent, feel that you didn't fit in as a kid, stumbled off of your path at some point. Who cares that you once fell in with the wrong sort, fell off some ledge, or society says you're too old, young, fat, thin, tall, short, odd, or a misfit, frail, or eccentric. Never mind your illusions of what you've lost. Forget if somebody told you, you lack money, pedigree, backbone, style, education, home-training or common sense. They didn't know who they were talking to. Their opinion wasn't accurate and isn't welcome in your mind. You are neither responsible for, nor defined by, the most careless words other people say. They are who they are. You are who you are. You are self-defining. You are real. Nobody but you must declare you're valid. You are a shimmering masterpiece. You are a standout like no other, claiming your rightful place in the evolution of the universe. You are a child of the One Love, and as such, you have everything you need.

You lack nothing. Everything's in your grasp.

Own your uniqueness and run with it.

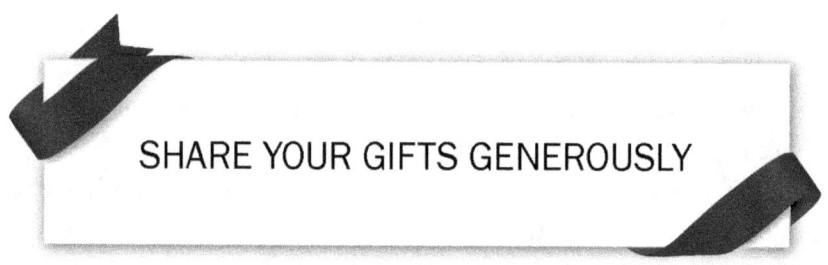

SHARE YOUR GIFTS GENEROUSLY

The qualities, skills and accomplishments you've listed were afforded you so you would share them with the world. Their potency is designed to increase in direct proportion to the extent that you employ them for the good, and you selflessly give their fruits away for the benefit of others. As you give freely—without expectation, anticipation of reciprocation, hidden agenda, defensiveness, or attachment to a particular outcome—happiness is a result. A positive outcome is assured according to the scope and measure of your positive intent.

Contrary to common belief, the road to the netherworld isn't paved with good intentions. Quite the opposite. Ill intent, no intent at all, or a lackadaisical application of intent, produce the bad results from which society sometimes suffers. Good intentions produce the best results. Good in, good out. Good multiplies. Good can only beget more good. Though we may not always see or experience the full measure of our work for good, we can trust and believe that our will to do good will produce good results somewhere along, for somebody, and in some way. We need not belabor the optics, or take credit for the good we do, and we needn't preoccupy ourselves with the benefits we effectuate. All of the good thoughts, words and deeds that flow from our hearts are producing goodness. We just need to ask for good, believe that good will come about, and be ready to give and receive pure good as the main objective of our lives.

Breathe that in for a moment: You are good. Conceiving yourself as an arm of goodness causes you to enact good works, and *be* the good you hope to see more of as you interact. You're an outcropping of the goodness others long for in their lives. You realize other people's dreams of how the world should really be, of what the world is in its purest form. When benevolence is the way of the world, narcissism falls away. You reignite hope in the cynical, and lend breath to the proposition that the good guys are winning, love conquers all, and each of us has full access to the power of goodness through our thoughts.

Doesn't it feel wonderful to know good intentions bursting from your good heart evidence themselves in ways you haven't seen, but do exist. The false belief that no good deed will go unpunished has caught on, but nothing is further from the truth. Though there may be a price to pay sometimes for doing what you know is right in the face of a system that seems to be going wrong in a manner you deplore, rest assured that the goodness you yearn to call up in the world increases and expands with your positive vibration.

You are changing the world for the better in ways outside your comprehension, once you share the gifts you're given. Your gifts are the pride and joy that make the world a pleasant place to live, regardless of the appearance of things at any given place and time. There's no limit to goodness, nor to your capacity to imagine it. Employ your skills and talents for it, be a conduit for good, or simply allow it to happen through you because you're given lots of good, and you're living to pass the good along. From this enlightened perspective, you can generously apply your gifts—whatever they are or however numerous—to the situations, circumstances and events that continue to shape your life, and the lives of others you do, or don't, know. You can create change for the better, from the tiniest of instances to those that rock the world.

It always amazes me—cracks me up, really—how sometimes I can smile at someone, perhaps someone wearing a frown or grimace, and all of a sudden, that grin lights them up with an unexpected surge of joy. It's like magic, and I love love love it. And then again, on the other hand, I can smile at another person and only deepen the scowl they're committed to. I'm the same person smiling at each. It's the same smile, basically, though perhaps in a slightly different setting, under different lighting conditions, at different angles, different times. The only real difference is, one spirit believes that seizing on any good thing can change their world for the better in an instant, and the other decides there will be no smiling here, thank you very much. That, that one smile they could have returned might well be the last smile allotted to their mouth. That grin would be one less grin in their grin account which their grin budget says they should not spend, especially on that occasion. Random smiles aren't affordable. They never know when they might need to flash a strategic smile to get something. The next thing you know, every stranger they encounter might expect a smile. And wouldn't that be unsustainable.

It's all a matter of attitude. A smile is just one tiny gift we can all give away, to anyone.

We each have a calling, a job to do, and our gifts are the tools to do them with. Some of us are inventors. We can change people's lives by fabricating new gadgets that make things easier. Some of us are healers who are able to save others' lives. Some of us can sing like angels. Some of us can paint a scene, and make every soul who sees our work behold a particular beauty. Some of us plumb the human mind to comprehend its mysteries. We're given what we need to do these jobs, and thereafter, it's up to us to understand what we must do, and tap into the means we've been given to do it. This means being self-aware, deliberate and magnanimous.

Your gifts are not yours to be meted out in a miserly manner. They're miracles. They're a hammer to nail down core beliefs, a spoon to serve up kindness and compassion, torches to light the way. Give of them with intensity, as if they were water to quench a desert traveler's thirst, to save her life. Pile them on like frosting on a birthday cake you just baked. Let them explode like fireworks. Give them as if they're unlimited. They are. They will never give out. They will only be redoubled every time you use your gifts for good. The universe will see your giving, logically give you more to give, and bless you with exhilaration, as you speak your brand of truth by using what you have at hand.

Whatever your gifts are, flesh them out, meditate on them, and soup them up. Cherish them dearly, with all your might. They're your way to make things happen. Protect them from those who would tell you, you don't possess them, they're useless, or aren't good enough. Work talent like a fulltime job. Half-stepping can lead to regret. Make sure you avoid being stuck in a dead-end job where you don't use your gifts, working day after day in a place that doesn't deserve you. You don't deserve that fate. Keep your dream from becoming a dream deferred by working at what you're best at, enjoying your labors, and being stretched by them. Hone your gifts until they are consummate skills, and work them into a plan. Be the penultimate best at whatever you do. That is its own reward. There is no functioning outside of excellence. Make the best use of your gifts by setting your goals with them uppermost in your mind. Act upon them with diligence, decency, dignity, drive and determination. Persevere. Trust you've been sent for the job. Believe in your ingenuity, and be not afraid of it. It's your friend. Wield it like a mighty sword, and apply it like a soothing salve to any and every dilemma you're faced with, any opportunity. Trumpet your talents with certitude. Be egoless in your humility.

Above all, utilize your gifts for the function for which they were intended. Employ them with passion, wisdom and abandon. Even as you do, you'll be making the world a better place.

COMMIT TO BEING A BENEFICENT SPIRIT AND HIGHLY BENEFICIAL FORCE

You might be asking, how do I go about doing all these lofty things with gifts that I'm not sure I have? With talents I haven't identified, or don't have confidence in quite yet. Or if, because I see failures in my past, I have come to convince myself that I am not gifted at all.

The answer is, realize that's not true. You know you have gifts, and you know what they are. Instinctively, you feel their strength each time you employ them. You know what you love. You know what brings joy. You witness your effectiveness. You see your capabilities every time you act decisively, because you believe in yourself instead of giving way to doubt. Confidence in your ability to make a connection and make a difference is yours for the asking by changing your thought patterns. If you think you can't, you won't. If you think you can, you will. A little reverse engineering can go a long way toward overcoming doubt. Banish your false belief that others have more than you have to offer, and instead, catch hold of the axiomatic truth that you're gifted, competent, and finely handcrafted by the Source to be a beneficial force. Commit to being beneficent and benevolent, and you will be. Empower yourself to engage with others in ways that benefit you and them, and you claim your rightful mission.

Your gifts are the *how* of what you want to do. That's why they're called 'know-how'.

Even more important is the *what* that you decide to do, the what that you're designed for. Some of us—including me—seem to know what we are meant to do. We're compelled to do it constantly.

I am a creator. I write. I'm an actress and voice over artist. I produce video, work in graphics arts, make jewelry, paint, draw, sketch, sew purses, pillows, clothing and other items I can barely fabricate before the next notion comes along. While creating, I feel most alive. I'm the happiest me I ever am, other than when I'm loving loved ones. Creating is my Meant-To-Do. Creating a thing that wasn't there, from an idea into something palpable, is a thrill that's the cornerstone of my life, and I know it's what I'm meant to do.

Some of us claim to have no idea what we're meant to do, but that's not true. Inside, we know. We're coded with it. We tell ourselves we don't know, so we don't have to take the risk of doing extraordinary things. But to live is to reach for high-hanging fruit, for it is the sweetest and juiciest. We're not meant to live blandly or moderately. We are meant to give over to doing our best for others, for giving of who we are. Some of us reach this conclusion halfway through life, others when life is near its end. Isn't it better to have this revelation out of the box? Now is the time for everything good. Poet Geoffery Chaucer seems to have been the first person to say, "Better late than never". I think, better never late.

Do you know what you're committed to? You can, at any stage of life, elect to make a conscious determination of what you want to do, and do it, by thinking it into being and thereby producing some awesome results for you and everybody else.

When we devote ourselves to probing our inner selves for answers, we engage the entire universe to provide them, and to promote us into being the answers we seek. We're self-fulfilling prophecies. We can use the power of asking to bring meaning to our lives, and to make of our lives a contribution unlike any other.

Pondering our lifework is a paramount function of our consciousness. It's far more important than pondering what laundry detergent will give us cleaner clothes, what gasoline gives us more mileage, which clothing store gives us more bang for our buck, or what color to paint the bedroom. Yet often, we randomly concentrate more on our trivial choices and tiny struggles than on what we're here for, in this passing incarnation. We oughtn't to misappropriate our time as to let this priority slide. We must center our thoughts in mindfulness in order to be effectual. Our growth depends on knowledge of who we are, and what we are meant to do, so this should be our first concern. Absent a focus on where our lives are leading, we subject ourselves to groupthink, wasted energy, boredom, loneliness, and feelings of uselessness, anxiety and angst. Devoid of what's meaningful, we risk inaction or acting without direction or effectiveness, and we may acquiesce to drifting through a life that is unrealized and unfulfilled.

Imagine just taking off in your car with no destination whatever in mind. Even if you go for a day of sun and fun, you decide where it will take place, and you set your course to hit that spot, proceeding on a trajectory that will get you there at a certain time. So why would you do any less with your life's aims? They're much more crucial. They must end up somewhere rather than nowhere, or worse, relinquished, vacated, backtracking, or veering onto a collision course.

Without aspiration, we are unable to prioritize. We are unorganized. We are prone to poor decision-making, because we lack a foundation upon which to base a decision.

On the other hand, focusing on our Meant-To-Do keeps us productive, centered, interested, happy, connected and energized. Our

Meant-To-Do keeps us in the now. Understanding that now is all there is, we choose to engage in what's happening in the moment. Rather than trapping ourselves in the past or letting ourselves be daunted by the unknown future, we are free to use our life force for the good of all, known and unknown. In Meant-To-Do mode, we can maximize our power of one by doing our part and being present.

We cannot move forward if we frame our focus on the past. Rather, we have to be forward-thinking. Just as driving the highway gazing into the rear-view mirror poses the danger of plowing into anything that lies ahead, so goes it with our impulses. Though our past may teach us lessons, we are not meant to dwell in its confines, taking up residence in its darkest corners, letting it cage our minds and plague us with stagnation. We gain wisdom and guidance by setting our course toward being a beneficial force.

Naturally, we are free to shift our focus as we learn and grow. The *what* of our lives is dynamic. It may change with the tides, in a natural flow. There's no rule dictating we must have the same *what* guide our preferences from the cradle to the grave. Our *what* may shape-shift according to gained abilities, altered perceptions, renewed perspectives, unforeseen opportunities and life stages that arise. We may fulfill one *what*, and need to move on to go after a bigger one. But without any *what*, there is nothing to change, no growth and no progression.

The essential thing, above all else, is our progress into the *who* we are meant to be.

Who you are, and who you're becoming, is the point of your existence.

The good news is you don't have to prove your existence. Unlike the Who creatures who struggle in Dr. Seuss's *Horton Hears a Who*, the popular children's picture book, you need not shout your beingness into the world in order to become a reality. The *who* in your scenario is YOU. Your you-ness is more than sufficient. Your you-ness is undeniable. Your you-ness is needed, wanted, loved and cherished.

Your you-ness is a throbbing heartbeat thrumming to the rhythm of the universe. You have something to do, and you're fully equipped with everything you need to do it. You are an entity, whole and complete, with sovereignty over your soul and spirit. You're free to be whoever, whatever and however you wish to be.

Here's the special, secret sauce—because you're a spiritual being, you can live a fully realized life by simply becoming your highest self, and committing to serving others in a way that serves to foster change for the better. This is a noble goal.

You just have to be yourself at the highest level you can see at any given point in time. You are a beneficial force from the moment you commit to be. As you grow, your thoughts and actions will improve in quality. To be a beneficial force is not a pipedream, it's your nature. It is how you want to live. Commit to it. That's all it takes. For once you commit, the whole universe will recognize that's who you are, and shape itself to form around this concept, turning the twist and turns of every situation in your life to match your pure intent, to help you be a blessing. Circumstances will arise consistent with your will to give.

It is within your power—*right now*—to have your being, aura and very presence on this planet shed such bright, transforming light that it alone will change the world with its power to ignite and inspire change. Like Mother Teresa. The Dalai Lama. Martin Luther King.

So, close your eyes now. Breathe in deeply. Take a moment to go within your *self.*

Let go of any fear of commitment you may have accrued along the way, and commit to loving, commit to giving, commit to radiating goodness. Doing so gets you halfway there. As it is with everything you do, the most crucial step in contributing to a better world is deciding to. To invest yourself, you must decide. This isn't a rudimentary step. You have to organically take this on, revising the contours of your life to make room for more than just your needs, wants and aspirations. You have to be willing to sacrifice. You have to be open to being a channel for grace and abundance to funnel through, to seeing your personal evolution in terms of its utility within the greater scheme of things. You have to come to realize that your growth into your highest self is intrinsically linked to what you're willing to give without reservation. You're giving, because you're so grateful for the innumerable benefits you receive from a cup that's overflowing.

Your intuition tells you that the being that you most wish to be is not just an individual who is living a singular life. Though it's great to be independent, and not needy, you are not alone, and there's never a reason to feel you are. You are not separate or detached, you are a part of the one true love that lives and thrives in all of us. Your viewpoint may be singular, but you are not companionless, abandoned or forsaken. Your characteristics are distinct, and your being is complete and whole, but you're a big part of a larger picture. This incarnation of your life is a part of the perfect wholeness that is unveiling itself through all creation. We are all one, so the good we do redounds to the advantage of everybody. It's easy to commit to being a blessing to everyone you meet, and to having them bless you in their way.

Like the spherical planets, everything in the world is conceived to be circular. What you send around will go around, and be returned to you in kind. See yourself as an ever-stronger, ever-widening conduit for good, and a steady stream of ever-increasing good will be revealed to, and through, you.

Commit to being a giver, and you will surely receive abundantly more gifts with which to change the world.

HOW CHANGE REARRANGES

YOUR THOUGHTS CREATE REALITY

Every thought you think contains energy. It *is* energy, in a potent form. Your thoughts create your world, and your experience therein. That which you are experiencing as your reality right here and now, whether you've known it or not, is a reflection of what you thought before, of what you believed about your life, your world, and those around you. Your reality is what you believed would happen, and how you would respond to it. Absorbing this truth is critical to any change you wish to make. The quality of your life depends on taking responsibility for the content and quality of your thoughts. Their energies will permeate and formulate the essence of what will unfold as actuality. It is vital to your life force to think of only what you want to see.

What you think about, you will experience.

If your thoughts are focused on what you do not have, you'll garner even less, and experience loss at every turn. If your thoughts are filled with fear, you'll soon be afraid of any and everything, and your life will be limited to a narrow, negative experiential framework, filled with hapless circumstances that are avoidable. If you're thinking the world is against you, you will engender enemies far and wide bearing ill intentions towards your life. If you refuse to trust others and fill up your mind with suspicion, only untrustworthy folks will be magnetized into your realm. If you wake up dreading your day, your work, the traffic, the weather, your family and friends, and problems you will never have, your day will unerringly head in the direction of that vision.

If, on the other hand, you awake with wonderful expectations, you will draw from the universe a match, and events, circumstances and people will formulate a very fruitful day. If your mind is filled with thoughts of thanks, an awesome array of goodies will arrive to reward your gratitude. If you think happy thoughts about who you are, what you do, and what you are capable of, your happiness will be reflected back to you as if by mirrors, and your life will fill with joy that overflows to those around you.

Your thoughts can create a better world for everyone you touch.

Your thoughts need not ramble on out of your control, as they may sometimes seem to. You think your thoughts. You—and no one, and nothing, else—control all the thoughts you will ever think, and you must manage them with vigilance. Only if you fail to command or take responsibility for your thoughts can any outside force think for you, and they surely will. If you abdicate thinking for yourself in ways that benefit you and others, you effectively surrender your control and your power to shape your life.

Have you ever watched, say, a football game with one TV commercial after another pumping out slurp-worthy images of hot pizza dripping with melted cheese, only to develop an intense desire for pizza? You might not even notice your craving jumped out at you from your TV set, inspired by a pizza seller trying to sell more pizza. That is how commercials work, to hopefully cause you to want what you don't need, may not be good for you, or might be just a waste of time or money you don't have to spend. Unconscious desires, ideas, even stubborn beliefs can be thrust upon you by the outside world, from different sources, some of which do not have your best interests at heart, but rather their own.

If you don't control your mind, then any outside force can do so by default. For instance, the media you consume—Internet, radio, newspapers, books, magazines, films, music and social websites—can input your subconscious mind. Even your conscious mind can be programmed with terror, war, poverty, loneliness, disease, discontent, disillusionment, deficit, limitation, fear of loss, hate, violence, pestilence, a sense of impending disaster, stress and other crippling ills. Parents, siblings, aunts and uncles, and other relatives may pass along their own beliefs and anxieties unsolicited, for better or for worse. Significant others will train you to their ways of thinking—good or bad, filtered or perhaps unfiltered, intentionally or unintentionally—without realizing what effects they have upon your mental, physical, spiritual or emotional health and well-being.

This can only happen if you allow it, if you aren't monitoring your thoughts, or if you are noncommittal about employing your thoughts to improve yourself and change the world around you. The thoughts in your mind are treasures that no one, and nothing, can usurp from you, and no one should be able to. Your mind is not just some depository in which any old random conceit may perch. Your mind is a sacred, solemn place, designed to create amazing things.

Isn't it best to avoid arbitrary baggage floating through the ether, letting no one but The One Love be the source of the content of your thoughts, pervading them with loving kindness, goodness, positivity, generosity and bliss?

Your positive thinking equals your positive life, and nothing short of that. Think happy, be happy. Think healthy, enjoy great health. That's how it works. See the world as abundant, with plenty for everyone, and assume abundance great enough to give away. As you harness the power of your thoughts for the goodness you want to experience, you formulate a better world.

You can do this in many ways, among them meditation, affirmations, prayer, religious studies, yoga and other exercise, and training with those who are crackerjack in the art of positive manifestation.

It's easy to hear, direct, and re-direct our thoughts when we listen to them, channeling thoughts in directions we want them to go in a morphing mindscape. "I can't" reverses to "I can", and leads to increasing empowerment. Thoughts of loneliness and isolation transmute into thoughts of solitude that bring self-knowledge, peacefulness and calm. Rather than being content to think "How dumb of me", "I love to learn" can build the framework of a ladder up. Our minds are our dominion. We can let go of the thoughts that don't currently serve us in an instant. It's easy to make this decision. Consciously changing the thoughts that diminish us into the thoughts that transform us recreates us into higher beings. Within this, is our power to change our world.

PROTECTING A POSITIVE THOUGHT ZONE BY TRANSFORMING THE NATURE OF NEGATIVE THOUGHTS

Experts agree that humans think fifty to eighty thousand thoughts per day. That means you're thinking really fast—at the rate of about two to three thousand thoughts per hour (forty-six times faster than you can legally drive on the highway) or thirty-five to fifty-five thoughts per minute. That's a lot of thoughts. And at the speed you're thinking thoughts, they could get out of control quite quickly.

If you don't control your thoughts, your thoughts will be controlling you. As thoughts can come from anywhere—from fear, from stress, from media—ordering and re-ordering your thoughts should be your preeminent occupation. Fortunately, it's in your hands. Any negative thought that comes to you can be easily turned around. You can stop thinking any thought, at any time, in any place, about anything you think about. You can replace a dull thought with one that shines, and brings you what you want. Thus, it pays to consciously elevate your thoughts until doing so is habitual, and a negative thought feels out of place. Your thoughts develop patterns, and those patterns spring from who you are, and the quality of your core beliefs.

When you believe that everything works for your ultimate good, that's your dominant thought, so indeed things work out for the best. Your positive thought pattern springs from hope. Your hope generates what you're hoping for. If your thoughts are infused with abiding hope, things will tend to go your way. Hope wants to externalize itself, to evidence and substantiate the thing that one is hoping for, provided the hope is a true belief, the believer herself works to bring it about, and especially if the thing hoped for is an element of the greater good. Hope implants in you the ethos of a winner. You don't accept defeat. You triumph in your every thought, and your winning thoughts increase your hope. Winners hope, and hopers win.

Hope springs from the notion that everything that happens leads to your highest good. With hope, you are able to practice persistence, let passion propel your pursuit of your purpose, have confidence in your own personal power, and rest in the thought that your mind can create a dream that's bigger than yourself, and usher it into reality for the benefit of all.

Hope is your mind on rocket fuel, expecting good things to happen.

When you expect good, good shows up.

On the other hand, lacking the fuel of hope, errant negative thoughts fueled by fear undermine. They can spark timidity, inaction, pain, regret, anxiety, doubt and constant worry. Worrying places your dearest resources and energies into a gloomy void that contemplates only what's working against you, conjuring dangers surrounding things that seldom, if ever, occur.

Once you're able to get it in your head that nothing is working against you at all, your vibratory atmosphere won't match any horror that worry depicts. Your vibration will match only positive scenarios, and bring them forth. The universe is on your side. Every positive scenario your positive mindset conjures up is infused in your limitless consciousness in concert with the Universal Mind that wishes good for you. Your positive thought spectrum is the mother of every positive experience stretched out before you as your life.

On the contrary, fear births the consequence of magnetizing what you *don't* want, subsequently attracting that, so your fear becomes real circumstances, situations, and more fear. As fear can only bring about more fear, and more to feel fear of, fear is the most fearful thing of all. The best thing to do is to let it go, and resist preparing a home for it. To engage in indulging your fear is to burn every bridge and lock every door to you.

You're brave. You aren't a fearful person. You are filled with hope and light.

Eliminate fear with positive thoughts, and there are no doors. No barriers.

If a negative thought should come to mind, banish it immediately. Your thoughts are yours alone, so you can think a thought, un-think a thought, and turn your thoughts around to face the direction in which you wish to go. You can replace any negative thought with a positive thought in an instant. *Bam!* Your thoughts are your own. They can turn on a dime, because you are the thinker that thinks your thoughts, and you are at the helm. You're pushing the buttons. You make every change. You are the ultimate programmer of your mind, and you control its diet. You feed thoughts into your mind, and ingest the nourishing benefits of the positive thoughts your mind cooks up. No one can invade that space unless you give away the key.

You can change your mind with one good thought, and change everything that happens next. Isn't that good news?

If, say, you happen to be in the shower, worried you "won't get there on time", and you find yourself programming thoughts of lateness into your expectation zone, you are working at cross-purposes with the thing you claim to desire. You are sabotaging the very appointment you want to keep, creating the very thing you want to avoid by focusing energy on it. That is not a plus for you. Instead, consciously vanquish those lateness thoughts, and tell yourself—repeat the words—that everything's working together for good.

The universe will manipulate traffic, retool the appointment prior to yours, and each appointment after yours, enhance your efficiency, speed you up, inform every action you take, and micromanage every little thing, coordinating everyone. It'll turn back clocks—and time itself—to get you where you need to go in total perfect timing. And if you do perchance arrive some minutes behind your scheduled time, that time will become the perfect time. Ask to get there at the perfect time. Believe you will. Open up your heart, and receive your prompt arrival. See in your mind every item of clothing slipping easily onto you, the perfect color, perfect fit. Start to visualize green lights ahead, and no one traveling in your path. See smiling faces, shaking hands. Watch yourself leaving the meeting pumping your fist, and viscerally feel the win. Dive into the wave of happiness. Feel the fresh connection to the people, and to your unfolding dream. You're the king or the queen, not a victim of chance. Not a hapless, hopeless voyager entrenched in the muck and the mire of minor mistakes or random quirks of fate, or even your own untimeliness.

If a negative thought creeps in unbidden, let the errant nature of it signal you to stop and think again. Rethink the thought immediately, to think about something affirmative—something you consciously avow is a thought that can change your life. Allow yourself a second thought. Think better of what you are processing through your mind, for it will design your future. Bid a negative thought to go in peace, for to sweat any negative thought will only give it power over you, and you don't want that. Decide instead to spin negative thoughts into positive ones which ignite your fiery passion for the next fruitful new idea. Implement this technique on the very next occasion you become aware you're thinking an unproductive thought. No frets or condemnation, just intensified awareness. Continue to do this until it's a pattern. Second nature. How you roll. Your thoughts are the tools that build your personal history. Keep them pure.

Make a habit of transmuting any and every thought that does not serve into one that serves you and the greatest good, and you yourself will change, and change the world.

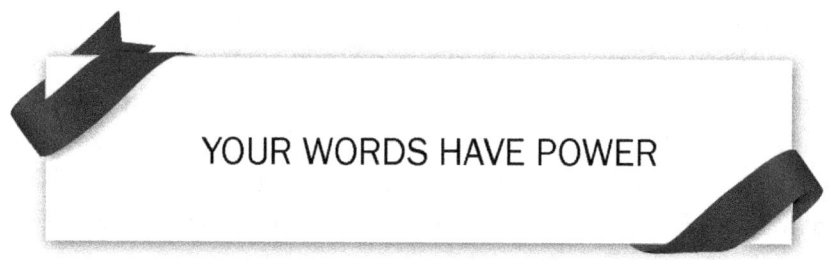

YOUR WORDS HAVE POWER

Our thoughts become the words we speak and write. Words matter. Words construct, destruct, and are powerful and immutable. Once uttered, a word cannot be unspoken. It can be apologized for. One can attempt to "take it back". One can speak countless words to try to undo the consequences of a word, but words themselves remain as echoes in the mind.

Words are like missiles sent into the stratosphere of other people's lives.

Once spoken, your words transmit energies. Sure, others can respond to these energies in a myriad of ways—and certainly how they respond is on them—but the energy you send out through words, the content and context of your words, and the choices you make when you utter them, are yours alone to reckon with.

I would submit that not only do words matter to anyone hearing them, but that words *are* matter in themselves—as real, effective and palpable as any material thing you own. Words have a particular resonance unlike any other substance known. You can uplift or depress with your words. Your words can be healing, or strike almost fatal blows to another person's psyche. Words take on a life of their own. They have presence the instant their meanings leave your mouth as sounds that carry your intent. Your words have long, strong, sturdy lives. They recur, reflect, reverberate, and they never, ever, ever die. Words are seldom forgotten, often recalled, and have nearly unparalleled power to alter everything they touch, and everybody at whom they're directed.

Think of the lyrics to popular songs that play in a loop in the heads of millions of music lovers around the world, moving many generations, stirring memories, bringing tears, making couples fall in love again, causing people to laugh, dance, sing, and recall the best moments of their lives. Bringing people together at parties and weddings. Comforting mourners at funerals. Inspiring church-goers to pray and praise. Words become memorable dialogue from classic movies viewed for years, making actors into movie stars fans watch over and over and over again. Words crackle in poison pen social networking messages that go viral, sending shock waves all around the globe, destroying reputations. Words make up love notes that join faithful lovers, and poems that school children memorize. With words, we express our emotions, communicate thoughts, and chronicle history.

The spoken word is pure vibration. Like music, the words we speak are physically felt by those to whom we speak, transmitted by sound waves. It is undeniable that people and creatures that listen to, or overhear, our words are either enriched or assaulted by phrases with which we are thoughtful or careless, generous or miserly, tactful or injudicious. As the bodies of others hear and feel our every spoken syllable, their emotions are buffeted this way and that in ways we can't imagine. This means our words come with a tacit responsibility for what they cause, the well-being of those who receive them, and the universal consciousness which depends on our words being positive, so it can do more good.

We cannot toss words about, because they are tangible, and the sound of them is either noise or music to our ears. Our speech is audible thought that has sound, cadence, tone, pitch, acoustics and resonance all its own.

We say what we believe—or what we want others to start to believe—and we know that believing is the beginning of what's going to happen next.

The written word has its own wizardry. The written word is visible, and an image has huge impact. Written images last in forms and formats spoken words do not. When somebody reads what's written—maybe many somebodies—merely the fact it appears in writing may make it seem more credible, even if it's not. People tend to give written words far greater gravity than they may deserve sometimes, believing what they read in books, magazines, newspapers, blogs and online posts is gospel truth. Written words are often consumed without questioning. The content therein is memorialized, repeated, resent and regurgitated.

Repetition of words can lend opinion, conjecture, or even slander, a muddy, misleading veneer of veracity, turning one person's iffy conclusion into another's concept of reality. People are prone to decide to trust certain sources, then to suspend disbelief to the point where whatever issues from that source is not only believed, but becomes a fact, even if it does not ring true.

Research by the University of Western Australia's Stephan Lewandowsky may explain, in part, why this is so. The study concluded, "Weighing the plausibility and the source of a message is cognitively more difficult than simply accepting that the message is true—it requires additional motivational and cognitive resources". In other words, people prefer to accept a message as true, because it's easier to believe a statement on its face than it is to examine its wisdom, veracity, logic, or even how it came to be, or from whence, or whom, it issued.

When we admire the characteristics of writers, politicians or celebrities, their words hit home. We may give value to what they say, and tend to subscribe to what they write. In fact, we may even depend on it. Celebrity bios, memoirs and advice books fly off bookstore shelves. In addition, our personal social spheres offer friends and acquaintances we respect, and thus, their written words and the subtext underlying them, influence us in many ways. In this context, words can wound or heal, distress or soothe, enlighten, dumb down, clarify, mislead, condemn, praise, add, detract, inflame, transform, or educate. Such is the power of the words we generate with our potent thoughts, and transfer to the minds of those who read or hear them as the truth.

Let us be transformative with words, their intent, and their inflection. We who wish to change the world for the better declare that our far-reaching words—whether written or spoken—are meant to uplift, and to be positive, caring, kind, inspirational, thoughtful, motivational, and, most of all, rooted in wisdom and truth.

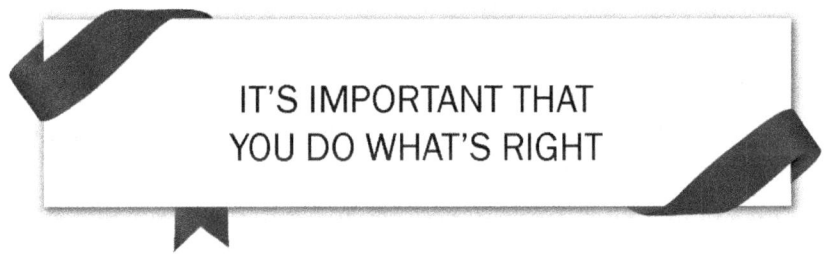

IT'S IMPORTANT THAT YOU DO WHAT'S RIGHT

Every action you take is important to someone. Every deed you do has weight. There's no *Oh, it won't matter if I just...*, pal. Yes, it will. Your actions count. That's why your moral compass directs you to do the thing your conscience says it's best to do. And to do it because you want to, not because of some shame or guilt you'll feel, or of fear you'll get caught if you do the wrong thing. You don't know who you'll hurt if you're driving drunk, or who your donation check will save. You just know drunk driving is dangerous, and giving often works wonders.

Do right for the sake of doing right, because goodness matters in the world. You're either on the side of goodness, acting from it at every turn—or you're not, and what happens is on you. You can charge like a bull in a china shop, oblivious to what you break, or decide to be good, and do good, because your goodness is effective.

One smile. One hug. One unexpected gift. One lie. One unreturned e-mail. One slammed door. One rolled eye. One hand-delivered casserole. One invitation. One hospital visit. One back turned. One warm handshake. One apology. One blocked driveway. One admission. One act of forgiveness. One love note. One thank you. One omission, inclusion, exclusion or insensitive act of thoughtlessness. Any of these things can change a life.

Just as we are responsible for the ways in which we react or respond to the situations and circumstances we encounter, we're defined by those we manufacture with each choice. It may be hard to predict what will happen next, but it's easy to do the right thing. Well, not always easy, but when we do the right thing, the world takes it from there. Our input is affirmative, and that's all anyone can expect of us. Rightness. How a gesture is received is something we can't control or moderate, but we do have the option to act in a way that furthers the causes of peace and love.

Our actions give rise to reactions and emotions we can't prognosticate, regarding others or ourselves. A slap to the face. What sensations does that provoke? On the other hand, foot massage. What quite opposite feelings does that invoke? Or betrayal. Desertion. Sudden loss. Somebody holding your hand. It's not just larger actions that send shock waves rippling through the world. Simple everyday deeds change the world for the better—or worse—and they begin with us. They start with one simple decision. One does not have to start a world war to disturb the peace or destroy the calm. Nor does one have to cure cancer to foster environments that motivate, improve, relax, encourage, inspire, or bring about esprit de corps.

If you want to change the world, make up your mind to do right. That's what it takes.

Every right action follows intent. We advance in the direction we point ourselves toward. We plot our course. We act from the depths of our character. We do the right thing from a right frame of mind. We humans are congruent beings. Who we are, shows up in everything we say and do. Any effort to separate our words and deeds from our native temperament or disposition fails, because it comes across as false. Nobody buys what they don't see emanate from a likely source. Good people do good things because it's their nature, because they commit to goodness. All they produce outflows from that. Malevolence drips from maleficent preoccupations of the soul. Just as roses don't bloom from a poison ivy plant, the seed of the positive change we seek doesn't bud in a murky mind.

Focus on being your highest self, because positive changes hinge on that.

When you know who you are, settle who you'll become, and decide what you want to exemplify, all choices begin to be facile ones—you just do the thing that's right. You make the choice that comes from love. You think, speak, and act in accordance with your vision of who you want to be, and that vision takes shape before your eyes, and in the view of others. Talk the talk, and walk the walk. That's it. Believe, and behave like you believe, and you're a believer. In kindness. Creativity. Beauty. Oneness. The wonderful dream you have. The supremacy of agape love. Love everyone. Love all the time. Love with all your heart. That's my motto. That's my story, and I'm sticking to it. Your life can be a love story, too. Don't you hear the love song coming on? A song as purple as Prince's rain, as booty-licious as Beyoncé, as anti-gravitational as Michael Jackson's Moonwalk and as passionate as The Beatles want to hold your hand. Everyone hears in the music of a musician, who that musician is. That's what makes us sing along.

People will sing along with you any time your music speaks to them. So be who you are, and sing your song, no matter the cost. Sing loud and long, so nothing discordant drowns you out, and the clang of mediocrity and derision cannot silence you. Do what's right, and your life is a love song played to everyone you're fortunate to meet, because good creates more good, and more goodness can only spread more love. And, like the Burt Bacharach/Dionne Warwick song says, goodness knows that now more than ever "What the world needs now is love, sweet love".

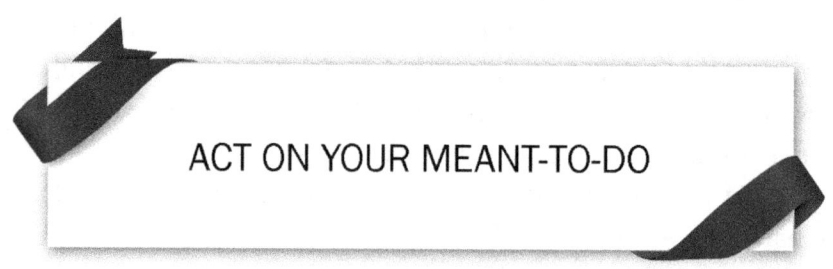

ACT ON YOUR MEANT-TO-DO

Once you realize your Meant-To-Do, act on it. It is why you're here. Resolve to allow your choices and priorities to center around the cause for which you're living. It's fun to do, because acting on your Meant-To-Do brings endless joy and mirth.

Doing what we feel we should, or must, can have a just reward, but doing what we're meant to do may be the greatest thrill of all. Our interests, talents, abilities and skills are custom-designed for us, to help us achieve our Meant-To-Do in a way that's satisfying. The elation we feel when we use our gifts to further what we're meant to do can push past any obstacle.

When we're acting on our Meant-To-Do, and doing it for all it's worth, we're giving and receiving love. We're loving life, and giving thanks for it by living out the dream the universe has placed in us. We're going for all we can be, and all we can do to change the world, as it evolves. We're creating a thing through mindfulness that would not exist without us, using what we are entrusted with to reshape the parameters of life, for all that exists and will exist.

What you do, only you can do in the way you do it. Period. Even if someone else could conceive and formulate something similar, your creations are direct extensions of your own uniqueness. Whether you create some text, a mowed lawn or a tuna sandwich, only you can do it in that manner, in that space and time. Only you can think what you think moment to moment. Your words and actions are also yours alone. According to a study by the University of Arizona, the preponderance of people speak about sixteen thousand words per day. At that rate, whose words can possibly be the same in any given day? Far less week, month, year or lifetime. Think of the possible permutations and combinations of those words. Add languages, slang, dialects, regionalisms, buzzwords and emoji's people translate into various verbiages, and who could say the things you've said, in the way you've said them, and to whom you've said them. Who will in the future? Anyone? Of course not. And your speech is just one way in which you are unique.

No one can do what you do, the way you do it, because no one else is YOU.

Let that sink in for a minute. Ruminate on it. Let it marinate.

You have a position that's solely yours.

Take a simple example. Think of a dish your mother cooked—your favorite when you were a child. Can anyone cook that dish like she did? Think of the way your mate kisses you. Can anyone kiss you just like that, and cause you to feel the exact same way? Think of a Picasso, or a Rembrandt, or a Van Gogh painting. Who can paint that same way now? Art forgers may attempt to, but they are pitiful imitations. They're merely copying someone else, not creating originals. They're infringing on someone's copyright, and stealing intellectual property, not advancing the cause of art. Even then, their so-called "tour de forces" don't contain the same paints, brushstrokes, lighting, canvases or ingenious concepts the genuine artist used, regardless of how hard they may try. That's why fakes are, more often than not, found out.

Is there another Marilyn Monroe, or Dorothy Dandridge? Certainly not. How many performers dress like they dressed, move like they moved, sing like they sang, mime their every sexy move, and never get close to being them, or doing what they could do with an audience? Not one. It's not possible. These are just extreme examples. You aren't any less unique. You're the best you, and that's a fact. Only you can be you with your singular purpose. Only you can do your Meant-To-Do, and make it work. So, act on your Meant-To-Do relentlessly. When you do what only you can do, you harness the force of the universe, and you act with its mighty power. When you pour on your SuperYou with sincere intent to improve conditions within and around you, you become unstoppable. You are living and working outside the realm of time, space and limitation. You become possibility. You become unbeatable. Your Meant-To-Be becomes the only thing that can happen, and will. Your Meant-To-Do does wonders, because it must.

Focus your thinking and core beliefs on your Meant-To-Do, and believe in it, and all that exists will reconfigure itself to conform to that idea, and to bring it into being in the now. Atoms and molecules will move to make what may seem impossible to others inevitable for you.

You can literally rearrange what is, and make it what it's meant to be.

In the way you tap into your higher self, the whole world yearns to do that too. The entire universe seeks to generate whatever it needs to be at its best, and you're a crucial part of that.

The universe wants to see peace and beauty shining out from everywhere. The cosmos is creativity wanting to fill the world with love, through you. It is goodness and light exclusively, and when that's not reflected back in the actions of us humans, it perpetually tries to achieve that state, and make it last eternally. The universe is on our side, but we have to commit, and we have to believe, and we have to act on our Meant-To-Do, because we all are part of what the universe wants to communicate. It will take every erg of energy from all life to hear the messages the universe delivers. So we must act purposefully, in ways that are different from what has gone before. We have to innovate. We have to go forth unafraid, with a mindset of willingness and unity. We have to be primed for miracles, knowing they can arrive at the strangest times, and convinced that we're each a miracle bound to happen anywhere. Miracles live in everyone.

Merely saying that you are committing and believing, and doing other than what will make your purpose meaningful, is not enough. Act on your Meant-To-Be and Meant-To-Do, or there's no point in having them. You have to act. If you're meant to write, write every day. If you're meant to be a mother, you can't smoke, drink, idle, and leave to chance your health or your role modeling. You have to be in the mommy groove. You have to be doing what it takes to get from A to B, and on to C, and so on up the line. If you want to be a quarterback, you'd best be tossing the football every second you get a chance, and learn to be quick as a wink on your feet. If you want to be a tech or game programmer, just playing games won't lead you to achieving goals—you'll have to learn how to code, and get into marketing what you create. You have to do the things your Meant-To-Do quietly demands of you. You have to be heading to your goals, and taking steps to realize them.

When you leave your home and walk outside, you're en route. You plan your route out in your mind, and unless something untoward occurs, you usually see it through. If you're off to the bank to secure a loan, you head to the bank, or you won't get there. Heading to the grocery store will not complete the task. You shower, shave, shampoo, and brush your teeth. You put on proper clothes. You might assemble documents.

If your aim is instead to get exercise, you may don some walking shoes, and head out in the sunshine. Even then, you know where you will walk, or what gym you'll go pump iron in. You know what you want to do, and you prepare yourself to do it. You have an aim. You take action toward that aim. You believe in it. Sure, you could slide by, marking time, never having that thing that drives or moves you, never believing you're meant to do that thing you're created for. You can get a job that bores you, roll with a spouse that isn't your perfect match. You can go along to get along, live a life of mediocrity that's really just a compromise. But is that the YOU who is reading this book? That isn't the kind of person who picked up this book to up her game. That isn't the guy with the kind of juice you bring to everything you do.

You're aware there's more in the world for you. You know what you're doing counts. You're alert to the signs that direct you toward an endeavor bigger than you or me. You know you can do what has never been done, and succeed at what others dare not try. You can invent, revise, and reimagine almost anything. You can give the world the next iPhone, Internet, Amazon or Google. You can turn politics on its ear. You know you were born to do something incredible, born for whatever is driving you, for what's making you want to jump up out of bed in the morning and get after it.

Once you detect your Meant-To-Be, there isn't a soul on earth that can keep you from doing what you're meant to do. No one assigns it to you. It is as rooted in you as you are in it. You are the one to discover and determine what it really is—not what someone else told you it must be, or what happens to seem most practical, what earns the most money, has status pinned to it, or implies security.

You're working to externalize the reality you desire to see. You are the catalyst. You are the spark. You are the change that's ready to happen. You do what you sense are the things you are personally suited to actualize. Once you discern that what you're doing matches what you're meant to do, and you're acting on what you believe to be true, your investment of time and energy can bring the best result. You are the arbiter of your truth, and once that truth is clear to you, it is only for you to act upon it, and to live your truth to change the world for the better in whatever ways you can.

If you haven't determined your Meant-To-Do, begin this with an open heart. It is never too early, nor too late, to fully appreciate who you are, and to take on the reason why you're here. The timing is always perfect. Let it come to you naturally, like a seed that grows into a sapling, then the sapling into a mighty tree. Everyone feels the need to know their Meant-To-Do. It calls to you. It springs out of your Meant-To-Be. It will tap you on your shoulder, yell to you through your expanse of experience, or flat-out bring you to your knees. If you're listening, you can't avoid its nudge or fail to overhear its voice. If you haven't been listening, tune in now. It is urging you out of the box, not just for out-of-the-box thinking, but for action too. If you wait too long to heed its call, you will feel the current framework of your life is way too small for you, constricting, like an undersized belt. Life will force you out, if need be, so it's best to expand yourself willingly. This is the sweet spot—willingness. You want to transform from your conscious free will, from your highest potentiality, where transformation happens.

Michael Bernard Beckwith (*Life Visioning*), founder of the Agape International Spiritual Center in Los Angeles, California, urges his congregation toward higher self, employing the analogy that when a chick feels her shell is too small for the transformational being she can be, or for her current stage of development, she feels the shell walls closing in. Yet the chick doesn't ask for a bigger shell—she pecks out, to a whole new paradigm. She evolves into a chicken.

Now, I'm not suggesting that you be a chicken—you need all the courage you possess—I'm just saying that when your shell feels tight, be courageous enough to burst out to the larger paradigm that beckons you. Behave like the person you know you can be, the even more expansive character yet to be exposed. Let him, or her, start to take the stage—the next stage of your maturation. Put faith in your capacity. Molt your old ways of thinking, like the creatures evolving around you shed their feathers, teeth or skin. Replace your old views with new patterns of growth, and help the world grow as you do.

You are not the only one counting on you. The world is awaiting your debut as a fully realized spirit. You are limitless. You are needed. You're an essential part of a whole that's so humungous, it's unfathomable. You can alter the course of world events just by acting out your Meant-To-Do, and being who you're meant to be. Realization of your highest self is a pivotal part of improving life for everyone. Accept this fact, it's key to your development. You are already the hope of the world as you are, and as you evolve, you're living out your piece of the cosmic puzzle. Avoid waiting until your shell explodes into shards sharp enough to hurt not only you, but those you love, and all your fellow travelers on this plane.

Peck out, establish your Meant-To-Be and Meant-To-Do, and spread your wings. You know you're meant to fly. Maybe you're an eagle, maybe a dove, or a hummingbird, or seagull. Whatever you are, keep your eye on the sparrow. Learn who you are and what you're meant to do. Live out what's inside of you that's grown to be so spectacular that it can change the world.

If your Meant-To-Do has been clear to you, yet if, for reasons you may not know, you haven't been acting upon it and making it your joie de vivre, start NOW. In this moment. Make up your mind to go forward as you are meant to proceed. Avoid wasting time in a life that's not yours, alive but hardly living. Change direction. You can make that choice. For you, the time is anytime. Plan what to do right now that plants you squarely in your Meant-To-Do, and propels you into the substantive change that kindles metamorphosis in you and those you affect.

Start small, if you have to, just moments a day of figuring how to turn your current priorities and Daily Do's into stepping stones on your true path. You can segue into your Meant-To-Do by finding time in every day to do what your spirit cries out to do. Take time for it. Make time. Do what feels right. You can fly cold turkey immediately from the humdrum aspects of your life, into living out loud in intentional ways that encompass all you believe in and color all you tackle from here on out. That fluttering sound is you taking off.

KNOW YOU CAN HAVE WHATEVER YOU WANT AND HELP OTHERS DO THE SAME

You can, and you will, have whatever you want, and you can help others do the same, if you believe that you're here to be happy, healthy, free and loved. Believe, and it will become the foundation of all you do and all you have. Make belief your basis for changing the world, and act on the beliefs you hold, and they will become your abundance mindset, bringing all you want to you, and blessing all others that do the same.

What you want, wants you. Okay, take this in. You're linked. What you want derives from who you are, so the dream you desire already exists, and it's tied to you like an umbilical cord. What you're dreaming about—perhaps yearning for—is your energy match in every way. It is the energy match of the fully realized you, however, not just any ole version of you that you might have become in the process of living unconsciously. Mindfulness is the umbilical cord.

Just as you desire your dream, your dream desires your evolution.

You become the person you're meant to be by making that your goal.

No matter who you've been, or who you are, the higher YOU is untouched by any negative energy levels you may have encountered in your life, because their rate of vibration operates lower than your own. Your psyche is pristine, because you don't live in peaks and valleys. Everything is a blessing when you function in your Meant-To-Be and do the things you're meant to do. The swings and sways of daily life can't pitch you to and fro. You aren't available to them. You're available to gratitude. You're inoculated from negatives, tucked into a sphere of energy that can only register positives, because that's your own polarity. Negativity doesn't match your vibe, so on it goes, elsewhere. In fact, your energy is so strong, it can dissipate negative energy and transform it for the good. Believe, devote, and dedicate your life to doing the good you seek, and any bad news may look for you, but it won't be able to find you.

Your power to create and change things brings you everything you want, and nothing you don't want, and it influences others to bring whatever change they want to them.

In fact, if something you don't want somehow manages to cross your path, the universe will reshape it into something in your favor. Count everything that happens as what's meant to bring some good to you, and that is what will coalesce, for you and all whose lives you touch. What you're thinking about is on its way. What you're feeling, you will feel more of. Choose to feel anger, and you become an angrier person by the day. Choose love, and you become a lover courting the love of the universe. Believe you're a king or a queen, and you are, because you will experience royal treatment, royal goods and royal transformation into your highest self. You will treat others royally, recognizing all beings as kings and queens.

You can have what you want, and help others do the same. That is your superpower. Put on your cape. Write an 'S' on your chest. Focus on who you want to be. Determine what it is you want. Act on what you're meant to do. Materialize your vision by asking, believing, and being open to receive all the good that's aligned with your energies. Know that the life you dream of, and the world you're working to transform into one that's best for everyone, exists, and is ready to manifest through you, at a time called now.

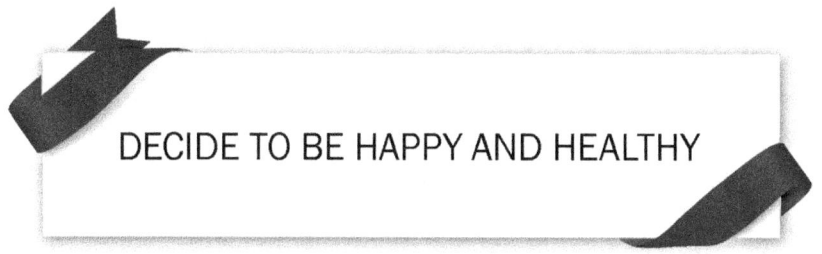

DECIDE TO BE HAPPY AND HEALTHY

When you decide to be happy, and stay happy, you're a happy soul. You don't ever have to search for happiness anywhere outside yourself, or expect anybody to make you happy. You are your source of happiness. Your happy smiles and attitude add to the happiness of others.

Happy is not a designer purse, red sports car, fancy clothes, boob job, or even a vacation home, although we may sometimes think it is, and falsely equate any happiness with the attainment of things or the lack thereof.

Happiness and health are states of being, and they are our natural states. We don't just feel happiness in a moment due to happenstance. If that were the case, then all the same things would make all people happy. Yet we all know, there are those of us who have no worldly goods to speak of, and they're happy all the time. On the other hand, there are those of us with all the riches in the land, yet they never have a moment's peace, or a smile on their face, or a second of joy, and may even seek destruction. What we perceive as happy moments come from the realm of happiness which we decide to, or not to, inhabit. We are happy, or we're not, because, to be happy, we have to choose it. We choose happiness as a cornerstone of who we are and are meant to be. Being happy is part of what we're meant to do, of the life we lead to make a contribution.

Conversely, sadness is a choice. Some of us rationalize sadness as a condition imposed from the great beyond. If that were the case, then the same things would make us equal sufferers. Yet some of us scarcely suffer at all, and some of us go through the tortures of the damned on a regular basis, no matter how much goodness comes our way. No matter who, or what, we're given. Sadness isn't a function of unequal luck, or good or bad fortune, or beating the odds. It results from individuals choosing what they wish to feel. Once they choose, they feel it. Simple.

Happy is a choice.

Let's say, two individuals get the same news. One of them sees it as good news—or bad news from which good can come. This person filters it through a happy outlook, sees the upside of what's occurred, and then gets even happier, sensing new possibilities. The other person sees the news as another heavy cross to bear, strains it through their sadness filter, processes it as unhappiness, and only becomes more miserable, hoping to spread their misery around like a viral pneumonia. Either way, it's all because of choice. Choose to be happy, attract more you can be happy about. Happiness brings more happiness. Sadness begets more stuff to be sad about.

Happy people are generally healthier, both physically and mentally. Happy people tend to stay healthier over time as they age chronologically, and are far less likely to get sick. Disease is just that—dis-ease. Unease. Thus, even if illness befalls happy people, they tend to recover more quickly, and go on to lead a happy life. A happy mind-body connection signals our cells, body parts and antibodies that all is well, and will be well, and we tend to experience wellness as a predictable result. Happiness can be a buffer if and when difficulties come along, and this provides great benefits, including lessening stress and pain, increasing creativity, and clearing the way for ideas and solutions that unhappy minds may not access. Therefore, happiness isn't just a feeling, it's a complete modality.

Sadness is stressful and painful in itself, and it is debilitating. We can decide to avoid its effects by clinging to all of the good in our lives, and steeping ourselves in our happiness and gratefulness, no matter what. Physical and psychological pain are dependent upon us feeling them. They must have our permission to rule our lives and make us react instead of responding in ways that might improve our lot. When we center our psyches in happiness, we refuse to give pain a home in us. This isn't to say we will never feel pain, for we may, but in our resolve to be happy, we gain such a positive footing that a negative episode will likely pass rather than take hold, because it is anathema to how we want to feel, and to how we're accustomed to feeling.

Resentment, anger and despair cannot exist within the framework happiness provides for us. Happiness is a barrier to deleterious input from without, as well as a magnet for the good we wish for in our lives. Love animates our happiness, and love is inexhaustible, so happiness replenishes with every good vibe that comes our way, and every good feeling that we arouse.

When all of your energy sparks from a happy, healthy outlook, your light shines so brightly that it alone can change the world.

FOUR

THE COAST IS CLEAR

> YOUR PASSION IS YOUR PURPOSE

Whatever is waking you up in the morning eager to get out and go, go, go—this is what you're meant to do. Good to know, right? Effective, too. Even if you haven't wrapped your arms completely around your Meant-To-Do, or you're into the concept but haven't yet claimed exactly what your function is, deep down inside, you know why you're here. Your Meant-To-Do never hides from you or becomes a complex riddle. It is a persistent urge, and it's poised to take over the tedious aspects of your life and make them zing. You were not born to trudge through a life that bores you out of your mind each day. That's not how it's supposed to work. You are designed for greatness, and you are outfitted for your particular brand of greatness with each tool required. You have all the talents, skills and traits you need to do your part in making the world a better place.

If you're working at something that doesn't work for you, it's time to change. If you're miserable, or feeling resentful, unproductive, or depressed, you have only to process the fact that your life is dynamic. It's always changing. All you must do to improve your life is to implement change that works for you and makes a contribution.

You'll be delighted with your efforts if they suit you well and bring about the kind of change you want to see. What you contribute is so specific and such a key factor to progress that you cannot afford to while away your time in colorless pursuits. You are constructed to live full out, to see your dreams come true in ways you never dreamed of, never could, and can hardly wrap your mind around once they blossom from nothing to something that wasn't apparent until you created it. Do what you are meant to do, for what you do is what no one else can. Not in the way, and at the time, you do it. In the continuum, you are the perfect messenger for the message burning in your heart, in the time and space it's gestating. Once it's in your mind, and past your lips, and into the work of your hands, it's not only the joy of your life, but the glee of the world. Your dream is meant to be.

You are intended to feel the privilege of working and playing at what you love so much that the very thought of it can make your body tingle. If you're thinking that isn't your life right now, the good news is you are already changing. Conscious change is occurring in you right this instant. Considering change, and reading these words, and expanding your thoughts into how you will change is already reworking who you are, and what you will be doing next.

You have the power to change yourself enough to change the entire world. Believe it. You are engaging in that now.

You are changing right before your eyes. And from now on, you're going to change for the better with every single change you make—because that's your imperative. You're not going to let outer forces change you willy-nilly anymore. You're going to change deliberately. You're going to change as you're meant to change, to evolve to the person you're meant to be. You have already taken a major step toward the center of your bailiwick by seeking means to change yourself and in so doing change the world. By striving to be all you're meant to be and do what you're meant to do, you're remodeling the design of your life, and re-building it from the inside out. You're constructing a new reality brick by brick each time you formulate an unconventional thought to advance the cause of civilization.

In the time you are spending with me in this book, in the mind meld we're forging now, you're transforming your life, and transforming mine as a writer wanting to share my truth with you in our effort to change the world. And you're changing all around you, just by acting out of good intent, and infusing insights into the Zeitgeist that would not break through without you. You are gifted, and you are a major gift. When you channel all your energy into the funnel of your true blue gifts, what you can achieve is immeasurable.

You have a function, a mission, a why and wherefore. You yourself are a dream. You are an aspiration of the Universal Mind. There is a reason you were created, and why your heart is beating now. You are a big idea, my friend. An idea so big, it has taken the form of a body, a spirit and a soul. You're here in this life with premeditation, something implanted within you that is destined to come alive. You are a force majeure so irresistible and incomparable that you cannot be controlled or repressed by any earthly force. Whatever good you believe to be your Higher Power, it's your source, and you are one with all there is. The universe, in all its wisdom, has planned a very special locus for you, as a singular possibility. You have potential that no one else has, and yet you are able to up the potential of all that is and is to be. You are a truth that has yet to be told as long as you are drawing breath. What you achieve in your human incarnation is a giant step in not only your own transformation, but the evolution of the cosmos.

Whatever has happened in your life, whoever you've been, wherever you've gone, whatever mistakes you may have made, or not made, while getting to where you are right now, in this moment, you're on the road to a great unfolding destiny. Nothing past can hold you back. Your future is what you make of it. You are headed straight upward toward the stars, the sun, the moon, and all there is. You need only open your heart and mind to the endeavor that awaits you, beckoning you with open arms. Ahead is every possibility for exponential good for you, and for others through you. Collectively, we are the greater good eager to happen.

You are an opening into the heavenly world of all the good there is. You are a part of every single being in the universe. Who you are, and what you do, is rippling throughout every subatomic particle in creation. You are in the nucleus of every atom that exists, because everything in the universe comes from the stardust of that one Big Bang that created all the galaxies. You are in all, and all is within you, so your potential is off the charts. You are all the good there is, and all the good there is, is you. And me. And every one of us. And just like the stars and every grain of sand, you are unique. There is no other you, and there never will be. The universe makes only one-of-a-kinds. This is how custom-made you are. Even if you have a twin, or a doppelgänger, or a clone somewhere, it will never be you, and you'll never be it.

You do not have to compare yourself with any other person on the planet. You do not have to reach for what others reach for, or attain it. You can set your sights on targets no one else can see, and bull's-eye them. You are not meant for what others are meant for, and others are wasting their time if they should seek to replicate the incredible character that is YOU. You have a solitary Meant-To-Be, an expectation in you, placed there as a sacred trust. I, along with everyone else, am hoping to see the divine in what you become. We know there is something imprinted in you that bears a gift for all of us. We know there is something in each of us that constitutes a gift for you. We know that together we can conceive a world that works for all of us, and we're willing to give our all for it. We know hunger, war, disease and homelessness are not meant to plague anyone. We know corruption, greed, and the ravages wrought of inequality aren't meant to be, and need to change. We know love should rule the world in all the places it does not. We know terrible things aren't meant to stand, and good comes through us all. We believe we all have what it takes to facilitate change. We know that we each have a Meant-To-Be. We understand you have a Meant-To-Be too. And we know that you have a passion for what is needed to accomplish yours, because we have passion driving us.

Feel your passion. Follow it. Examine why it's come to you. Give over to the many ways your passion can make things happen. Believe that your passion is guiding you to do great deeds your rational mind might once have deemed impossible. Know that whatever it is you enjoy and thirst to accomplish is calibrated for magnitude, that your passion derives from who you are, and from what you'll contribute as you realize your ultimate potential.

There's no separation between what drives you, what you decide to achieve in life, and what you must do to transform yourself into living your best life in the now while helping others do the same. The highest level of what you desire is no doubt what you're supposed to enjoy.

Your most elevated self-image is the hero you'll soon become.

The thrill you feel when you paint, or draw, or lecture, design a fantastical structure, write, cook a sumptuous gourmet meal, teach a searching young mind how to think for itself, fly a helicopter, plant a garden, surf, sing songs, invent, be a carpenter, or click a photograph is with you in your heart of hearts for a reason—to propel you. To cause you to do what you're meant to do as you become who you're meant to be.

Ignoring your passion stunts your growth and deprives the world, and deprives yourself, of your wonder and magnificence. Treat your passion like a loving friend. Sink into it. Let it envelop you. Let your passion drive you through each choice and moment. Let it guide you. Heed it. Feed it with your actions. Act not out of willfulness, but from willingness to do your part, to allow all good to come to you and through you. This will aid us all. Cherish the good your own goodness creates and brings to you and everyone. If you hide your light under a bushel, it will smolder until it eventually overheats, bursts into flames of passion you cannot control, and consumes the bushel and your light. Avoid letting your Meant-To-Do lay to waste. Let passion fuel your gratitude and ignite your flame of happiness. Let products, services, new ideas, creations and connections gush forth from you like a fountain. Claim passion as the origin of perfect timing, deals and offers. Let it devise your master plan.

Surrender to your passion, and the world will open like a lily.

The passion you feel for your Meant-To-Do is the key to opening every lock. Let it be the beacon that lights the way, and doors you once perceived as closed will turn into magic portals. You'll no longer be dredging up things to do. You'll no longer be subject to boredom. You'll no longer be searching for who you are. The evidence of who you are will appear all around as what you do. The sage that you are meant to be will work to flood the atmosphere with a steady stream of miracles you tenaciously facilitate. You will materialize who you are. What you are able to actualize will speak for itself with grace and ease, constituting your offering to the world. And your works will foster a cycle of growth in your ongoing metamorphosis.

Whatever struggles you have had will vanish to the full extent that your resistance wanes.

Take care to avoid wasting energy and passion on what you do not want. What you resist, you feed with your energies, making more and more of it, causing undesirables to persist, remain strong, and frequently recur.

If you are frustrated with anything, letting it weigh on your mind and heart, you can put a halt to all of it by realizing just one thing: The universe doesn't recognize that the energy you're investing into what you don't want to happen is expended to make it stop. The universe only sees your attention directed to a certain point. Energy flows where attention goes. If you focus on what you do not want instead of investing your energy into what you want to happen—even if you consider yourself to be focusing on it to will it away—you are energizing a negative, and in doing so, bringing more of it. Unwittingly, but nonetheless.

Though resistance is the opposite of passion, they employ the selfsame energy, and that energy is gleaned from you. So if you're resisting something, change your course and turn that ship around. Or better yet, bail out of it. Launch a new Love Boat with passion and purpose, and sail into your future using your energies to create a life that works for you and everyone.

Once you are centered in directing your passion, resistance ebbs and progress flows. No more resistance, no more pain. No more judging what has brought you pain. No resistance, no judgment, no more pain. You end one cycle and start on another. Your Meant-To-Be/Meant-To-Do Cycle is attracting all you want to you, and your feelings of love and gratitude are all you need to change the world.

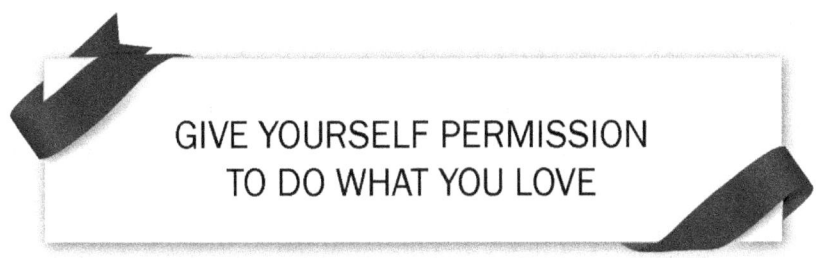

GIVE YOURSELF PERMISSION TO DO WHAT YOU LOVE

Now that you know your passion has prospects, how do you go about acting on it? How can you do what you're meant to do, and become more of who you're meant to be?

The first thing to do is to grant yourself permission to do the things you love.

Oops! Oh, my. Did that strike a nerve? Are you thinking, *do the things I love?* Are you kidding, who has time for that. What with the 25-8 wacky schedule I'm forced to be holding down at work, and the spouse, and the house, and the louse I work for, my great kids and all their needs, and my parents with their declining health, and the bills, and the hills I've had to climb. Enjoy? Don't be ridiculous. Get a grip. Do what I love? Ask me if I can even remember the things I like to do these days. Liked, I mean. Back in the day. Past tense are the times I heeded what I need and what I truly want.

What self-respecting professional doesn't dread her job and rue a life that didn't exactly turn out right and isn't what she thought it'd be. It's a requisite, being dissatisfied, isn't it? Isn't everybody? Isn't it just a part of life to see everyone else's grass as greener? Isn't that what I'm supposed to do, regret the life I'm leading and the cage I've built around myself. Shouldn't I long for what I don't have, and all I haven't accomplished in my semi-conscious trudge toward who-knows-what and who-knows-where. Who can keep up with the Joneses. I might even *be* the Joneses now, and still my life ain't cutting it, because something is missing, and I don't know what. How in the heck can I change the world when I can't even change myself?

When I can't even change my Internet service provider, or my flat front tire, or my voracious appetite, or my lack of an appetite at all, or the fact I hardly sleep at night or feel like I want to sleep all day. When I can't stop the neighbors from making noise, or that driver from cutting me off on the freeway, or how the bank constantly rips me off. Huh? Go on, then. Answer that.

Well, I hear you, and I can answer that.

You can change anything in your life.

You are The Changer, and you are The Change.

Try it today, and you'll see what I mean. Decide how you want your day to go, and see if it turns out just that way. Decide you won't have to wait on a line anywhere you go for business. Decide it's going to be peaceful in your neighborhood while you work at home. Decide whoever you thought was back-stabbing you actually is an ally now, maybe always was a friend, and that working with them will be easier. Act on that, expecting change.

Maybe the reason things seem off-kilter is you're not doing what you love. You're not acting on your Meant-To-Do, to become more of who you're meant to be. That's right, if you do what you don't want to do, you are cloaked in clothes that do not suit you, asking the universal source to give you more of what you don't want rather than what you want. Your life is taking its cues from you. It isn't happening *to* you, it is happening due to what you think and do, assuming it's what you wish. The universe wants you to have what you need, and it wants you to be happy. It figures what you do is what you love, and what you think about is what you want to come to pass. It doesn't deal in fear and doubt. It knows naught of worry. It doesn't perceive you feel downtrodden because you have compromised your ethics, sacrificed, or made mistakes. It doesn't compute in success and failure, it only circulates energy. When you do what you love, it responds to that by giving you more and more to love.

If you continue to do what doesn't work, you're effectively building more of it. You're rejecting all possibilities beyond your current paradigm, and you're limiting your experience to the punishing aspects of your life, complaining as if they are all that can be. If you focus your thoughts on what you wish were different, while you remain the same, you are asking for more of what you don't want, believing it won't, and cannot, change—and you're drawing that into reality, making it into the headspace that you live in, choking off your good. You are closing your fist to both giving and to receiving. This isn't who you are. You're a lover. Flip the script.

Do what you love, and the spillover from it translates into more self-love and agape love for and from others. Practice love in everything, and love becomes your driving force. Pure love becomes your Meant-To-Be. When love is your Meant-To-Be and your Meant-To-Do, you're energy is in sync with the consummate substance of the universe.

You can't help doing what you love when love is who you are. And conversely, when love is who you are, you can't help doing what you love. This is the state of blessedness, the paradise of Utopia. Being love and doing love. This is the heavenly rapture from which global change erupts. Here, you will find euphoria.

You can climb to this plane of beatitude quite easily, and in the blink of an eye. Let go of the guilt, and the shame, and the blame unhappiness and ill will contain. Drop what you're doing right now, if you have to, and bring your actions into balance with the center of your love. Be in your love, and do from your love.

You aren't alone if you're thinking it's impractical to enjoy your work. It seems to have crept in as pack mentality that whatever turns you on can only be an avocation, a fly by night hobby rendered to weekends, something you must set aside for vacations, or entirely. No serious person seeking success could possibly turn bird-watching or a love of knitting into cash, right? Why in the world would one even try. Be a doctor, a lawyer, a banker, a thief. Otherwise, live on the ragged edge, and have everyone think you're a dud. Get a real job, or be ridiculed and chance living cast out on the street. You may be exposed to this value system through family, friends, professional peers, fellow students, teachers, colleagues, bosses, government, neighbors, or the like, but that doesn't make it legitimate. You define what constitutes success. Only you can decide what's right for you, undeterred by what would your colleagues think should you ditch your illustrious career to become a horticulture buff or work to save the planet.

You aren't alone in a cycle of dissatisfaction or frustration with the way the world seems to have turned to hate, if that's what you think, or what you've thought, even though it's just an illusion. For hate is confined to a twisted few. It's not just the lyrics of a song that love is what makes the world go 'round. It is the reality. It's the unvarnished truth of life. Nor are you alone in the thought syndrome that what happens in life comes to you from without, and not from a place within yourself. Many of us feel certain shifts, but we also sense our power of one, our ability to direct our lives and affect the lives of others. Many of us want to change the world, but far fewer do something about it.

You know you are built for change. You know you are here to uplift and inspire.

Only you and your Higher Power get to guide your passion to your dream. Only you get to act on your Meant-To-Do, and become the full breadth of your Meant-To-Be. No one is the boss of you. Give yourself permission. You are the captain of your ship. Guide that sucker out to sea. Steer your vessel through choppy waters. Guide it past the rough seas to a calmer strait where you can float your boat and feel scot-free. Dock if you have to, to get your bearings, but chart your course with your moral compass. It's your choice. So make it. Now. You'll have no one to blame but yourself if you don't, and the blame game isn't fun to play. You know that. It's played out. You're the best judge of what's best for you. You survived to go on to triumph, right? You're smart. You're aware. You're intuitive, baby. Do it. Make your move.

Meditate. Take some yoga lessons. Go within. Educate yourself. Read at your library. Haunt the bookstore. Watch free videos on the Web. Take time to give yourself a chance to remember how awesome it can feel to do just what you want to do. Ooh ooh, doesn't that feel good? Pursue what you're made for. Go for it.

Make a list of the times you've felt most free and known the greatest well of joy in the last ten days, ten months, ten years. Go at it train-of-thought. You might be surprised at what comes up once you open your mind to the fact that you can do anything you want. Maybe what you've been thinking was upping your happiness isn't the same as it was. Maybe your bliss has relocated far from its last-known address. You've changed, so maybe it has too. Or maybe it hasn't, but it's been ignored. Explore it. See where the passion is. It won't bite. It's waiting to hear from you. It's looking for you. It's missed your smile. It can't wait to hear you laugh. Take the time you need to scratch the itch, to heal the hurt, to open up, to tickle your fancy all you want, to search in the deepest parts of you for what's trying so hard to peck out.

This isn't just for you, it's for the whole world you contribute to. You aren't the only searching soul who'll benefit when you fill in the gap between who you are now and who you can be. What you're meant to carry out is so much bigger than any task or individual. It's an exoplanet way beyond this solar system, off in space. It began before spacetime, has no bounds, and stretches beyond our Milky Way galaxy into all eternity.

Doesn't it warrant the hours ahead to come to grips with who you are, and all you're meant to be and do? I certainly think it does. I think you're worth much more than that. I think you're a singular, priceless creation. I for one am longing to embrace your finished product.

Engage with the things you love to do. Grab the hall pass, a big bunch of gold stars and the key to the recreation room. You can enjoy the things you love, and believe they're what you're supposed to do.

What you love is subject to shift and change, and that's more than okay, it's everything. It means that you're evolving. Your priorities may reorganize, but the constant of knowing who you are, and that you're meant for something big is the central focus of your faith that what you are doing is going to work well, and lift yourself and others. So, grant yourself a security clearance, trust yourself to get after it, and give yourself some room to breathe. Let go of the notion that work isn't fun, and go out and find, and live, your bliss.

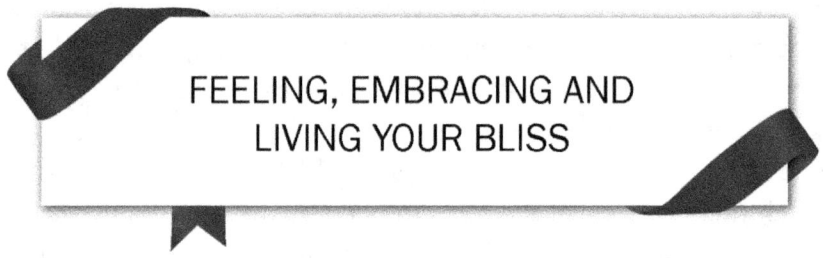

FEELING, EMBRACING AND LIVING YOUR BLISS

It isn't a matter of finding bliss for many of us, but of following it. Of letting our bliss guide the way we live and how we make our choices.

To upgrade your level of happiness, let your bliss infuse your work and imbue your life with meaning. There's a reason certain things feed your bliss. Your bliss is there as a leading indicator of what you're meant to do, and the space you're meant to occupy. Bliss arrives when you're on course and behaving in sync with what you're meant to do. Think. Why does sex feel so good? It exists to help us procreate, so we thrive and survive as a species, right? Orgasms rocket us toward that end. Well, our bliss is meant to do the same—to lead us to doing and being that which will help us to thrive and survive singly and together as Team Humanity. Our bliss cannot come from the sorrow of others. We are one, and our bliss is interdependent.

We often put aside our bliss, or shroud it in guilt and recrimination. Shame it, as if it were something shameful, shocking, bad or self-indulgent. Bliss isn't meant to help us escape any real responsibilities, or shirk duties in favor of selfish whims. And yeah, if one's bliss came in serial killing, lying, cheating, greed or theft, eschewing such bliss would be apt and necessary for mankind. Those kinds of feelings accompany sickness. That isn't genuine bliss at all. Nor are the temporary ups that come from indulging harmful habits. Most of us find a healthy bliss in helping others, moving forward, working to build a better future, and living moments gracefully. Most of our bliss comes from what we create, from families to works of art. Bliss urges us to be our best in everything we think and do. Our bliss is here to fuel our drive and passion for our Meant-To-Do. What brings us happy feelings helps us know why we're alive.

If you have been stuck in survival mode, unaware that your life deserves ecstasy, you're in for a treat from here on out. Operating as if on a treadmill is a compromise no blissful person wants to accept or tolerate. It's wasteful to spend your life force and good karma mired in a dreary plight. Your body is just going to last for as long as it does, so though you're an eternal being, you don't want to be left with what-if's in an hour from now, far less in your waning years. You were born in bliss, and in bliss you are meant to remain, so accept nothing less than bliss.

Your bliss is for you to define and declare. For some, this may simply mean ultimate peace. For others, no less than orgasmic euphoria meets the definition. The meaning of bliss may depend on the personality you bring to it. There's your theory of bliss as a concept, then there's your concept of what constitutes your bliss on a personal level. Bliss is golfing, for one. Bliss is kids, for another. Maybe the word *bliss* sends the right person into the state with the sound of it.

The Merriam-Webster Dictionary defines the word bliss with the short and sweet phrase "complete happiness". What makes your happiness complete? Do you know? Have you ever considered it?

Whether or not you have pondered such thoughts, let's consider right now if you're happy at all. If you are, is your happiness complete? Could there be such a thing as an incomplete happiness? What could make happiness incomplete? Does happiness have different levels? Is it measured on a sliding scale? There's no doubt that some people consider contentment as happiness. Is that complete? Isn't it enough to be content with the miracle that is life?

When I think of bliss, I think heaven. Valhalla. Everything that is paradise. And I have explored and been in this state of being for prolonged periods, for years and decades at a time. I've felt bliss in spurts in more difficult incarnations of my life. My life seems to have spanned several lifetimes at this point, and I'm certain I know what bliss is. Is that enough? Or is bliss a condition, once reached, that must endure throughout a lifetime. Like Zen mastery accomplished through deep meditative practices and study. So it never wavers, never ebbs.

I believe we are meant to live in bliss, to find and own what makes us blissful, help other people live their bliss, know bliss as a function of knowing ourselves, and ride bliss like a wild stallion. I believe we are meant to live the full spectrum of hues of what bliss can mean to us, and evolve ourselves to embody bliss. I believe bliss is unlimited in its ability to revolutionize, to transmute whatever energies we've transmitted across the world until now to reconstruct our paradigm, so life can be lived as a whole new experience, singly and as one.

Living our bliss changes everything. Dropping all pretense of what we are trained or advertised into thinking is a prerequisite for our happiness propels us into the genuine arena of examining what bliss is, and what it can do for us.

What would you rather be doing right now than what you're doing, anything? If so, go out and do it! Nobody's stopping you, but you. When I see bumper stickers, license plates and other signage stuff that proudly declares: "I'd rather be fishing", "I'd rather be flying", "I'd rather be in this place or that", I think to myself, "Well, go for it, pal." Why on earth would you brag about feeling trapped and unable to do what you want to do. Why advertise to the whole wide world that you feel you can't go where you wish, when we all know you can. Why would you plaster all over your car your apparent inability to accept responsibility for your life, and what your life can mean. That's no badge of honor. Rock your bliss. Bliss is your birthright.

There are those still searching for their bliss, and you may well be in that spot. That's cool, you're laying groundwork. You'll find bliss in unexpected places, people, aha moments, priceless gifts and musings. You put out an APB for bliss. You know it's out there somewhere. Maybe not on that dating website, easily accessible. You might have to dig around for a while on your own to determine where bliss lives, but discovering bliss can be bliss in itself, because bliss dwells inside you. It might not be stickered to your ride or emblazoned on your forehead yet, but it's coming, and when that gift arrives, tear into it. Wear it like a mantle. Keep bliss closer than your skin. Let nothing come between your bliss and you, for it explains your life. Define exactly what you want your blissful dreams to lead you to, and go for it wholeheartedly.

Determine the Who, What, When, Where, How and Why your bliss is yours to keep, and be sure not to settle for anything less.

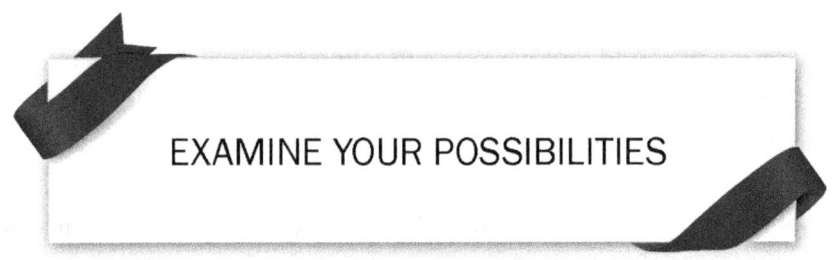

EXAMINE YOUR POSSIBILITIES

Your life has possibilities beyond what you're imagining. Possibilities are unlimited for you and everybody else. The pool of possibilities has not one limitation. Limitations are only in the mind. You can do all you imagine, everything on which your heart is fixed. So much more than you might be conceiving from your current unfolding perspective.

If a doubt arose when you read this truth—*The Truth of Unlimited Possibles*—examine where your doubt came from, then release it to the stars. It's imperative you believe in *The Truth of Unlimited Possibles* in your life, for only with this staunch belief can you realize your dreams. Your Meant-To-Be and Meant-To-Do reside in *Unlimited Possibles*. You're going to have to rely on them to build the bridges you will cross. The U.P.'s are your closest friends, and they can take you anywhere. They're like forceful sci-fi heroes come to rescue you from a ho-hum life. But U.P. heroes are for real, they aren't science fiction. You have their supernatural strengths. You can walk through walls and shatter glass ceilings, fly over mountains, breathe underwater, heal, time travel, and see in the dark. Believe in possibilities. They are omnipresent. All the time. Anything is possible —and that means every dream you dream.

Any and all you're hoping for is a dream *because* it's possible.

You yourself are a possibility.

You once were a *Possible*. Now you are. And what's possible through you is already real, providing that's how you perceive your potential and use it for the good.

You dream the possibilities in which you are the major player intended to spin a possibility into a narrative that plays out. You are the star of the movie in your mind, because you've been cast for it by a universe working perfectly. You are the perfect actor for the role of the dreamer of your dream. You are set to produce a story that will have a happy ending.

Root yourself in the fundamental truth that anything is possible. And it is—and I mean, anything. Any anything. Including yours. You have the power to bring about good in ways and shapes unknown to you. Know that the universe works with you to bring about such miracles as no one can conceive of now. Who pondered the scope of the Internet before it came to be? Once only the germ of a great idea, the idea was pursued, and fed, and grew into something beyond the dreamers field of vision. It took on a life of its own, the duration and ultimate fruition of which has yet to be revealed.

Examine your possibilities. Look around, and inside, you with gratitude, and plumb the depths of all you are, and have, to make a dream come true. A dream bigger than you. A dream so big that it will take a stand, make change, and bend the course of history. A dream that is born from your self-love, and the love you harbor for all humanity, creatures and your Higher Power.

Use what you have to get what you want—for yourself, and to bring change to the world.

Our dreams become our future world when we pursue them bravely, and with love that's all encompassing. Love everyone. Love all the time. Love with all your open heart, and a gamut of possibilities will reveal itself, take hold of you, and make you a vessel of pure potentiality that translates to fact.

With everything possible, you must choose. Your moment-to-moment and daily choices of where to place your energies determine outcomes far beyond your one life. All you do is huge. Pebbles you toss in the water we all swim in ripple out in waves. Gentle waves that tug along the shore and feed the ocean's life, or tidal waves that can destroy.

What you do with your possibilities is on you, and that's a simple fact.

No matter who you are, or where you came from, or whatever's gone before, there's a range of possibilities for what you can do and who you can be that can be curbed by only you. Nothing can make you finite but your own decision that you are. Decide right now to be all you can be. Believe you can do anything. Make up your mind to put your faith and talents to a worthy task. Call upon your U.P. to display your alternatives clearly, so you comprehend all that is doable. Decide in this moment to do all you can to be an inimitable force for change that must, and will, arise from you. Be matchless in determination, unwavering from discipline.

Examine all of the possibilities revealed to you.

What first step do you want to take?

Take out a pad and a pen, or whatever you have at hand, and make a list. You can jot it in your phone perhaps, write it down on the back of a store receipt. Whatever you've got. Just do it now. Make a list of the thoughts you are having of things you want to do, or feel you must. The visions you see when you close your eyes. The places you go in your daydreams, have a passion for, adore. The people you think of consistently and feel you have a connection with, connection to, or want to meet. The activities you want to do at times your mind goes numb with boredom watching to-do lists grow with tasks you feel an increasing aversion to.

Just look at the wonders you can pursue. Contemplate what feeds your bliss, stretches you beyond your bounds, and might most alter things to come. What's most suited for you, and calls to you? Listen as you write your list. The impetus for what you write is your Meant-To-Be and Meant-To-Do. Write freely what your soul is seeking. Meditate, and go within. Quiet your mind of external and internal voices that may chatter to you about far less vital subjects than the meaning of your life. If any voice tries to censor you, instead hear what your instincts say. Tap into your peace of mind. This is your time, and these are your choices.

Your choices line up in a daisy chain to formulate what happens next. Today's thoughts are tomorrow's reality. Let your higher self write your list for you. Experiment. Write down fun things. Whatever you find you're afraid of, list with a star, and determine to tackle it first. That's likely to be the move that takes you to your highest peak. Keep jotting until you sense your list contains all the elements you need. However long it takes, keep at it. Nobody owns your time but you. You know how best to spend it. If it takes a few minutes, wonderful. You're in touch with your needs, and you know what you want, even if only peripherally. You think about your destiny. You pretty much know where your passions lie. If it takes weeks, well, that's swell too. You need to take time to find your way forward with increasing happiness. Your list is your opportunity to take a look at where you are, and where it is you want to go. You can benefit from solitude. Take whatever time you need to consult with yourself, take stock of things, learn about your current state, and plumb the full depth of your true desires.

If creating your list is difficult, start by thinking of what you enjoyed in your past, or perhaps what drives you nuts right now, so you can let it go. Take a few strolls down memory lane, to the places where memory lane is filled with light, love, likes and satisfaction. Think of a time in your life when you felt fulfilled, refreshed, renewed, enthusiastic. What was happening then? Who was with you? Where were you? Someplace different? In your same locale? What were you doing? How did it happen? Would similar circumstances bring you happiness again, or still? Have you grown out of it, or might you want to revisit what made you happy then? What made you discontinue it? Is it worth giving another go? Or might it be best to clear the cobwebs, start off with a brand new slate?

Did you replace some activities, persons, challenges or interests that could stir good feelings up again? Did life's demands delay your course? Did responsibilities weigh you down? Is your source of joy unknown to you, or dormant now? Or are you just putting the good times off because you concluded life sucks? Are you convinced your past mistakes truncated your possibilities, relegating you to a blasé life? At what point in your progress did you lose your passion for something that made you, you? Did someone talk you out of it? Or did you go at it and merely give up when success didn't happen as fast as you'd like? When did you stop, and where did you stop, if you did, pursuing your higher calling, knowing you are meant for greatness?

You are meant for something BIG!

Is there something you feel could be holding you back? If there is, it is just an illusion. Nothing is holding you back. You're a star. You're an idea whose time has come, and nothing is more powerful. Not a hurricane wind or an earthquake tremor. Nothing can possibly stop you, but you, and you're all systems go. Start by freeing yourself from the sad misconception that any tie is binding you. You're free, and if you're not feeling free, that hiccup is worth examining.

Is there something you see others do, that you wish you could do and think you'd like, that you feel you could ace if you gave it a go, and yet, for some reason, you didn't check out?

The parade isn't passing you by, my friend. You're passing it by, if you feel unfulfilled, and aren't yet pushing past that point. You aren't meant to stagnate. If you're passively standing on the sidelines, actively avoiding change and bringing change into your life, there has to be a reason. You need to know what that reason is, so you can debunk its hold on you. Do you figure you're not the parading type? Could it be that you convinced yourself you don't, or can't, march forward, sing, ride floats, play music, celebrate or revel in being alive? Of course, you parade. Put parade on your list. It's your list. It's a definite possibility. You can parade anytime you want. And no one can rain on your parade. Get to the bottom of what's going on inside you, then come out and play. Parade like there's no tomorrow. There *is* no tomorrow, there's only now. Tomorrow is now when you get to it, and let's face it, that's not guaranteed.

This is your life, and your life is a party. Break out the balloons, and the cake and ice cream. Open presents. Have a blast. Touch what you love, and make note of it. Explore what makes you happy. Open up to a different *Possible*. It could well be your ticket to ride. It's likely it could change the world. It's meant to. It's your all-access pass.

When your list is chock full of delicious possibilities that bring you joy, take a look at your likely priorities. Which of the possibilities do you want to be probabilities—the things you probably will pursue as professional goals or pastimes. What is a probable vocation? What is a probable avocation? Picture your days as you want them to shake out. What are you doing?

You might want to evaluate your list with an eye to balancing various elements—your career, professional lifestyle, physical, mental and emotional health. Your personal life, your home, finances, where, and for whom, you might volunteer, a diverse and thriving social life, your spiritual development, romance, the whole shebang. It's your world, buddy. Cram it with meaning. Meaning for you, and your family and friends, your community, and those you'll never meet who'll benefit from your choices. Choose the biggest and boldest effect you can have. The best effect. The loftiest. You can make the world a better place.

Go on, narrow your list to a Top Ten List. It can change, of course, but begin it now. You have favorites, you know what they are. Favorite pastimes, people, places, things. Let passion drive your every choice.

What was the thing you wanted to do when you grew up? Remember it? If you feel some resistance, indulge yourself. Do you recall how adults used to ask you, "What do you want to be when you grow up?" Is your answer on the list? If it is, is it at the top? If it isn't, why? Do you want it there? Were you going to be an astronaut? An Olympic skater? Santa Claus? Santa runs a non-profit, has for years. I bet you could do the same. Maybe skating could get you off the couch and into a gig teaching underserved kids. It could be their leg up. As an amateur astronomer, you might be the one to discover a new exoplanet, sun or solar system, changing our view of outer space. You could be who discovers life there. Or, let's see, were you going to be a nurse? Then go get your nursing certificate. There's nothing standing in your way. Not your age, or your sex, or your current gig. You can change a lot of sick folks' lives with your special brand of healing.

Possibilities loom for a reason, and the reason isn't only you. A *Possible* is meant to give, and share, and light the world. Bliss isn't a temporal feeling. It is a place where you take up residence. It's the opening to possibilities that spur us on to giant shifts in the tectonic plates of connectedness that move us forward as a people. Possibilities point out our piece in the puzzle of life that works for everyone. Possibilities aren't just fantasies, they're the stepping stones into the garden of life that feeds, and grows, and guides us all.

Now you're ready to pare down your list to three, among which a grandest *Possible* will speak to you, inspiring you to form a plan, make definite goals, and take action regarding the tasks you must do to complete your goals in a set timeframe.

One thing is for sure—your greatest and finest achievements are yet to come, if you only believe that's true, and you set out to make your dreams come true with the greater good in heart and mind. It all starts from the place where you feel your greatest bliss, and see possibilities with no limit to their depth or breadth.

"Follow your bliss" isn't just a saying. It's a doorway to success, the key to all things possible, and a pillar of everlasting change.

When you love without limits, you change the world.

FOCUS POCUS

LOVE YOURSELF AND LOVE OTHERS

Choose to be love itself, and everything good will naturally follow.

Do everything with love, and you will see your world change before your eyes.

Love is the beginning, the middle and the end.

All things start with love, as it is the substance of their creation.

Love creates, and continues to expand, the universe and all things in it, including us human beings. Love is the life force that sustains us. Love keeps all things going and growing. Love is the most potent, poignant, productive entity and energy. Love cannot be superseded, destroyed, reduced, nor in any way compromised. Love is the answer to every question, solution to any pressing issue, spark of every new idea. Love is the nadir and the pinnacle. Love is the uniting force that draws and assembles us into one. Without love, we humans cannot survive, interact, transform to our highest selves, nor reimagine negatives in our society into positives. Love infuses our lives with mission and meaning. Love is the basis of all good feelings, creative impulses and constructive communication streams. Love is the glue that binds us together. Dreams, goals, beliefs, work, play and family life subsist on love. Love is the motivator that compels us to be more than we've been and do more than we've done.

Love is the catalyst for change, the means by which we change the world. Love and change are inseparable. Love changes us and makes us change. It is because we love that we want the best for ourselves and others. Love moves us to action, and therefore, we strive. To bring about change, we must love as our first, last and only order of business.

When we do everything with love, the world becomes a better place.

In your quest to be a Change Wizard, it is essential that you achieve and sustain your highest and best vibration. As the highest vibration is love, your heart and mind should be set on loving everyone all the time, and doing so with all your heart. Center your thoughts, words and actions in love. Living within this framework, your choices and priorities are a simple matter of deciding which alternative brings the most love to the world, and thus creates the utmost good.

Center your focus on not only what you will do, but more importantly, on what you will ultimately become—which is love itself. What you do is a natural outcropping of how you now believe yourself to be, what you think, the collection of words you say, and the soul you're evolving into. Decide your true nature immediately, for character is significant. The results of your vision of yourself will manifest surely as night follows day. Debase yourself, you'll demean the world. Decide to be more like Jesus, Buddha, Krishna or Muhammad, and you'll spread peace and loving kindness wherever you go. Leave this to chance, and you're subject to dim vibrations and low energies attacking your vision of yourself. Who you are, and what you stand for, is for you to decide and stand firmly within for every moment of your life. Your beliefs and convictions define you, and our collective beliefs and convictions decide the course of world events, the vibration of the universe and the spiritual progression of all future generations.

As a person rooted and centered in love, radiating love at every turn, you change the world for the better with the strength of your existence. Osmotically giving and receiving love, you co-create with the Creator, increasing righteousness and ethicality in all beings.

In order to change the world for the better, strive to be love at your core by practicing love with such relentless passion that your presence drives out any negative emotion, condition or circumstance, and transcends any negative situation. Be an uncompromising lover, for there's no substitute for love, no shortcut around manifesting love in all corners of your environment, and in all endeavors, large and small, with every soul you contact. This is your primary goal.

Being a Love Ambassador is not only crucial to your inner peace, it is essential to the progress and proliferation of world peace. First, represent love, and your love will infuse all else. Even your biggest mistakes will rise and lift others, and your worst instincts become impeccable.

Close your eyes for a minute and envision this: Imagine everyone in the world doing every single thing they do with love. Isn't it incredible? Think of the grocery store checker loving you, packing your grocery bags with care. See drivers in traffic on your commute traveling safely, yielding the right of way. See your co-workers cooperating, pitching in, drumming up ideas, pulling their weight, being thoughtful, considerate, each respecting every other, committed to you and your clients or customers, dedicated, fulfilling needs. Envision every person who crosses your path flashing you a smile, speaking encouraging words to you, performing acts of kindness. Visualize neighbors banding together, being supportive in times of need, celebrating moments of adulation, looking out for each other because they care. What if loving made manufacturers crank out safer products—well-engineered, convenient, affordable, nicely designed, long-lasting. Doesn't the thought of that lift your vibe?

The idea of everyone doing all they do with love as motivation, guideline and intent isn't some fantastical notion. It is real life as it's meant to be. And it can be had for the asking, just by each of us setting our hearts on it. Doesn't this boost your spirits, flood you with hope, encourage you to trust? It's lifting the world as we speak, because possibility is reality, and love is absolute.

One thought can change reality.

A doctrine of life as love is quickly shifting us onto a higher plane. We are lifted by jointly adopting this scenario right now. Living from love animates belief in yourself and others as principle. Adopting this fundamental tenet, you believe you can do anything. As you love, you decide to do only good. As you love, you live an authentic life, because there is no separation between the lover that you claim to be, and the by-products of your loving. Your being is a benefit the instant you set your heart and mind on loving unconditionally.

Love has a beneficent social effect, wide-ranging and all-encompassing. From love springs respect. From respect, comes connection. Connection spawns integrity. Integrity ensures that ethical principles guide your every thought and deed, and direct your moral compass. Love applies your ethics at all times, based on your concept of right and wrong, and what you believe to be true and correct. When the jagged terrain between right and wrong is paved with guidelines you have set for what you will, and will not, do, as a matter of integrity, you bring change where there is no integrity, upgrading discourse and behavior. You bring goodness where goodness has not been valued, strength where there have been weaknesses, logic where thought patterns were unclear. You bring peace where otherwise strife would exist, and might prevail toward no good end. Loving is the right thing at all times, so love makes you a hero, standing tall for what you believe in, which is the application of love to everything and everyone. Love makes you a leader. Love makes you a light. Love makes you a solution. Love makes you a symbol and source of change.

Changing the world takes you changing you, me changing me, and everyone changing as a choice, so the world works better for us all. The unvarnished truth is, you are change. This fact is inescapable. You are change, and change is you.

As we change ourselves, we change each other. We lead by example, association, thoughts, words, deeds and lives well-lived. We interact, and through synergy, we combine our energies to reconstruct the dynamics of our world. Let your essence reflect the kind of change you seek, for this is the only way the swift change you demand may come about. Let YOU uplift the human race and every living creature. Let your associations be among those of good will, for this is your mission, whatever walk of life you choose, whichever path you take. Transform, and be transformative. Your self-transformation is laser light. Your light lights me. My light lights you. Like the rings of Saturn, we light the world when our inner light radiates outward with such brilliance and ferocity that it creates peripheries of light far-reaching and wide enough to stretch beyond the presence of our physical bodies, over miles, around the circumference of the Earth, and into the span of the universe. As spiritual beings, this is our gift. This is our capacity.

We need not be perfect—only perfectly us—to bring light into shadows and overcome what shadows may have fallen on our inner selves as a result of our experiences, the ways of the world, or our own flaws in judgment. Change comes from lessons learned. Become a brighter spirit, and you change the world in increments or leaps and bounds with every breath.

Be grateful, for when we are grateful for all we are, and have, we feel more love. We give out more love from happiness, and a healthy body and wholesome mind.

Love everyone—especially you—through easy and hard times equally. Love all the time, beginning now. Love with all your heart and soul, for the love you give will change the world.

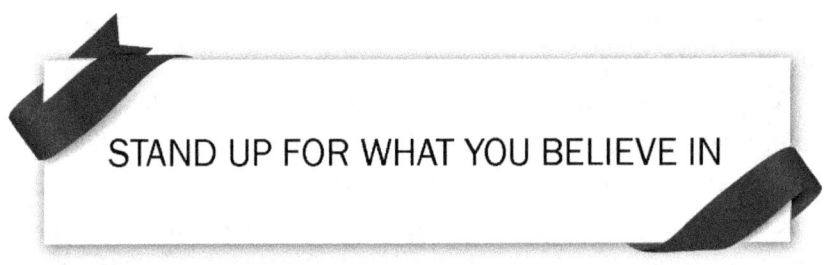

STAND UP FOR WHAT YOU BELIEVE IN

Know what you believe in. This is essential. Belief leads to manifestation. What you believe is going to externalize. To be without beliefs is to be ineffective, inefficient, ineffectual, and inept. Believers become achievers. Non-believers become an afterthought, and wrongly believing thwarts progress because it's disengaged from truth.

You must know what you believe in, and plant your energies into the fertile soil of belief and your own belief system. Your beliefs are the spongy material it takes to achieve your hopes and dreams. Beliefs are readily subject to growth as you transit toward enlightenment.

As we learn more, we do better, but we have to start off with a firm foundation of how we believe we ought to live. What we believe, we act upon, so it's pointless to leave our beliefs to chance in the turmoil of subconscious thought. We live, for the most part, to evolve, to rise higher with every thought we think, into loftier states of consciousness. We achieve higher consciousness largely through the grace of increasing love. As we love one another, we discover beliefs we might otherwise never know we hold. We're compelled, as we love, to assert beliefs in acts and conversation. We trust, or we don't. We are sure love works, or believe that love is for suckers. We are loyal, or we're a fair-weather friend. We gossip, or we believe that others do their very best. We're convinced that people are basically good, or inexorably sinful and bad. We believe in being fair and honest, or we're persuaded we're free to cheat.

None of us can be expected to know everything in a human incarnation, but we can know what we believe and cause it to show up in our lives. We are not omnipotent, but neither are we impotent. We have the power to create, and we're using that power all the time, for better or for worse. We are not omniscient, but neither are we blind to what is needed in the world. Only a power higher than ourselves can make a claim to truth, but, as we our sentient beings, we can seek truth with all our might. We can commit to purveying truth and portraying it in our daily lives. If we start with no beliefs about the world, about life, about what is good, about what we are and are meant to be, we have no understanding, no direction and no precepts. If we fail to form beliefs about how the world should function, what beauty is, and how best to use creativity, we become barbarians at the gates of each other's cognizance. We must believe what agape love can do to afford each other dignity, equality and sanctity of life. We must believe in peace.

Positive change requires of us relentless belief in openness, unbound belief in good, belief in unlimited possibilities, in love, in ourselves and in those around us. Belief in our inextricable link to the source of good from which we come, which resides in us, and in which we live. World change demands this positioning more than ever, for our survival. We cannot leave goodness hung out to dry. We have to actively take its side. We have to take each other's side, and take each other's hands. Let those who wish to divide us, try, but the ultimate truth is: We Are One. No person, nor group of persons, can cause us to lose this reality of our existence. We are one entity, born in love, to live in love eternally. We must make this belief conspicuous, apparent, revealed, unmistakable, crystal clear, big as life, detectable, and evident in all we do.

It's our belief, our vision and our creed that we can change the world. And that we must change it for the BETTER, not just for the sake of change. Change is not random currency. The change continuum thrives to transform, to evolve our souls and uplift our spirits to heaven here on earth. Change results from our beliefs. We are centered in positive beliefs, for what we believe will sprout like herbs once planted as seeds of conviction in the rich terra firma of our minds, spicing up life with blessings or reaping bitter consequences.

Who you are meant to change into is speaking its message to you all the time, because change is a process that comes from *you*. It can be difficult to fathom the full extent and varied content of your beliefs as they formulate, but you are in control of them. No experiential factor, lucky or unlucky thing that occurs can dictate a belief unless you subscribe to it. On the contrary, your beliefs determine how you process what occurs. One cannot blame one's childhood, spouse, "bad breaks", or regrettable episodes for allowing unfortunate cells of beliefs to congeal. One believes as one wishes to believe. Believing everything works for good will cause you to process all that occurs in a manner that only leads to growth, and to something good coming from every event that transpires, no matter its innate quality. You are the master of your beliefs, not a slave to them, or anyone, or anything that happens. You can turn adverse beliefs around. You can birth a belief in an instant where a vacuum stood void in your psyche.

Sometimes, we don't know exactly what we believe, or how strongly we believe it, until our beliefs are put to the test. Situations and circumstances we might never imagine we'd find ourselves in can be catalysts to our greatest growth. They cause us to act out our beliefs. They display our connection to our convictions, and reveal the content of our character in stark relief for all to see, and for us to observe as new self-awareness. Sometimes, this comes as a shock or surprise. Through opposition, beliefs take shape. It is often in moments of direst doubt that we stumble upon a clarity we might never have otherwise achieved, but for an unwanted challenge. Destiny seems inescapable when our back is up against the wall, and wisdom blares as bright as sunrise blazing a trail across the sky. Beliefs can be nearly fatal to earn, so they're priceless in value, and they must be safeguarded if they're to survive others' disbelief, and the rigors of our own internal wars with what can be crippling doubt.

What we consider to be a belief can be challenged by the beliefs of others. We can be lifted by others' beliefs, or we can be dragged down into the dirt. We sometimes have to dig deep to determine whose belief will lead to greatest good. We have to rely on our instincts to discern what constitutes the truth. Our beliefs can come under constant assault by those who would seek to manipulate and undermine societal mores for their shady purposes, be they social, political, economic or personal. Even peer pressure can render one's beliefs more malleable, and thus, even at an early age, our beliefs must withstand false promises, inequities and iniquities. We have to know how to tell right from wrong, and believe in standing for righteousness.

On a macro scale, there are those who stand to profit from convincing us to buy things we don't really want, crave things we will never need, and engage in activities that bring harm to us or others through the development of unhealthy habits. We have to choose what we want to believe, and not assume our beliefs by default, neglect them or leave them vulnerable to any will of the wisp. We have to sense what change we need, and judge when change is for the better.

Those who wish to persuade us due to their thirst for power must not sway our thoughts, nor may those possessed by greed or other self-interests contrary to greater good. Those who promulgate hatred and animus over love, respect, equality, kindness and cooperation should not be able to penetrate our consciousness with their beliefs, nor substitute their base concerns for our hard-won moral stance. We don't have to judge them, put them down, or directly oppose their influence upon us, we only have to trust our core beliefs, and act them out. We must only know what we believe, who we must be that's consistent with that, and what we must do affirmatively to cause our beliefs to take hold in the world and provide mankind a forward leap.

We are all evolved in different ways, and to different degrees of enlightenment. Some of us make a life's quest of working to make the world a better place. Some of us quietly live a life that causes this to happen. Some of us plunder with reckless disregard for what is good and right, eschewing the cause of righteousness, poo-pooing others' needs and wants, unwilling to proffer any belief, except in their selfish desires. We do not have to develop any ill will or bad feelings toward those who would diminish the causes of peace and love. Those who are self-aggrandizing in a manner contrary to greater good, or who speak or act counter to our beliefs, are perhaps best left to heaven. Instead of adopting opposing positions, we choose to be affirmative by exercising utmost care in adhering to our own beliefs and the boldest behaviors they mandate. We go about our daily lives with dreams, goals, tasks and priorities reflecting the nature of our beliefs, using our gifts and abilities to work at peak performance.

Remaining true to our beliefs is instinctive. It is second nature. It is encoded in who we are. The voice that guides us knows what's right and keeps us on a proper course. It is when we come in contact with destructive beliefs and their bitter fruits that we most vigilantly adhere to the core beliefs that keep us whole.

We are aware that forces exist inconsistent with our belief in goodness. They must not ever access our thoughts and feelings to our detriment, whether they are individuals, institutions or other elements that are subversive to our society. Though others may try to exert their will to corrupt our discernment of good and bad, and to subvert our sense of right and wrong, we let no one reduce us to less than our highest selves as individuals or as a collective.

Our beliefs—insofar as they are rooted in truth—should be wholly unassailable. No manipulation of laws, diminution of dignity or decency, downgrading of our learning centers, governmental or political institutions, proliferation of corporate news, mishandling of facts, false advertisements, vile speech or lurid language can degrade our virtue in the least, unless we give it our express permission. We do not give permission. We hold fast. We maintain our standards. Period. And we raise them higher all the time. We maintain the sanctity of our beliefs, and retain our governance over them. We know our beliefs will come to pass. We know that attempts to divide us are untenable, and will not work. We know that all persons are equally created and meant for greatness. We know it's not right to lie, cheat, steal, or take advantage. We know love, truth, beauty, creativity and light rule the universe eternally, and we live according to this belief.

Living according to our beliefs requires courage, discipline and faith, and we possess these traits, strengthening them at every turn. We believe in ourselves, and in our Higher Power as we perceive it to be. We believe in others too—from each stranger we meet to those we love, for no one is a stranger to us. We are all family. We are the One Love. This is the basis of all our beliefs, and we stand up for what we believe in regardless of the strength or size of opposition.

Throughout history, it has been those who have been willing to stand up for what they believe in who have changed the world profoundly, often with the least power and resources with which to bring about change.

Think of boxing great, Muhammad Ali, who stood up against what he viewed as an unjust war in Vietnam, consciously objected, and nearly lost his hard-fought boxing career for doing what he believed was right. Look at Abraham Lincoln, whose mother died when he was nine years old. He was a farmer, rail splitter and soldier, but in spite of his humble status, he freed the slaves in an atmosphere that led to America's Civil War, and became President of the United States. Rosa Parks, who the U.S. Congress dubbed "first lady of civil rights", was a hard-working secretary at her local NAACP (National Association for the Advancement of Colored People), but her decision to stand her ground by refusing to surrender her seat on a segregated bus became a clarion call to all who believed in civil rights. She changed the course of history.

Standing up for what you believe in can be a difficult, costly road to hoe. But it is the key to advancement of civilization as we know it. Those of good will and good intent have the guts to imagine a future that is better than the past, the present and even their wildest, most wonderful dreams. You are this person, and you have your dream, your heart and the personal power to be all the change you want to see. You bring change, and change brings you where change is due.

You can stand up for things you believe in, whatever the cost, because you are willing to pay the cost. You believe you are meant to lend a mighty conscience and consciousness to your workplace, school, neighborhood, community, every place you're fortunate to find yourself.

You're effective the moment you choose to get involved, and to be a tide of change. You don't have to stand on a soapbox, preaching to others and fighting each micro-battle that comes your way, but you can advocate for good, and never shy away from it. This is your duty and your assignment. You have been placed in uneasy spots to defend what's right. You know you're sent to do this with aplomb. You can be loving, tactful and kind, and you easily get your point across. You can sow peace where there's discord, seek understanding where there's divisiveness. Your beliefs are the guide to right action, and you take right action when it counts. You have the right words, just the right touch, and the right temperament to bridge the most gaping gaps in logic.

When you feel in your heart that something's wrong, you understand you've been given an opportunity to correct that ill with measured grace, and to bring things into balance. With your upright example, words and deeds, you hold steadfast to your core beliefs. You follow wherever they take you, with the knowledge that all will turn out right, because everything's working together for good, regardless of how things may appear. To not stand up to advocate is to give in to fear and self-doubt, and let low vibrations rule the world. This isn't what you're meant to do. It isn't who you're meant to be. You're meant to change the world. Your spirit and soul depend on it. You aren't a fluke or a victim. You're the hope of things to come. You're alive to mean something immense to the world, to be someone so cool that you do such huge things that their impact travels around the globe. You lend to the world the unparalleled grace of the shining star of who you are, and take your place on hallowed ground with heroes and sheroes of days gone by, upleveling your life into miracle status, upgrading yourself into greatness.

Your beliefs reveal your Meant-To-Be, and the glorious things you're meant to do. Your Meant-To-Be and Meant-To-Do comprise your greatest gifts. Go out and give them. Do it. Now.

Nothing comes to us by accident. There's a reason for everything that happens. Every challenge we face is a cutting-edge chance afforded us by destiny. We are part of a whole. We're not alone. We're a segment of something bigger and better than what we see, hear, touch, taste, or smell with our five senses. We're part of the great experiment that births potentiality into reality. We are each responsible to forge the change that leads us to a better world.

Our beliefs are the guideposts on the path to fulfilling the promise we came here for. Fortunately, we're helped in this by every twist and turn of fate, and all the ways we change and grow. When our beliefs are questioned, ambiguous notions tend to crystalize. What may have seemed like a nebulous tangle of unrelated principles or conjectures becomes a manifesto.

What you believe is yours alone, customized by the life you are privileged to lead.

Your beliefs have been forged in the hottest fires. Own them. They belong to you. You have them for a reason. Your beliefs are combustible. They flare up. They spread. Spark them into incandescence. Be the person they require. What you believe lights the path as materially as a hand-held torch. Make your luminosity the brightest it can be, for all our lives depend on it.

When you stand up for what you believe in, you are the butterfly leaving the chrysalis. You are doing what you are meant to do, and delivering your gifts into the world. Spread your wings, take off, and fly!

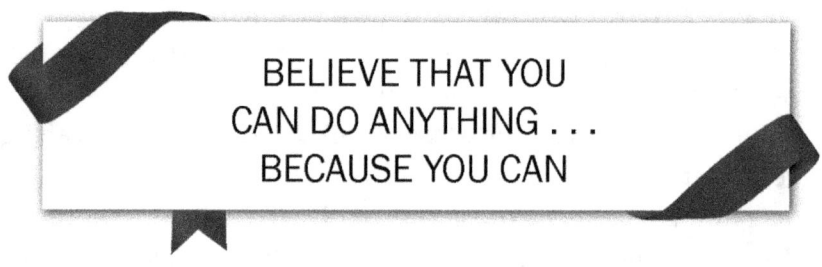

BELIEVE THAT YOU CAN DO ANYTHING . . . BECAUSE YOU CAN

To do anything, you must first believe you can do it. Seems elementary, right? But people dive into all kinds of stuff without truly believing it will happen, that they can be successful at it, and it can make a difference. You have to believe in what you're doing, or else you'll be out of sync with it. You won't have what it takes to persevere when the going gets tough. You won't carry the matching vibration to jump it off, if you don't believe in it.

Harbor the absolute belief that anything is possible. Remember all the "impossibilities" that are realities today. Air travel, cell phones, the World Wide Web, the list goes on and on. If it's possible, and it's on your mind, go ahead and believe you're designated for it, that you are equipped with all it takes to take it on and see it through. You can do all you set your will to doing, once you believe you can. Believing you are capable, and believing in what you're meant to do is the main ingredient added to your recipe for success.

The famous American industrialist and founder of the Ford Motor Company, Henry Ford, once uttered the axiom: "Whether you think you can, or you think you can't—you're right."

You have to believe. Your mind, your spirit and your soul unflinchingly execute what you believe. The universe cycles back energy to you in keeping with the energy you generate with your beliefs, providing you with talents, strengths and skills that combine to empower you to perform whatever feats you believe are within your capacity to achieve.

Believe you can, and trust you will. That's it. The magic of believing lies in the fact that the universe clears a natural path from belief straight to reality, such that beliefs are experienced. Believing also generates the energy, enthusiasm, plans, poise and persistence needed to start, pursue, and complete the tasks you undertake to make your dream come true. If your belief is unshakeable, even the moon and the stars will root for you. All of the solar system will rally to orbit and transit its vital parts to fit your mental picture.

It is easy to believe in what you want to do when you have faith in YOU, when you recall what you've already done, and how far you've come since you were born. If you're really honest with yourself, your achievements are voluminous.

You may have survived tough trials and tribulations requiring great character, whether or not you've acknowledged it. You may have survived being orphaned, for instance, or widowed, divorced or abandoned. You may work with a disability, or still be recovering from ill health or injury, fraught with pain. You may work at hard labor, or hold down a difficult job that demands your concentration, stamina and diligence. You may toil for years under adverse conditions, for not enough pay, with a trying boss. You may be gripped by homelessness, or be overwhelmed with eldercare. You may have a child who tries your nerves, or tries to destroy your family. You may be living in poverty, burdened with lack of education, racism, sexism, religious intolerance or physical abuse. You may be enduring domestic abuse or sexual assault. You may have spent some time in jail, or been hooked on drugs or alcohol, and had to retool every aspect of life.

When we give ourselves credit for pressing on and working past what has gone before, we see our way clear to believing in our ability to do anything that lies before us at this point. We're stronger, more resilient, wiser, seasoned, more compassionate. And when we consider our graduations, home life, innovations and donations, ways we volunteer—perhaps to help others help themselves—and the work we do as employers and employees to grease the wheels of change, strong belief in ourselves, and in what we can do, is a very natural outcome. Reviewing the ways we change others' lives for the better, in large and in tiny ways that may barely be perceptible, emboldens us to take on more.

If that doesn't do it for you, though, take a look at the many extraordinary achievements others accomplished—folks who began with resources far more paltry than your own, and went on to change the arc of global events throughout the ages.

Even when you're attempting to blaze a whole new trail—to "go where no man has gone before", as they say on the *Star Trek* Enterprise—there are figures, past and present, from whom you can draw fresh inspiration. People whose shoulders you stand on now, from your illustrious ancestors to those who toiled in obscurity. They're connected to you. You're connected to them. Tap into their belief and their self-confidence, their bravery, their store of good intent. Take time to read biographies, and you'll see their greatness lives within you, eager to take its turn at bat.

Research aces in your chosen field. Delve into the lives of performers, athletes, spiritual leaders, politicians, entrepreneurs and educators, scientists and pioneers. See who invented the technologies that are making life easier for you now. They started somewhere. You can too. They couldn't see the road ahead. They just took the first step and believed it was there. Read articles and interviews. Watch videos about their quests. Look at old pictures. Peer into their eyes, and you'll see the belief that drove them to success—to advancements the world was waiting for. Pin their photos on your wall. See where they came from and how far they went.

Precious few start out knowing where they'll end up, or even the next few steps to take. They begin somewhere and resolve to keep going. They grind till their efforts pay off. They believe in possibilities. They believe they can do, and will do, what they set their minds to, no matter the odds. No matter what other people say, or what bubbles up into the atmosphere. They believe in themselves. They believe in their families and friends. They always believe in love. They believe in their vision, their skills, their thoughts. They believe their dream is good and right, that they're working to make a contribution, able to do whatever it takes to rise to the occasion. They believe what they're doing is meant to be, and they are meant to do it.

They choose to take up a cause and champion something larger than themselves. They believe that they are needed. They believe in their Higher Power, and that its energy is alive in them. That all things are working together for good. They define themselves as they wish to be. They refuse to be circumscribed by others, traditional roles or shifting tides. They don't accept any limitations, go along to get along, feel restricted, get confused, or shrink themselves down for anyone. They avoid letting anger motivate them, letting their past control their future, letting complacency, laziness or apathy steal their days or nights. And rather than being ruled by fear, they tap into a higher source that gives them guidance, strength and zeal. They're healthy of body, mind and soul, and their spirit soars with eagles.

You're walking in their footsteps now. You are such a person. You're one of them. You know what you want, and you know you can get it. You know it will benefit more than yourself. You know what you're thinking right now will determine what's going to happen next. You can think anything you want, and it will flow into your life. That's how thoughts work.

When you believe in yourself, your belief is contagious. People believe in you, and they also begin to believe in themselves. They cause you to believe in them. Trust and belief break out all around you. You're like music people can't help but dance to, when you decide to believe.

Dance to your own tune. Do it now. Go within, and determine what you believe. Believe like you never believed before, and set out toward your vision. Let belief be the rhythm and rhyme of your life, and you will accomplish more with a thought than you ever imagined anyone could. People will start to tap their toes and clap their hands and sing along until what you believe appears in the real world, showing up as peace and love. Believe until your every thought creates blessings like none the world has seen. Believe, and the clouds and the planets will form a conga line to dance with you, making infinite possibilities into magnificent achievements. Stand on the rock of your solid belief, and it will become the foundation of change in groupthink that will elevate every soul you touch and shape our future world.

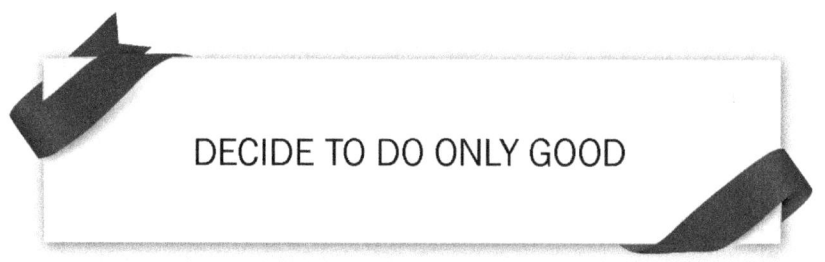

DECIDE TO DO ONLY GOOD

To be a beneficent force in the world, you have to do more than just roll with the tide. You may have to swim against it. Everything that you're doing now, will do, and have done in the past, has been a choice. You always have to choose. I'm choosing to write this book right now. I could be sleeping, or out for a walk, or feeding my face while I watch TV. I could be having sex instead, or cavorting with my buds. I could choose a bunch of things. I choose to sit here at my laptop, peer in my monitor, and look straight at you. None of those other endeavors or pastimes are now a choice I want to make. I want to spend my time with you. The lists on my desk, like, a jillion miles long, don't pull me like this writing does. I'm into communicating with you, loving you at this point in time, though you may well be reading this years from now. At least, it's my hope this will reach that far. That people will read these words decades from now and draw enormous strength and wisdom from them. This is my choice, to be present with you, because you are so special. You are my joy. You're my light and my love.

You are choosing right now, too. You're choosing to read these words for a reason. You are seeking something new, and that something is leading you back to yourself. You're seeking a path to a better life, choosing to follow your instincts to join the discussion of how to change the world. You're yearning for greater connection. You're looking for guidance with open heart and hand, and the will to improve your lot. You want to be gushing with positive vibes, so life on the planet will rightly evolve. You want to bring change, and to widen your sphere of influence. You want change to illuminate and unite, not debase, destroy or be craven. You're pursuing a trail of breadcrumbs to a destination seen in dreams, and yet you know it's real somewhere. It exists as a possibility waiting to happen, rising, a brand new dawn.

Every choice you're making now will count.

Choose deep in your heart of hearts to do only good. It's the point of your life. Choose now, and forever hold your peace. For the choice to do good will bring you peace, and spread peace all around the world. The choice to do only good is like a Google map in consciousness. You type in the address of the next good deed, and good will unerringly arrive. Your internal GPS will take you where you want to go. You'll see overheads, street views, one town to the next, because you'll direct your zest for change to the places it will do most good. There may be some detours, sure. Your route may be circuitous, but as it's determined by your thoughts, you can move in the knowledge your good intent will lead you to your goals. You may traverse some rocky roads, but your auto-pilot's set for goodness, so your path is paved with gold. Rose petals are strewn on the road ahead.

When you're determined to do only good, good will permeate your thoughts, speech, actions and results. There are liable to be mistakes and misadventures, but you'll learn from them. They'll come from the head, and not the heart. There won't be any missteps that occur because you left to chance your destination. You intend to do good, and that's all you can do. Just good. No more, no less. Radiate goodness, you'll attract it. You will be vibrating at good's level, oscillating at good's speed, and churning out more good with every heartbeat. As you surrender to goodness, even your faults and failings will give rise to goodness in the end.

Resolve to yourself in this instant that the highest good is your repose.

Breathe deeply. Feel tranquility. Relax. Close your eyes. Feel how good it feels, and how good it feels to feel so good. Good is the only way to go. Not everyone chooses good, but you choose goodness, and it feels so good, you know you'll choose goodness forevermore. Failing to set a course for goodness abdicates your throne in the burgeoning kingdom of creativity. Positive progress depends on positive people committing to do good. No one can make this choice for you. No one can make you an advocate, a creator or a volunteer. You are the one who decides for yourself what you're going to do with your gift of life, and what meaning you'll infuse it with. You must decide on its scope and scale, on whom you will touch, on how you will live, and on whether you'll lead or follow. Will you be an inspiration, or a downer? Will you speak truth or talk trash? It's a deliberate choice to make. Considering all factors you perceive, will you stand on the side of good, and take up the banner for a better world?

Meandering through life, abstaining from committing to reaching your fullest potential won't cut it. You are a spiritual being, traveling the Earth in a physical body. You are the essence of transformation, intended to enter the largest persona your soul can inhabit. You are the change we all want to see. You have to decide if you're yay or nay, else the world will be robbed of your skills and talents, void of the contribution you are intended to make, if you only believe. Decide it's your duty to work for good. You make the choices, moment to moment, of what you'll do, and where you'll go, with whom you will associate, what you're willing to take, and what you're not, what you stand for, what you'll give, what you'll say and what you won't, and how people will feel in your presence.

What will you lift up with your life, and what is beneath your dignity? How far will your compassion stretch, and who will it encompass? Stumbling in darkness with no regard for north or south in your moral compass doesn't work. You have to choose. Choose sooner than later to make your life an adventure including others. Not choosing results in a lack of direction, limited productivity and a dearth of reciprocity for all that you are given. Those who don't commit to good will crash, and if they're plentiful, the world will be crashing as they do. Without good at one's core, one is all but lost, because goodness helps one find true self.

You're the vanguard of society. Change accelerates. Whether it's steered for the better is in your hands. You're at its wheel. Change on its own speeds willy-nilly. Devoid of navigation skills, change can be lateral or for the worse. Since change is the only thing that doesn't, and it's changing constantly, why not drive it so it transports us all to where we want to go.

Stand for good. Commit right now. Before you make one other choice.

Choose good, and I will be at your side, and so will all the angels.

Good thinking will lead to right action. It always does. Choose good, and think good thoughts. You must direct your thought into what you wish to see spring up, not what you don't. You know your thoughts create. You're creating the future today, my friend. You're choosing, so choose well. Invest energy into the good you desire, for mighty change is on the way.

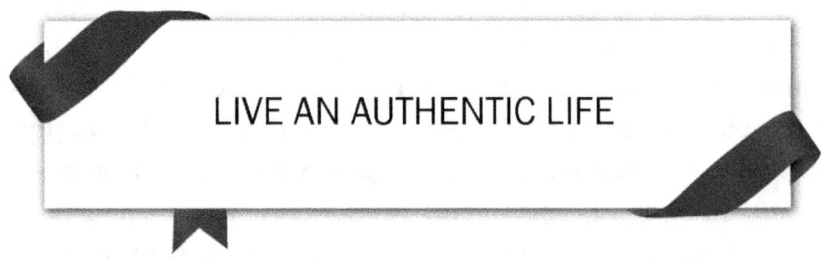

LIVE AN AUTHENTIC LIFE

Authenticity. We hear that word a lot. But what does it mean to be "authentic"? How can we live an authentic life?

Webster's New World College Dictionary defines the word authenticity as: "The quality of being genuine or not corrupted from the original...Truthfulness of origins, attributions, commitments, sincerity, and intentions."

That's a mouthful, right?

What does it mean to be genuine? How can one be uncorrupted from one's original self, one's newborn self, considering all the water under the bridge that flows since infancy. It's easy, when you think of it. We aren't merely what happens to us. We aren't what others think of us, if others think of us at all. We're certainly not our mistakes, and we are more than flesh and bone.

If we choose, we're the pure, uncorrupted original being that was born. If we don't portray any artifice, we are the genuine person we were when we took corporeal form. This isn't to say we haven't grown. It is only to say we were never harmed or mutated, unless we mutated ourselves. We remain quintessentially us, regardless of how many stones were thrown our way, or how many times we fell and got up, how many wrong turns we happened to take, or how our thought processes may have strayed. Nothing, and no one, dinged us. We aren't, and can't be, damaged goods. We're born to be perfected, spawned by a perfect Higher Power, into a universe that improves itself.

We can choose to hang on to the innocence, joy and pure potential that we were when we entered the world from our mother's womb. We can be authentic. We can be truthful of origins, attributions, commitments, sincerity, intentions and all that started our earthly journey. We are completely intact. We don't have to wear a mask to belong, court acceptance, solicit approval, be liked, or attempt to survive. We can be who we are at our very best. And that's a fantastic trait.

The only way to come across as authentic is by being so, and knowing that's enough. How, really, does one pull that off? Seems simple, right? Just be yourself. But it might be easier said than done for many of us these days. Living an authentic life can be tricky in a lot of ways.

First off, one must be in touch with one's true self in order to live from it, and to know oneself can be arduous, especially if one doesn't spend much capital on one's inner quest. To keep up with one's eclectic mindset, ways of dealing with the outside world, childhood sores, defense mechanisms, illusions and economic state is a job. A hefty and ongoing job too few are willing to undertake.

You must first learn who you are in order to fathom who you're meant to be.

So, who is the authentic you? Go within to find this out. Ask your High Power. It is the source of your wisdom, guidance, purpose, love and life. It is the origin of truth.

Second, to be *perceived* as authentic is yet another feat. You mightn't care who perceives you as being authentic. You might not hassle yourself in general trying to suss out what others think, and this is no doubt a healthy stance, considering you'll never know for sure, so it can't matter much. Yet to change the world, you need street cred. You need to be an influencer, seen as a sort of sage.

In order to be an influencer, you must have credibility. And for you to have credibility, you must be perceived as larger than life. So it kind of does matter what others think. To be a thought leader, you have to be seen as honest, respectable, trustworthy, kind. You have to be seen as a place of truth. You have to come across as real. No one's following Fakey Ms. Fake-Pants. Not on Twitter. Not on Snapchat. Not on YouTube, Facebook, Pinterest, even to the ladies room. Not out of the line of fire, that's for sure, or out of a burning building. To amass a loyal following, even the shallowest Instagrammer has to be *really* shallow, not a fake. Every post must be truly vacuous, authentically deep as a kiddie pool, or it'll be called out.

Being authentic, and coming across as authentic, can be two different things. Some people tend to be misunderstood. On the other hand, fake folks fool people into thinking they're authentic. That's problematic in the short term. Rarely can they keep it up. Politics is rife with it. Salespeople, tradespersons, financial advisors, and outright criminals all gain trust, though some may be wholly untrustworthy, conning people left and right, and doing folks in at the drop of a hat. There are lawyers, contractors and men of the cloth with long lines trailing after them, even though they don't have good intent, may be lining their pockets with caches of cash, and will rip off a donation box. Most people in these professions are honest and doing the very best they can, but who knows who's authentic. We can only be authentic, trusting we will draw our match.

People have different perceptions regarding whether others are genuine, or appear to be disingenuous. One person might think another inauthentic because they smile too much, while another may process a smile as a sign of goodwill. Smiling indicates friendliness, and is often a sign of happiness. But if, say, the first observer believes happiness cannot be achieved and friendliness is impossible, he or she could deem any smile "fake", and any smiler inauthentic. This could be far from the truth, but, hey, perception is reality. Misconceptions arise and abound. We can't worry about being misunderstood. We focus on being genuine, speaking our truth, and living authentically. This invites other authentic beings, prospects, and activities.

People perceive us according to their beliefs, which may be so entrenched that nothing we say or do can vault them past our gender, faith, accent or the beautiful melanin in our skin.

What we can do—all that we can control—is to know ourselves, and be ourselves, and get better at sharing our truth in ways that benefit others substantially.

Authenticity is a perception by a perceiver who has a staunch world view that might not include your particular brand of genuineness, and that's okay. Whether you seem authentic or not to other individuals, you can't let it bother you or stop you from *being* authentic. Authenticity isn't a label we tack on our foreheads or on others' chests. It exists, like all else, in our thoughts, words and deeds. It's conveyed in expression, comportment, mannerism and the inner space we explore behind our sparkling eyes.

How can you show up authentic, then? Tell the truth and refrain from just making up stuff to cast yourself in a better light than whatever the facts of *you* may be. Do what you say you'll do, and be where you say you'll be when you say you'll be there. Show up displaying your cheerful heart. Be present. Live in the now. Really listen when others speak with you. Don't coax your mind to wander off or cop out to come up with responses you want to put out there before you can hear what they say. They're sharing. Care about them. Leave things better than you found them. This includes other people's hearts and minds, not only clean sinks and full tanks of gas. Be open and honest with hopes and dreams. Work to get, and stay, connected. This is authenticity, not "This is me, take me or leave me. I'm not going to change, I am who I am." That's caveman talk. We could soon live on Mars. Let's converse like we're evolved.

No one can say who you really are, but you're certainly free to define yourself, and continue to redefine yourself, and to act from the dictates of your soul, and pursue your natural instincts. Authenticity has to do with growth, and the depth with which we participate as we interact, embracing change. It has to do with giving. It has to do with being a space that's safe for others, and secure. A place that's untainted, unjaded, unselfish, upright and acutely respectable.

Once you are right with yourself, and portraying the character uniquely yours, you do not have to compromise your ethics or your boundaries. You are authentic in *your* eyes, those that turn inward, revealing truths, assessing who you're meant to be, and striving to become her. In the bright light of your consciousness, the valuable asset of your values cannot help but be perceived as truth incarnate. Find this space. If, from anywhere outside yourself, you happen to be misperceived, such misconception can only derive from vibrations that don't match your own.

Be at peace when things don't seem to click. It means they're not supposed to. What isn't attracted to you, you do not need, and it does not need you. Show respect and decorum, bless that spot, and proceed where your authenticity shines. Ascend in authenticity, and people, places and things congruent with that will gather around.

Focus on being, and knowing, YOU, and sharing the full extent of your being wherever you happen to find yourself, and you will live authentically with others who are authentic.

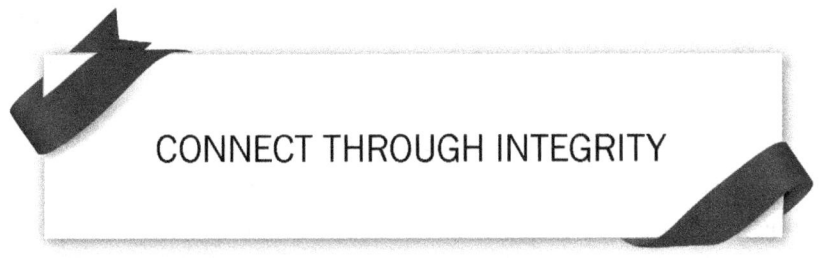

CONNECT THROUGH INTEGRITY

The key to connecting and staying connected rests in your integrity.

Integrity is an enchanting force.

You can connect with anyone when what you say, do, and believe in seem to act in concert. People conclude they can trust you, because they sense you'll do what's right. Nothing about you puts them off, because your ethics are intact, and your morals are clear and evident. They don't have to be suspicious of you. You're the real McCoy. They have no reason to fear you'll hurt or compromise them. They see who you really are. They can like you, or not. They don't have to build a wall to keep you out, or at a distance. Whatever walls they have already built come down, or you get through to them. People tend to let you in when they feel they can be at their ease. Because you communicate at deep levels, family relationships can grow.

You keep faith with all your friends. Co-workers conclude they can count on you.

Just as being authentic brings you the loving life you're meant to lead, your virtue and good judgment engender respect, because you show respect. When people respect you, they change for the better due to what you exemplify, and your rosy expectations. They model your kind behavior. You're an inspiration to them. You set a standard, raise the bar. Things improve, because everyone wants to step up in the company of integrity. You elevate everyone you touch, and do so just by being you.

If you lie, or cheat, or refuse to show up, or you're late or trifling in other ways, nobody's hopping aboard that train. It you're easily angered, discordant, malfunctioning, contrary, gossipy, selfish, or grumpy—or you just plain do stupid stuff—you'll find no place on any team. If you complain instead of solving, finding answers, being change, and upgrading how a system works, folks flee your company, put you down, and don't want to hear a word you say.

If you stab others in the back, or tend to down others to lift yourself up, that karma rebounds like a boomerang from the moment you do the dirty deed. If you don't care, nobody cares for you. If you half-step, it's only a matter of time before dragging your feet will trip you up. When you compromise your integrity, cut corners, make excuses, blame the boogie man for what went wrong, you limit what you can do in life, all the miracles you can be part of.

On the other hand, when you are true to your word, and conduct yourself in alignment with a towering set of principles, you attract others who do the same, and the bonds you create are unbreakable.

True connection requires integrity on both sides of any relationship.

Relationships are built on trust, and trust results from virtue. Virtue is born of integrity.

Integrity breeds excellence. Because you're committed to doing your best, and to being transparent with everyone, whatever you do takes on the sheen of legitimacy and value. Personal integrity grants solidity to everything you say and do, and every product you create.

Credibility's worth its weight in gold.

In the eyes of the world, what you produce is inseparable from your character. Integrity gives you authority. There's no faking that. It's second skin. You either have it, or you don't.

With love and integrity as your life story, the spine of your biography will never grow dusty on a shelf. It is all that is left of you after your tale is told, your final page is turned, and you become a memory. Or better yet, you make history.

You make history by making change that's vast enough to rock the world.

SPECIFIC IS TERRIFIC

THE LENGTHS OF YOUR STRENGTHS AND WEAKNESSES

Let's take a more penetrative look at who you are in your current phase, now that you know it's by knowing yourself as you are that leads you to who you can be.

Who you are determines what you do, so if you want to change your life—and have an effect on the lives of others—self-knowledge is a prerequisite. What are your strengths and weaknesses? Are you kind? Are you dependable? Do you take suggestions easily, and up your game because of them, or are you overly sensitive and defensive when you're criticized? Are you mentally strong, or prone to cave when difficult circumstances loom? Are you brave? Quick to action?

Confident? Do you take charge? Procrastinate? Are you open and honest, or secretive? Do you stay in touch with your emotions, or do you shy away from feelings, bury your pain, go numb, shut down? Are you a giver, or are you a taker who grabs and then comes back for more?

Remember, when you consider the various aspects of your character and examine your personality—every strength you possess is one side of a two-sided coin. Every trait has an upside and downside, so there's nothing about you that isn't terrific in one way or another. Realize this, it works for you. If you have to admit you're stubborn, you must recognize you're tenacious too, not easily deterred. If you're bull-headed, you're not prone to quit. If you're flighty, you must be flexible and agile when change comes your way. Gullible? Then you're apt to believe in yourself and the goodness of others. See? Two sides to every coin.

You must love the truth of who you are, so you can become all you're meant to be.

Lies are no plus on any count, but the last person you want to lie to is yourself. You have to face the facts. How else can you possibly change them? You have to be willing to change, but you can't change that of which you are unaware. Introspection leads to change. If you know yourself, you can transform. If you don't, you may be pretending. Without looking inward, you lack information. With self-knowledge, you're able to seize on the most useful facets of your character, and let go of what doesn't work for you or suit the person you've become. You can reconstruct any part of you with a blueprint drawn to your specifications. Isn't that alluring?

Why go around thinking you could stop smoking, drinking, or overeating any time you want, all on your own, if, in fact, you're in need of professional help? Why tell yourself you're not creative, when you never tried to draw, write, dance, or play an instrument. You could be a Romare Bearden, J.K. Rowling, Misty Copeland or John

Legend, and not know. You'll never know if you're not in touch with hidden assets and desires, or your true potential.

Are you a soft touch? A bigot? A genius? A rebel with a cause? Are you happiest when you rock the boat, or you're flying under the radar?

Just think of it—you can conceive a whole new person, once you take stock of your gifts and evaluate shortcomings. Not that you need to remake your whole self, but you can if you want to. You can become a different you. You can be anyone you want. Only, how can you grow more sophisticated, if you don't realize you act like a boor? How can you be a siren, dressed in Mom jeans and a flannel shirt you bought on sale in high school?

When you go within in silence, pray, and meditate or practice yoga, ask for your true self to be revealed. Check yourself out. Watch your behavior. Count the contents of your thoughts as if they were hundred dollar bills. Let your ears hear what your mouth is saying. Hear how you describe yourself. Hear what you're told by your Higher Power in the many ways it speaks.

Know yourself. And love yourself. Trust yourself. And grow yourself.

If you don't know you, how can anyone else? If you don't realize who, and what, you are, who's going to, Daffy Duck? Ronald McDonald? The Tooth Fairy? Who? It's your job to see who you are and determine who you want to be from here. To be cognizant of the person you've been, how she's changed, who she is, who she wants to become, and what she must do to shed her flaws, and pump herself up with the strengths that make her adorable is supreme.

Change is a choice. Change deliberately. If you do not change your world as a matter of choice, the world will change it for you.

Nature is changing around you. Don't you want to? Do it consciously. All kinds of trees are sprouting new leaves, or shedding their old ones with Fall colors that fall to the ground and fertilize it. The moon is cycling from crescent to full. Snakes are molting. Babies are birthing. Oceans are surging from low, to high, tide. Chameleons are living kaleidoscopes that morph and transmute in the blink of an eye. You can make things happen, let things happen, or actually *be* what's happening. You just have to know yourself.

Are you conceited, or insecure? Or both. They're flip sides of a coin. Are you a pleaser, or self-involved? Maybe none of these things is true of you. What is? Who are you? Where are you going? Do you like who you're becoming? Do you make good choices? That's a strength. Are you open, and like to try new things? That's also a useful attribute. Write it down. It's part of who you are. It's a quality others would like to have, that people who know you are crazy about.

There's so much about you to admire.

Be honest about your strengths, because you have to know what tools you have in your toolkit to help others. You can fix things that are broken. You can even fix a broken heart. You can help the world grow stronger. You can accomplish world-changing feats.

The world is in need of change more than ever. Change for the better, not for the worse. Change, to banish hate and injustice. Change, to defeat mediocrity. Change, to end war and be more united. Change, to spread peace internationally. Change, so all children get educated. Change, so no one goes hungry or homeless. Change, to counter climate change. Change, to conquer disease.

Since change within brings change without, go within to find the specific change for which you're uniquely qualified. Each of us has a position in the matrix of change that is to come. It's up to us. It's up to you, because change begins with you in a moment. Be confident, knowing whoever you are, change thrives in you. It's bursting out. Make friends with yourself. Avoid self-denial. Be interested in your weaknesses, because you can turn them into strengths.

You can change anything about you, because you're the sovereign of your soul.

You are the only one who can change you.

Changing yourself will change the world. Everything in the macro world will shift, if just imperceptibly, each time you adapt your micro world. The more you grow, the greater the shift.

You tune up your car, spring clean, mend fences. Now is the time to clean up your act.

Toss what doesn't function. Let go of old funky melodramatics. Embrace and shore up all that constitutes your incredible strength of character, your sense of humor, your resilience, all the excitement you arouse. You're no accident. No slouch. You're YOU! You're a who's who of excellent qualities, evolving and purging moment to moment. Realize this enhances you.

What are your strengths and weaknesses? To change them, you have to admit to them. Know them like the back of your hand.

What do you want to start changing about yourself, so you can change the world?

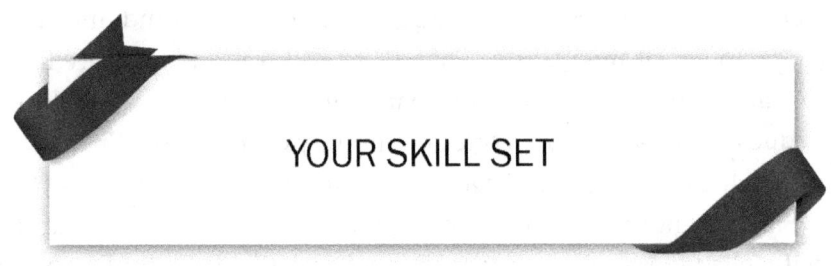

YOUR SKILL SET

A skill set is simply a set of skills. Everyone has one that's distinct.

What's in your skill set? Do you know? Since you earlier listed the things you can do, do you understand these are skills you can trade on anywhere you go?

We might not think about what we know how to do until we apply for a job, set up an Internet dating profile, whip up a resume or a bio, start to rehearse for an interview, design a website, ask for a raise or envisage a social networking page. But we all have skills that others don't. We all have skills others need and want. We do things that set us apart. We all have to learn things we didn't anticipate. We have certain specialties. They might not seem like much to us, but we come in the world with talents, and we pick up skills as we evolve through whatever challenges we may face, things we discover we like to do, specific know-how that is self-taught and formal education.

Look again at the skills you jotted down. You most likely have more than you thought. Let's organize them, so they work.

You might want to list your professional skills first. Those may be uppermost in your mind. Do you have a degree? If so, what did you study? What skills are involved in the job, or the jobs, you're doing at the moment? Do you have a trade? It means you're skilled. What skills does it require? Maybe you're now an executive assistant. What does that mean? What skills are involved? Fast typing? Filing? Scheduling? Communication? Organization? Do you book flights, hotels, rental cars? Event planning, do you do that? Do you organize meetings or seminars, possess sales skills or assemble teams? What about graphics art skills? Do you design brochures or business cards, flyers, announcements, email blasts?

All of these qualify as skills that might be applied in other fields, broadening your sphere of influence, upping your income, and widening your circle of contacts, any of which can change your life and help you change the world.

Think of the skills entailed in doing whatever you already do for a living. How can you apply those skills to other venues and scenarios? What are you proficient at that supersedes your job description? Appraise what it can do for you.

Next, take note of your other skills—things that don't currently earn you a living, but at which you're capable, ingenious or adept. Can you sculpt, cut hair, ace algebra, read palms? Do you mow grass like a pro? Do you design throw pillows, throw clay pots, blow glass, barbecue like Bobby Flay? Do you yodel or sing opera? Can you paint a house or fix roof leaks? Change a tire? Milk a cow? Do you have a green thumb? Can you talk a blue streak? Are you a coupon bargain shopper? Comedian? Horse whisperer? If so, put it all on your list.

Anything you're good at can be a game-changer. It can work for you.

Examine your skill set thoroughly, and be objective as you do. Outline in detail what you can do, and consider how well you can do it. Remember your skill set is a gestalt. That is, its whole is greater than the sum of its parts. Your skill set is unlike any other. Only you can employ your array of skills in the manner in which you're able. No one can even smile like you do, smell like you, or make a bed. Your skills are immensely meaningful. Every skill you possess is valuable to someone, somewhere, at some time, and it can move mountains if well-applied.

It may take days to construct your list and understand what your skill set means, and how you can use it to foster change. It may take minutes initially. More skills may surface over time.

Whenever a new skill comes to mind, add it to your lineup.

After you see what you know how to do, list all the things you wish to learn, and how you plan to gain more skills.

Your skill set resembles a fingerprint—and it's likely how you'll make your mark.

LEARN AND GROW FROM EVERY EXPERIENCE

It isn't what happens, but what you do next, that can change your world, and as a result, change the world around you.

Everything happens for a reason, and that reason is our growth. Life can seem like a puzzle sometimes, often with some missing piece that's vital to the bigger picture. This is an illusion. Feeling without, or living bereft, of something is a chimera. It's a mythological monster we make up if we sense some deficiency or hallucinate insufficiency. We lack nothing and suffer no limitations. Experience exists for change. Only we can block our good, if we let what happens thwart us. We're always on our way somewhere, always coming from someplace, always inside the urgency of now, which teaches us many things. Experience is always for us, not to punish us or spin our wheels. It's meant to lead to greater things, and reveal our higher selves.

We are children of the universe. The cosmos wants us to succeed.

Just as necessity is the mother of invention, experience fathers change.

We get to choose which experiences change us, when, why, if, and how we change, and whether a change will be a plus that furthers our evolution. We can regulate change as it occurs. We do so according to who we are, what we do, and what we believe. We are the arbiters of change. It is how we resolve to interpret change, and elect to make the most of it, that determines each new outcome. If we only choose to react to experience, rather than respond in upbeat ways that echo our dreams and goals, and harmonize with our Meant-To-Be, we cut ourselves off from the chance to grow. If we utilize change, we benefit. If we live for change and work for it, it has to work for us. We know this deep inside ourselves, yet we often fight against it.

Within everything that happens, there is embedded a seed of benefit. That seed must be nurtured in order to grow. We are the greenhouse that nurtures the seed so it always inures to our betterment. To nurture the seed, we stay rooted in an eternally flowering mindset. Whatever occurs, we grow from it, knowing everything has an upside. Events can be sources of revelation, if we're open to their lessons. Occurrences don't determine us. Conversely, we determine them by the manner in which we process them. Determine to grow from every situation, and you will. We are born to live totally free and absent any inhibition or impediment to growth. Toward this end, experiences stimulate growth. Therefore, gladly receive your experiences. They're needed so you might prosper. Believing this way will lead to greater freedom, health and happiness.

There is nothing we can't overcome. Fighting or flailing against what we may perceive as a negative incident can only lend power to that which seems to be trying to work against us. That is a waste of energy. What could irk is reduced to impotence, if we're grateful for it, let it go, and treat it as a blessing. If and when we see things through this lens, we eliminate tribulations.

Reinterpret negative energies with your power of positivity, and what others may see as disaster, to you, is another chance to grow.

As energy grows where attention flows, when we focus on growing with each experience, more good experiences seek us out. Even a lemon, though it is bitter, is filled with antioxidants and unique phytonutrient properties that interact to enhance our health. If we focus on its bitter taste alone, its vitamin C content is not just rejected by our taste buds, it may be harder to absorb.

When we grow and learn from experiences—no matter how rough they may first appear—we are lifted by the winds of change.

Headwinds become winds beneath our wings that carry us aloft. If we offer openness to growth, we're open to receive the good embedded in any event.

We're an experience in ourselves, and we want to be enjoyable.

We are Change Wizards enjoying change, helping others transmute their experiences into pleasant and propitious ones. We grow wiser with every twist of fate and stronger at every turn.

The added bonus of wanting to learn is that we learn something from everyone.

When you listen to each person you are blessed to come in contact with, it's a live-stream of their consciousness without any data overages.

Yes, we're accustomed to learning from our parents, teachers, spiritual leaders, mentors, coaches, and the like, but it's also the children, cab drivers, cashiers and elderly neighbors we randomly encounter who teach us lessons. Lessons we don't have to learn the hard way often change our lives. Because everyone has a story, every person has a store of knowledge ready to impart. We live a different life from theirs, so the plot twists in their storylines will teach them things we might not learn so easily through our experience. We are born of different parents, raised in another environment—a big city, small town, on a farm, in a different state or country. Perhaps they're married, and we're not, so they know more about relationships. Maybe someone or something they loved and lost reveals something to them we might not learn in any other way. Maybe some knowledge a stranger shares could someday save our life.

Maybe you'll learn from someone washing windows on your path today. Maybe you'll learn from the man that's asleep on the bus stop bench, or the FedEx guy, or the tech who comes in to repair your printer. Maybe the teen whose car breaks down outside your house has pearls of wisdom. Maybe a client. Maybe your doctor. Maybe a meme on a social network site will solve your problem. Your barista might know a thing or two, maybe a pathway to inner peace.

There is no chance encounter.

The people and things that come into your life arrive to teach you something good, and they're waiting for you to reciprocate with goodies they can contemplate.

There is nothing outside your purview, and not one thing that cannot speed your growth and fuel your transformation.

I learn from my garden, for example. How, for instance, plants are transplanted and keep right on growing nonetheless. They don't miss a beat, don't fret for bygone days when they lived in a pot in your kitchen with other plants they came to know. Or maybe they pine for a little while, but they quickly adjust to new surroundings, always bending toward the light. When they get planted in bigger pots, they expand and flourish all the more, unconcerned with the fact that their pot has changed, and the soil is unfamiliar. They don't hunker inside a comfort zone. They bud in unexpected places, let breezes scatter their seminal seeds, and provide us with endless beauty. They don't hate on the yellow flower in the adjacent bed because they're pink. They break out from under concrete, asphalt, tile, anything that may try to constrict them, growing together happily, adjusting to whatever watering issues they happen to be subjected to. Within reason, of course. All things may starve from neglect or the pain of abuse. We all need water, food, light, love. The whole world is a university. Life lessons abound for those eager to learn.

The instant you're ready and willing to learn, the teacher shows up, and the lesson begins.

You'll discover you're a teacher, too—a teacher and a student. Pass on what you learn with an open hand, and be prepared to teach yourself. Purify your thoughts. Keep an open mind and open heart, and check yourself at every turn. Take care to improve your behavior. If you see yourself procrastinating, tackle the hardest chore on your list as a number-one priority. Rout out any latent prejudice, selfishness or sloth. Look for ways in which to safeguard your health and advance your state of being. Turn bad habits around before they take hold. Assimilate information that can help you reach your goals. Read, read, read. Learn easily. Attract geniuses and sages. Lure wisdom, and yearn to be wise.

Remember, when the chips are down, and you really don't know what to do, go inward. Seek your Higher Power. Pray. Be humble. Ask for answers. Be rational. Think before you act. Find yourself a quiet spot. Close your eyes and breathe in deeply. Stay calm, and let your heart rate slow. Access collective consciousness. Answers will come when you need them most.

Learn life lessons when they're taught, so no experience goes for naught, especially if it's painful. The pain doesn't come to hurt you. It is just poking to get your attention.

And for heaven's sake, don't make the same mistake twice.

When you're open to learning from every experience, and your goal is constant growth, there is literally nothing you can't learn. All that happens is charmed and relevant, and you're able to let things go. When you live in the land of epiphany, your lens on life is focused.

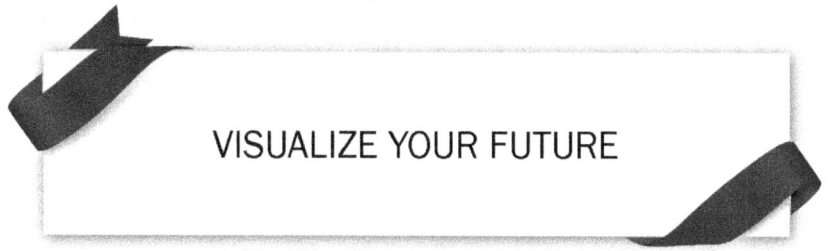

VISUALIZE YOUR FUTURE

What we imagine, we become.

Your imagination is infinite, and so is the good it can manifest.

Thoughts create, and so do you.

The simple act of visualizing what you want can bring it to you. Sounds kind of fanciful, but it is true. What you see in your mind isn't nebulous, it's substantive. It's real. It simply exists in another realm, until you will it to this plane of existence in this spacetime.

Everything starts as a pulsing idea before it becomes a reality.

Your dream is meant to be.

It's *your* Meant-To-Be that you're meant to do, and it's germinating in your mind for that reason—because it is part of you. It is possible *because* of you. It is inextricably linked to you. It is primed for you to bring it forth. Roll that around in your mouth for a minute. Taste it on your tongue. Tantalizing, isn't it. You and your dream, together as one. Inseparable. In love.

Here's an example from my world.

Several years ago, when I was married, and before my husband passed away, we lived in a teeny tiny apartment. We were deliriously happy there for years, never giving much thought to moving. We had an apartment in New York, from which we shuttled back and forth to our cozy cocoon with a mountain view in a chichi part of Los Angeles, smack in the middle of TV-ville and the major filming studios. It had amenities. It was low maintenance, suited our lifestyle to a tee, because we ran back and forth to work. We had to be where the work was, and acting work does not stay still. Our little place was safe and gated. Perfect, except it was miniscule. Suddenly, this became a "thing". We almost couldn't breathe in it. The walls were closing in. It was time to let go of our New York place and invest in a California home that wasn't designed for a Keebler elf. Time to move on to our next stage of adventure. We were desperate enough to move to Mars in order to land the perfect digs—and as it turned out, we almost did.

We—well, the truth is, actually I—became all but obsessed with the house-hunting guides, magazines, websites and TV shows. So, together we'd cruise through neighborhoods, on the lookout for errant "For Sale" signs, scouting for vacancies, trawling for fixer uppers, condos, anything. This was our date night. Every night. Dinner and looking for houses. Slightly weird, but sorta fun. Dreaming, and scheming about a home loan. Combing newspapers, our ears to the ground. *How much is that puppy in the window?* We were determined, focused, driven—almost out of our minds. We dreamed of our place relentlessly. But where was the house? It eluded us.

Then, one day—being the constant creator—I sat on the floor in our matchbox digs and conjured up a dream board. Basically, just a collage of houses that looked like they could be our dream house. I scurried around to buy poster board, magazines, markers, scissors glue. I picked up an IKEA frame, toted it home, and went to work. First, I snipped pictures of gorgeous manses all across America, visualizing one for us. I didn't know dip about visualization, but I definitely had an imagination on me (still do) that was fierce.

Well, long story short, in under a week, we landed a spanking new luxury home. It came out of the blue, unexpectedly. And the kicker was, it looked just like the houses I clipped out of those magazines, every one of which sat on a waterfront, which I didn't realize at the time. Our house wasn't in a magazine. It was on a real-live waterfront. A lake. It leapt from the pictures in my head right into our reality. We literally projected ourselves into that sucker viscerally.

We drove into an attached garage. We felt how it was to be living together in a spacious, modern home. We pictured the colors of furnishings, smelled the aroma of meals we could cook in the kitchen, experienced what it was like to look outside at a gorgeous view through a wall of huge glass doors. We lived there long before we ever arrived in our dream home physically. We cuddled in our master bedroom, bathed in the roomy en suite bath, washed our clothes in the laundry room, lolled in the shade on the sprawling veranda. We owned it, and it came to us.

This is the power of visualization. Visualization entices what we want with a flow of energy resulting from our focus. We draw what we want through the Law of Attraction.

The Law of Attraction warrants way more study than we will devote to it here, within the pages of this book. It's worth many books of study, and a lifetime's application. There are plenty of resources that delve fully into what it is. But what it means is simply this:

Thoughts become things.

We attract to ourselves matching energy forms, according to our vibration.

Focus on what you want—not what you don't—and it will come to you.

The mind is able to conjure up a universe of scenarios. We humans often squander this incredible capability—thinking of what we fear, and drawing that to us, instead of what we really want to populate our lives. What we think today, we experience tomorrow. What we believe and imagine, and what we feel emotion for, we attract to us. What energy we carry in our souls and spirits draws a match of energies that materialize things from elsewhere in the universe which enter our reality. Thus, choosing to be angry brings us more to be pissed off about, while opting to be generous brings us gifts from myriad sources.

When you visualize, for instance, that today will be smooth sailing, the whole cosmos will conspire to make life easy on you all day long. Conceive of gloom, and you compel every subatomic particle in the realm of possibilities to block your path and heap ill fortune on your head. The choice is yours. You think your thoughts. You can choose what to think, and therefore choose the reality in which you live.

Choose what you want to experience—all the good you desire to bring to your life and to the life of others—and then see it and feel it so keenly, with such positive intensity that you own it and make it manifest in your now as concrete reality.

Your thoughts are becoming substantive as we speak, because that is the name of the game. Thoughts become things. We become our thoughts. Who we become, becomes what we say and do, and what we act upon. What we act upon with energy and emotion shapes our world.

What we focus on appears. *Tada!*

So, focus on what you want to happen, not on what you don't.

You are the thinker creating with thoughts.

You can see who you wish to be, visualize how you want to live, and position your life for a makeover. Every cell in your body will summon your soul to turn on a dime and receive your command to uplevel your energy haste post haste. Higher energy will be returned in kind, because it is the nature of energy to seek out its match and reflect itself—and you will live the life you dreamed, and bring into the world all the benefits or detriments of your beliefs. You are doing this every moment of every day, perhaps unconsciously, co-creating collective reality by default in many instances. The key is to *consciously* create, to enhance and reveal the greater good. By conceiving, you make things tangible, experiential, nuts and bolts. Believe and conceive what you wish to appear, for your thoughts and emotions are conjuring it up right now.

This is a power you possess.

You change your world with your energy.

Know you have the ability to materialize all your mind's eye sees. Not only the material, also the priceless like world peace. Focus your mental imagery, and you will be able to actualize phenomena as you would have them be. This is what you are meant to do—to visualize the future as an increasingly brighter hue of light, and make an ideal world tangible, for you and every other being.

Your mental ability goes beyond any physical limitation. From a biological perspective, whether you actually skydive or just picture yourself parachuting from, say, thirteen thousand feet in the air, you trigger correlated nerve cells—relevant neural networks—that connect your body's actions to the nerve impulses in your brain that control your actions. Thus, thinking and doing can feel the same and, in fact, create the same result.

It is no wonder that some folks are content to talk about what they'll do instead of really doing it. The act of chatting up their dream, behaving as if they were taking steps to achieve it, and seeing themselves in the role of a busy entrepreneur, for example, can initiate the same brain functions as really being their own boss. Many people stop right there, and never make it happen.

Whereas, if they took time to visualize the specifics of a business life, asked the universe to deliver it, sincerely believed that their dream would come true, became open to truly receiving it, felt gratitude for having it, and took action commensurate with its success, imagine what the result would be.

Many successful athletes, performers and people in all walks of life utilize visualization to see and feel their achievements before they occur. In so doing, they program themselves to achieve at higher levels. It can work for you just like it works for them.

Employ visualization as a technique to immerse yourself in the imagery of the perfect world you want to see and your life when that vision is achieved. Visualization increases self-confidence. It can boost your creativity. With it, you can program your brain to excel. You can use the Law of Attraction to not only lure your wants and needs, but create the world of which you dream.

Perception is reality.

You can elevate your reality by perceiving from higher consciousness. You can use your creativity to visualize what you want to see and what you prefer to experience, and actively mold that Yet-To-Be—that heightened, new reality that benefits all beings. Use your imagination wisely. Let your limitless mental agility help you imagine a more perfect world, and leave the world better for your having lived. This is your desire, right? To fulfill the function for which you were born—to lift up the world with your special gifts. Gifts that only you can give.

Visualize exactly what you want. Ask for it. Feel what it's like to have it. Think of the good you intend, and only the good. Focus on it faithfully. You are the thinker. Your thoughts create.

Believe the vision you see is real. Believe it can only materialize.

Feel what it feels like to be in your dream once it manifests as reality.

Open up to receive it with gratitude, and do all you can to substantiate it.

Your vision is even now coming to life. I believe in it, and I believe in you. I can feel your dream is coming true, and I know you can make it happen. Let it happen. Be its conduit.

Your vibe can reverb around the globe, and make of you the change you seek.

VISUALIZATION

Visualizing is super easy, really. It's what you did as a child. Perhaps you had an imaginary friend. I know I did. Oops, maybe that's way too much info, but, oh well, you catch the drift. Maybe when you were a kid, you had some fun tea parties when your guest was an empty little chair. You imagined. You saw what you wanted to see, and felt how you wanted to feel about it, preparing yourself for social soirees later on in life. You believed you were having a real tea party. You were, because you perceived you were. Maybe you even sashayed around, like I did, both legs in one pajama leg, the other trailing behind you, as if you were wearing a ball gown or wedding dress. You dreamed of being a fairy princess or a prince's bride. Maybe you had a cardboard sword, and you were the prince on a rocking horse. You projected your spirit into your future using the same access to creativity you have now.

Visualizing is viewing a picture in full detail, zooming in, walking into it, and feeling the way it makes you feel, from joy to exhilaration. Go on, roll the movie in your mind. Step into it. Enjoy your role. This will generate the energy to propel it from your dream world into the real world as a change. You will project yourself into it real-time using your power of thought. You will fake it till you make it, until you are literally living the dream.

Use the power. Close your eyes. Situate in a comfy position.

This method of visualizing isn't the only way, of course. There are many methods. You'll find yours. The one I am sharing with you here is what comes easily to me. I am a creative. I live by my imagination, always churning out ideas. Fantasies, imagery, insights and inspirations come alive in me in perpetual motion, day and night. I believe everyone is creative. We all co-create with the universe. No one's left out of the process. That means you're a creator, too. Whether or not you believe you're creative now, believe it from this point on. Your imagination is your friend. It can take you places nothing else is willing or able to go.

I am happiest when I'm creating—characters, stories, voice overs, artwork, video, photos, jewelry, crafts, my music. This all brings me joy. Some of us work as creative professionals plying our trade and artistry. Others engage in more left-brained mental activities such as tech and math. One way or another, we all create. We exercise this power just by implementing what we think.

You are creating all the time. The last e-mail you wrote was a creation. So is the outfit you're wearing now. Even if someone designed your shirt and slacks, and someone else sewed them up, it's you who assembled your ensemble. You, who created the fashion statement people experience when they're with you. What you wear is your creativity reflecting your aesthetic and displaying your personality. Maybe you're featuring boots, or a scarf, or a hat or some other accessory. Maybe you tucked your shirt just so, or tied its tails into a knot. You create your look.

If you code, then you created software, coded a videogame or made an app to generate workflow. If you cook, you created a meal. Even if you styled your hair, you created a hairdo all your own, as no one else has the self-same hair, or flair, or combo of things you used. Face it, you're creative. It's a fabulous thing. Be proud of it. And you've only just begun.

Take charge of what you create by visualizing what you want:

1. Unplug—Turn off music, TVs, phones and other electronic gadgets
2. Find a quiet, peaceful place
3. Make yourself comfy
4. Close your eyes
5. Take a deep breath, then a couple more. Smell the roses, blow out the candle.
6. Picture the place you want to be when the dream you're dreaming happens. After it turns from a goal to a series of tasks that are completed. What's the result? Where are you now? Maybe you're in a trendy office space where your startup business thrives. Maybe you're in a house you built. Maybe you're in your restaurant, or studio, gym, or the magnet school in which you love to teach. See it clearly in your mind. Play it like a movie. Move from the panorama of it. Zoom in for a closer shot. Crank up the surround sound. See in Technicolor. Go 3D. View it in Super Hi-Def. You're the star of this film, so make it good. It's destined to be a hit. This is becoming reality. Design the production as you go. Write your lines. Direct your cast. Leave out all the drama. Sniff the scents and hear the sounds. Are sea waves lapping?

Hear birds chirping? Is there a song playing in the background?

7. Step into the picture. Look around. Relax. Take in the 360 view. You are at home. This is your place. You own it now. It's real. You're more comfortable here than you've ever been. You're unflappable. How do you feel? Are you in a blissful state? Are you happy? Excited? Thrilled? Elated? Probably a smile plays on your face. Maybe you're feeling tingly. *Feel* how you feel. Is it safe and secure? Of course. You can let your feelings flow. Your emotions are key to unlocking your creativity. Let this new world be. What are you doing? How are you doing it? Is someone in here with you? Someone you know, or have yet to meet? A new love interest? Business partner? Child you'll bring into your life? An entourage for your album tour, or book tour? Maybe a loyal friend? Is it a pilot flying your private plane? Or the residents of the village you want to help bring water to? It's all about love here, isn't it? You don't have a care in the world. You are meant to be here. It's your palace of peace. Nothing can keep you from living here, not any obstacle in the world. The universe is working for you. You're connected to this place. It's your very own Utopia.

8. Stay here as long as you like. It's your world. It exists because of, and for, you. If you have an epiphany while you're here, resolve to remember to write it down.

9. When you're ready to move, keep the images playing, realizing your dream is already true.

10. Wrap the movie in your mind around you. Relax in it like in a favorite blanket. Wear it like a well-worn garment. Continue to let it embrace you, feeling it hug you like a second skin. Cuddle up in its arms. Rub it onto your legs, head, neck, chest, face and body. Absorb it like a creamy lotion. Lounge in it. Feel it seep in through your pores and rush into your

bloodstream. Let it energize your joints and muscles. Take from it superhuman strength and infinite stores of energy. Massage it in like fragrant oil. Imagine it filling you up with light, as it courses through your veins.

11. If it's nighttime, allow it to lull you into sound sleep and restful dreams. Imagine it being a part of you, as much as your heart or lungs.
12. If it's daytime, let it propel, protect, and motivate you through the day.
13. Open your eyes and feel renewed. Jot down the thoughts that come to you.
14. Repeat this process often. You will attune to this discipline naturally. Repetition of perfect practice can make you a wizard at realizing dreams.

As you see the change you want to be, be grateful your dreams are coming true.

PREPARE FOR THE JOURNEY

KEEP AN OPEN HEART AND MIND

Information bombards us all the time. It's up to us to assimilate it in a manner that triggers creative processes and fresh perspectives. For this, we need an open mind. An open mind quickly accepts unfamiliar concepts, works to facilitate change, and seeks unusual, untrodden routes to a goal through original thinking.

Change is the natural order of things, and change is happening constantly, but often we don't understand what we contribute to the course of change, for better or for worse.

Since change for the better is mandatory, else there is no point in change, we have to commit to making change for the better to make progress.

Change, by definition, makes things different fundamentally—as to their nature, form, contents, relation to all other things, potential, future development and ultimate effect.

For changes to take place in us—because we have will, and exert our will, and because we have our consciousness—we have to be open to changes occurring in and around us for change to spur growth. This is because we change ourselves. We're not like the weather, changing from sunny to stormy, or like the changing tides which follow the phases of the moon.

Our changes emanate from thought. Our thoughts are things that we control. Change is up to us.

We perhaps cannot change an occurrence, but we control the way it changes us. Resisting the changes around us is fruitless. We often resist them anyway, preferring the familiar to the unknown to the point of counterproductive reactions to changes we view as unnecessary, abrupt or undesirable. We may, or may not, be aware of this. Change often invades our comfort zones. We sometimes feel victimized by change, and want things as they were.

A closed mind closes to lock out change, to block out possibilities beyond the status quo. If possibility is blocked, there is no change. There is no growth. There is no upward movement.

Change can be seen as a strike against our freedom, and this causes pain. As people are prone to flee pain and race toward pleasure, unexpected change can feel like an assault. Some of us perceive change as an imminent hazard, dangerous, a menace to our safety. Menaces to our safety threaten society as a whole. If we view change as a threat or hazard, we will, rather than welcome change, be likely to take up arms against it. This can cause our subconscious thoughts to assemble armies battling change, when what they really need to do is receive it with hope and gratitude, as a chance for expansion and growth.

An open mind embraces change, sees changes as opportunities, and every opportunity as a chance to reach peak potential.

Program your mind to be open to good, and you'll find every change in the outside world to be for the best in some way or another. With an open mind, changes lift you up, and as always, the best way to lift yourself up translates into lifting up others.

See your mind as an ever-expanding space, not contracting, but constantly widening. Your mind is a conduit for good. Like a pipe that fresh water rushes through, the wider the pipe, the more water can flow, and the more clean water the world can drink. Change is the ocean from which water flows. Oceans are made from the water from clouds. Clouds are made from ocean water. Everything is a cycle, and when your mind is open to cycle good, the more good there is for you and me, and everyone on the planet.

Along with your ever-expanding mind, you will want to develop an open heart. An open, tender heart is key to giving and receiving love. Love is the light that lights the world. Your open heart can light the world, because positive changes derive from love.

We tend to guard the entrance to our hearts, as an open heart can let in pain, and pain can be debilitating, physically, mentally, emotionally, and to a degree that's hard to bear, and we might find irreparable. We think people can easily hurt us when we open our hearts and let them in. When we open our hearts, we are vulnerable. When we allow ourselves to be vulnerable, we're effectively exposed. We see this as a liability requiring great strength and bravery, assuming it carries high levels of risk.

When we're in touch with our emotions, pain can come in from any source. But, to my open mind, the risk of an open heart getting hurt is far less than the impact on one's soul and spirit one sustains by guarding one's heart overzealously, and never connecting honestly with the heart of another human being. Lack of love is total loss. Not to love is the ultimate danger. Not to love is not to live. This is the greatest tragedy. It's positively Shakespearian. It is a self-inflicted wound deeper than any other cut. It can impale one's quintessence.

Cherish your open heart and mind, and the world will reward you with infinite potential for the good. Openness lets possibilities in. The change that can come from opening your heart, and opening your mind to accept new ideas is always a change for the better. It is the path to perpetual peace, to living a life that's free from fear. Openness leads to invention, re-invention, transformation into higher self, and changing the world with light and love.

MEDITATE TO HEAR THE VOICE WITHIN

The art and science of meditation aims at stillness of the mind.

Our daily hustle and bustle, and the ever-present, droning din of media and new media through which filters negativity, is a drumbeat of distraction from the inner voice that guides.

The meaning of life and the ways we enjoy it broadcasts at a lower volume than the cacophonous news reports, loud music, smart phone ringtones, doorbells, arguments, hassles and complaints.

Meditation is both an antidote to noise and a healing balm. It offers a direct connection to your Higher Power. It allows you to tap into the source by weeding out static frequencies like a radio antenna. In quietude, we feel as one, not just know it intellectually.

You may wish to meditate, as I do, to get closer to your Higher Power, however you perceive the power greater than your own. I meditate to still myself to better hear from God.

Whatever your religious beliefs, or the absence thereof, may happen to be, your spiritual connection is unbroken. You're part of the One that abides in us all, and in which we abide in eternal good beyond the bounds of space or time. We may define things differently, but the fact that we are one is undeniable and absolute. And the fact that the one is the substance of love is the mesh that knits us together.

I believe that, though we may reference the One Love praising its goodness with different names—God, Jehovah, Allah, Krishna, Brahman and the like—we all worship the same highest force of goodness, just in different ways, through varied means and customs that are more alike than different. The ultimate power of goodness is big enough to fit into more than one religion, as far as I'm concerned. We all seek love and enlightenment. You may do so espousing different beliefs, which I respect and seek to know more about. We agree on more than we disagree. God is not a bone to pick or a theory to rip us apart. God is all and everything.

Some tenets we follow are fundamental. That we treat others as we'd like to be treated is pretty much basic everywhere. That change is always possible. That there is a power greater than us that loves us unconditionally, that wants us to realize why it created us, wants us to reach enlightenment.

The focus of my meditation is to come close to God, to do God's will, to achieve inner peace, and be more like Jesus Christ in thought, word, deed, output and nature. I believe this is why I live—to create, enlighten and entertain while aspiring to my highest self. I believe I can change the world for the better, and that God is working through me to achieve that aim. I also believe God works through you, and everything there is.

You may wish to meditate for these or other personal reasons. Perhaps to achieve more inner peace, eliminate anxiety, or allay any fears and worries. Maybe you want to find answers to questions and challenges in your life, or to ponder the meaning of life itself. You might meditate to reduce stress levels, improve sleep habits, eliminate pain, increase well-being, let go of the past, or gain a more positive outlook. You may wish to improve career performance, maximize creative flow, garner lasting relationships, curb bad habits, obsessive behaviors, indulgences, judgments or character flaws, or enter relaxation. Whatever your motivation is, meditation will improve your life and benefit you immeasurably. Practicing it will make you smile.

Meditating on life's meaning can make you chuck your endeavors totally, steering your life in a whole new direction, shaking yours up and others' too. This is how grass roots change expands to a global level—starting with individual change that's bound to filter out.

When we meditate to reveal our purpose and how to fulfill it, we supercharge. We surrender ourselves to be guided to the people, places and things that help us do what we are meant to do, and be who we are meant to be, which is highest self. There is no higher calling than actualizing highest self. It's why we are here in our human incarnation. Meditation aims us toward this goal of realization. Plucked from a world of cause-and-effect, diversions, situations, circumstances and illusions, we aim straight at the truth of our existence.

As spiritual beings in a physical world, we are not to succumb to base instincts or reduce our thoughts and actions to the lowest common denominator. We are to elevate our thoughts, so when they materialize as palpable realities, they are of benefit. When we meditate, we are positioned for this. We let go of the trials, tribulations, blockages and low energies that bring about discord and strife, and immerse ourselves in our mission as emissaries of the peace. In this mode, we can better access our gifts and talents, and, with confidence, put them to work to change the world.

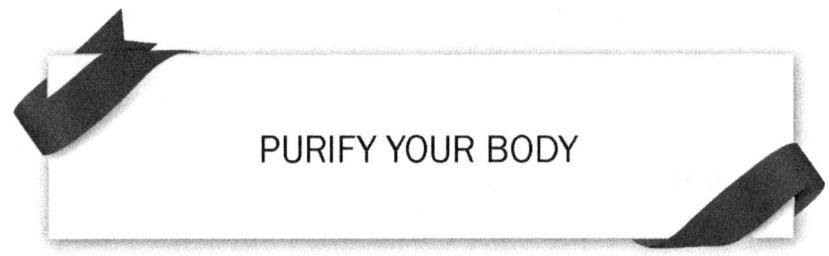

PURIFY YOUR BODY

Your body and mind function together. Your body takes signals from your thoughts and feelings, and responds to them. You are what you eat and what you think. You mind takes cues from your body, too. When it tires, it tells your mind to sleep. Now, whether you actually go to sleep can be another story. But if you don't sleep, function slows. Your body and mind are a unit.

As you purify your mind, take care to purify your body. Proper diet, nutrition, exercise, sleep habits, breathing, relaxation, hydration and hygiene regimens are essential to your overall health and wellness, as is your happiness. The energy, stamina and fitness required to see your goals through to completion isn't something to neglect. Olympic athletes train for their events. Change Wizards have to, too. We have to be ready to roll. We're in it for the long haul, so we need to be strong and hearty. Changing the world is not for the faint of heart. All systems must be go.

To be in tiptop shape, we have to take care of ourselves relentlessly. Well, duh. It might seem obvious, but it isn't always easy. We have to take care of others, probably work harder than we ever have, care for our homes and communities. And stressful input seems to come in never-ending streams. That is, if we process it as stress. Our time is consumed, like never before, in managing everyday tasks for finances, business concerns, domestic matters, careers and growing lists of chores, from phone calls, to errands, to paying bills.

We barely have time for relationships beyond our immediate family and friends, far less for accessing the calmness, focus, self-expression, mindfulness and balance comprising healthful life. Technology and electronic devices sit on the edge of consciousness every fleeting second of every day, and it's easy to get caught up in them and the sedentary lifestyle they engender, rather than go outdoors. Walking, running, hitting the gym, or playing a sport takes time and drive we may not seem to have. But we have to do them anyway, and we have to eschew superfluous smoking, drug use, overeating, fat consumption, salt and sugar intake, alcoholic beverages, fast foods, junk and processed foods, and the bevy of harmful additives. Artificial colors, sweeteners, flavors and preservatives can derail us as much as some pesticides.

Nutritional supplements such as multiple vitamins, green drinks, protein shakes, and plant and flower essences can help us achieve the optimum levels of nutrients our bodies need, and give us the vitality and alertness needed to work long days. A preventative beats a cure any day, and prevention goes a long way toward ensuring whatever we tackle, we complete.

When your body functions optimally, you're free to go about daily chores with the zeal, drive, toughness and get-up-and-go that effective people exhibit. You want your endeavors to be far-reaching. Good health allows you to persevere, persist, be resilient, exert yourself, even fight, if you must, for a worthy cause, more forcefully than the average bear.

The more potent your energy, the more you can do, and the more what you do catches on. You can avoid obesity, complacency, procrastination, lethargy and other ills, and pursue world-changing strategies with the power of good health.

By tweaking your diet, monitoring habits, releasing what doesn't support your health, sending your body strengthening thoughts, and enhancing your physicality with ample rest and exercise, you can literally embody change.

YOUR PAST IS NOT YOUR FUTURE

Whatever happened in your past, it doesn't have any hold on you. It doesn't loom over your future unless you drag it along behind you, like a semi hauling a heavy load. And it doesn't overshadow now, or have any claim on your present, unless you grant it permission by giving it a home in the here and now. If your psyche doesn't store it on the hard drive in your mental scape, it won't be even a blip on the screen of the movie in your mind. Not one pixel in your mental picture has to draw on memories. They're thoughts like any other thoughts. They are subject to your control. Not only control, authority. That's absolute authority. It is you who hold sway over memories, and no one and nothing else. Your memories can't flood into your head and remain there waterboarding you. You're a rememberer. They are memories. They must obey your will.

Any painful memories replaying as loops in the movie in your mind constitute a form of self-abuse. They're not pushing the playback button, you are. You've entered them into your playlist, probably posted them there unedited, uploaded them onto your Internet channel, and now those suckers are up on YouTube, live-streaming yesterday's failings, insecurities, negative programming, stale energies and debilitating feelings such as inadequacy, futility and distress. And for not only you, but a wider audience—spouses, siblings, co-workers, neighbors, dates, employers, employees, investors, partners, potential customers, clients and the whole wide world. This doesn't have to be the case. It is not an inevitability. You don't have to roll old footage, you can produce new memories. Great ones.

Bad memories are fleeting. Let them pass. They're not visions projected by outside forces, not like embarrassing family photos your parents can't wait to show visitors. They're pests you can eradicate by willingly shifting your focus to the abundant possibilities that grace your what-comes-next. Be present, and bad memories will never get a chance to form. The next good memory is taking shape as a wonderful possibility you are able to bring into now.

And guess what? News flash. Little known fact: Bad memories aren't bad at all. We've just tagged them with that keyword. A virus got into the metadata, causing us to mislabel them. Hashtag: #uhohigothurt. And when we get hurt, we want it known. We might not verbalize it, but we wear it around like a tattered robe, and dare anyone to notice it isn't the hottest runway couture. Hurt can cause us to get defensive, clam up, shut down, hurt other people before they hurt us, and block any good that comes our way.

You might even have an old website up—www.mistakes.com. You designed it on Windows 98 way back in the day on an old desktop. It updates automatically, posting new video all the time, archiving every dumping, firing, abandonment, betrayal, financial debacle, flu, loud neighbor, weight gain, insult, chore and bad hair day. Unpleasant flashbacks on demand. You're thinking of pitching the History Channel, or maybe the Smithsonian. They surely must be interested in the relics of your painful past, that terrifying horror flick. Doesn't everyone love to relive their pain? Well, no, they don't, and nor should you. Pain is a drain. You don't have to endure it. Ghosts don't have to haunt you. You can jettison what bothers you, and move on to the next opportunity.

Steeping yourself in bad memories and allowing them to creep up on you can effectively dog your every move. You don't have to live as if things don't change, like another swell thing won't come along, as though you must cling to what's gone before.

You're changing. Life's changing. Go with it. You're setting your course and direction. Don't go backwards, look ahead. The train's pulling out of the station, pal. You're no passenger, you're the engineer. Own it. Stay on track.

You can only do this if you're not tied to the past in a way that limits expectations for the future. Stay in the present tense. This is critical for the life you want to live, and the gift you want to give. And yeah, it might not be easy. It might take a bit of work. You might have to look at some things that aren't so pretty, and why you stuck with them, and work through them until you can cut them loose instead of repressing their affect effects. You might have to own up to certain things, or take responsibility for stuff you might rather blame others for. But you're the one who'll benefit, the one who'll be able to turn the page.

And there's more good news—you're not alone. The less time you spend with the ghosts of your past, the more love you can share in the present, and the more you proclaim your future.

If a painful memory crops up, you can short-circuit it with an uplifting thought. You can focus your mind on empowering images, sounds or other sensory data. A memory is just an extinct idea that has already had its day. It isn't a real experience, and it doesn't reside where you are now. It only exists as an echo on the periphery of your imagination. When it is good, let it lift you. When it stirs ill feelings, let it go. You're not a curator of artifacts from the past. You're the sculptor of dreams to come.

You're writing your script with your every thought. Your script isn't writing you. Letting thoughts regress wastes energy meant for the brave new world you're building, so, like the hands of a clock, you move forward, not back.

Direct the effect of your energies so they always progress and expand.

Tackle a memory that holds you back, come to grips with it, stare it down. Unburden your heart. Apologize. Drop it. Forgive. Forget. Concede. Let it dissolve or evaporate. Quit visiting it like an ailing friend. You don't owe it one minute of time. Don't drop in to see what it's up to now. Pay attention to what you're meant to do, and not what you did that didn't work, or what someone else did that tripped you up. Woulda, Shoulda and Coulda are not your buds. I mean, what have they done for you lately, huh? Introduced you to Oh-No and Regret, and they aren't in your corner either. They just drag you down.

Be where you're loved and appreciated. Love and appreciate where you are. Let go of the past, and hold hands with your present. Your future is brighter than you know.

Start believing that what is ahead is better than anything you left behind.

If it was important, it wouldn't be gone.

If it's gone, it isn't important now.

If it feels important, it *isn't* gone. It just feels like it's gone, but it's part of you. That it's lost is a fable you told yourself. The good doesn't leave you, it just makes you better.

The bad doesn't matter, it falls away. But only if you let it. And nothing is bad when good comes from it. Good can come from anything. And it does, when you're grateful for all that comes. It's all good, when you're grateful. A memory is neutral, just something that happened. What happened brought you where you are, and where you are now leads to where you will go. Be grateful, and keep moving.

Nothing can touch you that isn't good, because *you* are good, and you draw your match.

Only energy that you radiate comes back to you in kind. That is the truth of the Law of Attraction.

Whatever has happened, make peace with it. Carry on with the wisdom it affords. That is its only legacy. Your legacy is brilliance, and a future that will change the world.

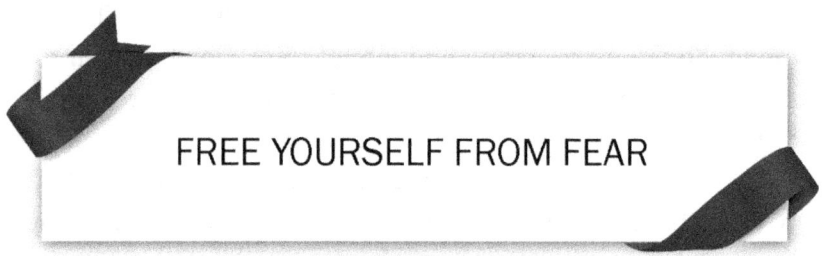

FREE YOURSELF FROM FEAR

Fear is a false and insidious enemy threatening to turn your dream from a reality into a nightmare. Fear leads to inaction and despair. Current culture is steeped in a media-driven web of fear, foreboding and anxiety that is unjustified. If you fear, you court paralysis. Fear misuses creative thought and emotions to bring what you fear to your life. Although logical fear must be recognized as a tool to protect us from actual danger, illogical fear blocks progress by subverting our will to try new things, making us adverse to change, and causing us to shy away from other living creatures. Fear can make anything look like it poses inordinate risk to safety. That's how it tricks and manipulates us. Fear is an all too common technique to divide and conquer, attempt to control, and arouse pernicious suspicions. Fear can only separate us. Ultimately, what we fear the most will result in a fear of each other. This is no way to interact. This is no way to bring greater peace. Fear of each other can only bring conflict, urge all sorts of bigotry, and keep people locked in a box smaller than the size of their potential.

To fear is to live inside terrible things that will likely never happen.

Nothing so truncates the lure of a fascinating life like fear. Genuine trauma can bring on fear, but we need to avoid having unfounded dread becoming an excuse. Fear alters our organ functions, and has our metabolisms doing flips. And many times, people don't know why it is they fear the things they fear.

We may be programmed to fear as children, by loving adults trying to keep us safe. We're persuaded to fear by advertisers wanting to sell us antidotes to diseases we're not sure exist. Some people get tattooed with fear of failure, others with fear of success. Still others with fear of animals, fear of commitment, fear of heights. These kinds of fears are phobias.

The Mayo Clinic defines a phobia as "an overwhelming and unreasonable fear of an object or situation that poses little real danger but provokes anxiety and avoidance". If it poses little danger, why in the world would we be afraid of it.

Though unreasonable fear is a paper tiger, claustrophobia, agoraphobia, arachnophobia and other phobias can be difficult to grapple with. Which is not to say they aren't real, but fear that's unsubstantiated can do more harm than what is feared. For instance, though fear of public speaking is proven to equal a lack of success, it's shown to be a greater fear than even fear of death. It sure doesn't seem to make much sense to fear talking in front of others more than losing one's own life, but if fear is allowed to get a grip, it holds on with a vengeance.

The good news is fear has a countermeasure—simple, safe and efficacious. Ready for it?

It's called faith. It is knowing that the universe is working for you all the time. That the universe is on your side—on all our sides—and life is good. It's called choosing to stick with the energy of hope and everlasting love, rather than giving in to fears you know are just delusions.

Faith and fear can't occupy the same space, so you have to choose. When you believe the universe provides, protects and pilots you, you cannot simultaneously acquiesce to the limiting counter belief that frights surround at every turn, commissioned and charged to do you in.

If you fear, you chose the noxious belief that bad is stronger than the good. You ally yourself with low energies, and you pull the feared thing closer in a self-fulfilling prophecy. Fear is respect for negative forces over respect for the positive. Such a paradigm is untenable. It is one that is in need of change, not one that can forge a better world.

I, for one, am all in with faith. That's my choice, and I'm sticking to it.

Faith, or fear. Which do you choose?

1. The Law of Divine Oneness

We are all One. We're all connected. Everything exists together. The whole of all things is greater than the sum of its parts. We're a great gestalt. Everything in existence emanates from a single source—an eternal, unchanging field of energy unifying intelligence, underlying all there is, and infusing all of life. The substance of it is agape love. Recognition of this reality, and its presence inside all of us, is paramount for realization. To be fully realized, we must come to see the divine in every being, respect and adore the ultimate oneness happening inside each of us, and know we're all part of an energy so infinitely bountiful and beautiful as to blows our minds.

Every part of the Universal Mind is within us all, and we're in it. Such is the enormity of our potential and connectedness. We exist within this endless creativity, and it exists in us. This consciousness created matter and gives rise to life. We are not individual tiny specks of a distant star in a murky sky. We each contain *all* of the universe, just as the acorn contains the oak tree. There is one force in the universe. It is goodness. It is everything. It makes all things possible. It is all-knowing, and from it, we draw all thought and every good idea. It is *for* us, never against us. It protects us, guides us, makes us inseparable one from another, and inseparable from it. It makes all things work together for good, no matter how things may appear. We come from this universal power, live in it, and are grateful it is the source of every change.

2. The Law of Vibration

All there is, moves, and has constant movement. Everything is, and has, energy, and these energies vibrate at varying speeds. Every being, creature and object carries its own vibrational frequency along an electromagnetic spectrum.

Just as a TV or radio station broadcasts on a specific frequency attendant to levels of sound vibration, we have our own unique vibratory signatures and patterns.

Nothing's as solid as it appears. What we see as a solid is made up of tiny subatomic particles—photons, leptons, electrons, neutrons and quarks that pop in constant motion. Thus, everything is an energy field. We humans are fields of energy consisting of particulates. Our vibration is determined by our thoughts, emotions and deeds. The more lofty our thoughts, emotions and actions, the higher the frequency of our vibe.

Love and happiness are high vibrations. Anger, hate and despair are not. Because like energies seek one another, our challenge is to match our vibration to that which we wish to bring into our lives as palpable phenomena.

We control our thoughts and feelings. We can change them on a dime, uplifting our vibe and environment. This is the key to maintaining a high vibration that changes our personal life as well as the shape of the outside world. We create change from the inside out.

3. The Law of Action

The Law of Action states that you must take specific, repeated and targeted action toward your dreams and goals in alignment with your feelings, thoughts, words, aims and aspirations. Merely wishing or chatting up alone is not going to make things happen. Take positive, swift, definitive action, keeping it moving with surety, for the universe values speed and rewards commitment, not just fancy talk.

This doesn't mean that hardship, stress, strain, struggle or strife need inform your work.

On the contrary, struggle begets more struggling. A vibration accompanying struggle will not match that of the thing you want. Instead, take action to do the deeds—that perhaps you've never done before—that will manifest your vision. Take the leap. Though you might not initially be entirely sure of the proper course, when you take that first step in abiding faith, the universe will back you up. Move forward with hope, belief and persistence, and doors will begin to open wide. What you're creating will magically take on a life of its own, and change the world in ways that are miraculous.

4. The Law of Correspondence

The law of correspondence says that what you experience in the world corresponds directly to who you are, and in sync with what you anticipate. What you believe will happen, happens. The outer world mirrors your inner world. What exists inside you will be evidenced as your reality. It will reflect in the outside world. What you think and believe, you experience. You are constantly in the process of physically manifesting fear or faith, your hope or doubt, your joy or pain, good luck or bad. You shape your life. Your experiences are not random. All the ups and downs you might have thought were thrust at you by an exterior force, beyond your control and against your will, were actually created by your will, whether you realize that or not.

The truth is *you* create your life, and the way every change affects it.

5. The Law of Cause and Effect

Good in, good out. It's as simple as that. You reap what you sow, as the Bible says. If you're generous, you reap rewards. When you're kind, much kindness returns to you. Call it karma rebounding endlessly, like a yo-yo springing back to you. Or, as the law says, cause and effect. The energy you generate returns to you in kind. Every change that happens has a result. We determine what that result may be insofar as we're concerned, and that result has a result.

Change can change you, and you can change, change.

6. The Law of Compensation

What you give is what you get. Giving is why you receive. To give as solely a means of receiving is outside the spirit of this law. Giving for giving's sake to benefit others, from a pure intent, aligns your vibration with plentitude and rewards you with abundance. Your prosperity is a function of how you help other people prosper. When you give of whatever you have to give, the universe favors you. You are blessed. Give of money, knowledge, time, unconditional love, a hug, a smile, or any of your gifts and talents, and the world will give to you. Just as the One Love gives to you without your asking, always present, coming through, so should you seek to do for others. As you give, you shall receive.

7. The Law of Attraction

This is how you make things happen. This is the key to living the life you may only have lived in visions. The Law of Attraction is perhaps the best known Universal Law.

Because you are basically energy, and energy always seeks its match, it's vital you align your vibrational field and the wave forms it entails, with what you want, not what you don't. You draw your match no matter what, so draw what you want to experience. Think, feel, speak, believe and act on only that which you wish to see materialize as reality, and stay open to receiving good. What you ask for, believe, emit feelings for, and are open to receive as fact appears. It doesn't matter what. The universe doesn't discriminate for you. You must determine for yourself. If you focus on fears, you'll bring them to you. Focus on winning, you will win. Your ability to attract to you the things that you desire most hinges on your ability to act in concert with them, behaving as though they are already yours. Act like you already have them, and you'll attract them. You will draw to you the people, places and things required to actualize them in your life, and exteriorize possibilities that were once just an idea.

8. The Law of Transmutation of Energy

You can change your energy in a snap by changing what you think and feel. Transmuting your energy instantly is achievable when you believe it is, and exert your consciousness to change your current state of being. Since energy moves to make wishes come true, and higher vibrations trump lower vibrations, you can set out to change your world by eschewing lower energies and adopting higher ones. Your dynamic energy field is raised the moment you shift your inner focus to higher vibrations of energy, such as positive emotions. Since energy flows where attention goes, when you pin your attention on greatest good, more good will organically manifest.

When you vibrate above the plane low energies live on, they can't locate you, move you to sadness or other ill feelings, or block what you desire. You're amped up above their vibration, above their pay grade. They can't mess with you. You're out of their league, and they're banned from yours, because they don't have your attention.

Focus on good to uplevel your place in the vibratory scheme of things by connecting with your Higher Power. Within the Universal Mind, all energies are the change they seek.

9. The Law of Relativity

Everything is relative. Experiences lack intrinsic value other than what you place on them by making a judgment born from your developing perspective. Your perspective is particular to you, and thus, is relative to every other point of view. A ten-dollar bill may seem like a fortune to someone fighting poverty. To a rich man, hardly anything. We assign value based on who we are, and our experience. We determine by analogy, deciding what is good or bad by comparing it to another thing. Situations and circumstances seem like a comedy or a tragedy relative to what went before, or what is occurring somewhere else, and our own set of expectations.

There's what happens, how you process it, and how you respond after processing it as a negative or a plus. This processing colors everything, though it's often done subconsciously. You interpret your experiences. Your singular interpretations stem from your feelings and beliefs—beliefs you might not know you hold.

If, for instance, there is an accident, say, with an injury to a foot or leg, some may process it as a warning, a chance to rest or indulge in self-care. Others may peg the incident as an exogenous turn of events that, though unfortunate, could affect anyone, and likely soon will pass. Others may barely take it in, continue like nothing untoward occurred, refuse to let it bother them, and decline to learn anything at all. And yet others may see it as more bad luck on top of the streak of bad luck that plagued them ever since they hit the scene and got diaper rash in a bassinet. Such persons may rant and rave, and rail against those they deem responsible—which rarely turns out to be themselves. Each of these reactions to the same, or similar, stimulus is a relative construct of the mind dependent on who the person is, and the value judgments they may make.

As everything is relative, you give change its meaning, its significance and its value.

10. The Law of Polarity

For everything, there is an opposite diametrically opposed to it. There's up and down, and young and old, rich or poor, and fat or thin. There's an entire spectrum in between these polar opposites, encompassing possibilities on an ever-extending scale. Very little exists at either extreme end. Most is neither black nor white, but subsists along the gray scale.

Regardless of where you may see yourself now, or how you have processed prior events, what happens is subject to your perception of it, and yours only—that is, as it relates to you. Therefore, you are always qualified to experience the polar opposite of situations, circumstances, people, places and all things by changing your perception. Ergo, contrary to popular belief, you can actually choose to change the past by looking at it differently, and thereby changing its effect on you. That's pretty cool. No, very cool. Revolutionary, really.

And that's not to mention changing your present, and altering the trajectory of your future life experience by shifting your perception. That's, like, a whole sci-fi thing there. Empowerment times a bazillion. That's capacity, privilege, accreditation and license to the max. Shift how you see it, that's how it is. How's that for a magical power.

Did somebody try to put you down? Interpret it into self-esteem. Down to your last, say, fifteen cents? Perceive it as more room in your wallet for riches that are on the way. Can you see how that thought will generate words and actions that will work for you?

You can reorient any thought, idea, belief or experience by switching your attention to its opposite and making it a touchstone. Turn any change 180 degrees if the flipside is opportunity, which is what all change is meant to be. You work with the law of polarity in a proactive way, constructively as you're meant to do, by using the power of opposites to be the light that shines the light, so others don't stumble around in the dark. In this way, you *are* the change.

11. The Law of Rhythm

Everything has a rhythm because all that exists is some form of energy, and all energies vibrate rhythmically. We feel them like our heartbeat. When scientists record the sound of stars, we hear an exquisite universal rhythm that enchants.

We most often experience rhythms that delight us when we hear music. Music is dubbed the "universal language" everyone comprehends. We all feel rhythms, and when we do, we immediately understand them. Hearing rhythm makes us want to move. Aligning ourselves with the rhythm of something helps us move in concert with it. Think of the rhythm of a basketball team, dribbling a ball and passing it. The rhythm of an assembly line or of an acting cast.

To stay in concert with the Law of Rhythm, listen to your heartbeat and your pulse. Allow them to quietly speak to you. You can modify your internal tempo such that it's not frenetic, syncopated or irregular. You can match your personal cadence with the high vibration of what you want through relaxation, concentration, imagination and focusing. You can employ a metronome to accustom yourself to a steady beat, listen to calming recordings, or fall asleep to a sound machine that, for instance, produces the patter of rain, the ebb and flow of ocean waves, or chattering city sounds.

Align yourself with the rhythm of upbeat energies your dreams contain, natural rhythms of the great outdoors, and the constant pulse of the flow of life, and adapting to change is as easy as hearing the next song on your playlist.

12. The Law of Gender

The Law of Gender indicates everything carries energies, both feminine and masculine.

Both genders have to come to bear in order to create. Like a male and a female create a baby. Achieving the balance of yin and yang is the crux of all creation. The balance of physical and spiritual, for example, or ego and soul. Masculine and feminine energies in combination produce the balance essential to live a healthy life. We develop this balance through knowledge of self. Self-knowledge can take time. Creating anything takes time. This is called a gestation period, the time from idea to reality. We need patience and persistence to accomplish any goal.

To know oneself is to realize the oneness of all energy, to know all things are possible, and that change is the natural order of things. We carry the seed of change within. By balancing the yin and yang of male and female energies, we create the change we crave.

EMBRACE CHANGE

Merely tolerating change ignores the appeal of making change ourselves or actually designing it. If change will occur, why not use it as a tool, like a kitchen utensil.

As change comes to help us evolve, we work for change and let change work for us.

Think of a personal change like a job loss. Downsizing or firing can hit like a brick and cause such immediate damage that it can be hard to imagine an upside. But job loss is often not personal these days. Stores go out of business. Restaurants close. Technologies render some jobs obsolete. Many jobs are outsourced. Or maybe a corporation is bleeding money because of lost customer base, a budget cut, a bankruptcy, or because it's been mismanaged. Often, such change can be devastating. Mightn't it be a blessing, though? What if it signaled a different phase. What if it led to the very development we've been hoping for, for years. Instead of lolling around in pajamas, depressed or angry, filled with dread, gobbling entire bags of chips as we frantically comb our list of connections trying to find a job just like the one already dead and gone, what if we looked at the change as something *for* us, not against us. What if we rested a moment in the quiet of our inner selves, listened to the still, small voice (which isn't ever small at all), and sought guidance as to how we could use forced changed to make a whole new start.

What if the change imposed on us resulted from not having made a change ourselves?

Think of the times a change occurred, that you might not have seen as a plus at the time, and yet thinking back, you can now see how, if you had been willing to change yourself, you might have avoided the hassle. In the case of the lost job, truth be told, you knew that job wasn't a fit anymore. Maybe it didn't pay enough, was part-time instead of a fulltime job. You weren't treated with respect. You were overqualified. The job was a millstone around your neck, and that isn't just sour grapes. Face it, it wasn't where you belonged. You were trying to squeeze that round peg into a square hole maybe for months or years. Perhaps you were too complacent or lackadaisical to take action to find a better job within your field, or start that new career that might require additional training.

Maybe the change was a divorce. Your marriage fell apart. You knew it wasn't working, but instead of admitting you were unhappy or seeking help to repair the breach, you waited until it was past all hope and eventually imploded.

Maybe the change was more rudimentary. Maybe you needed to tackle responsibilities more responsibly. What about that bathroom leak? Couldn't you have called the plumber before the pipe corroded to such an extent that it flooded the bedroom floor, and caused such extensive mold that you had that untimely move. Of course, you could. But if you did, you would've had all those workers in. And you don't like strangers in your home. You would've had to change your mind, change work schedules, change the pipe, and maybe change the faucet, too. And the look of the bathroom vanity. You're sure they don't make that kind these days. And you liked it, you didn't want it changed. Of course, it's too late to change it now . . . okay, maybe you shouldn't have resisted change when the bathroom leak popped up.

Change in your life can signal a change you're meant to make in the outside world. The leak you fix might show you things you can fix in your business or on your job. The marital breakup, as hard as it is, may indicate how to bone up on relationships way beyond romantic ones. The firing or downsizing could be the start of a whole new career and new chapter in life.

Change is your prerogative, so get it like you like it. Be the cutting edge of change, the forefront, like the seasons change. You don't have to get dragged along behind it, kicking and screaming about the change that happened when you weren't looking. You don't have to have change imposed on you from without to make a major shift. You can give yourself permission now to make the change you dream about. Dreams aren't nebulous musings in the ether, they're possibilities. They're more than possibilities. They're probabilities ready to happen, if you only let them. They're goals and tasks you can complete. They're actually what is supposed to happen, if you will only get out of the way and let positive change be what you love.

When we make change in the primal way of taking our cues from intuition, change brings inspiration. We see positive change as natural, and we're happy to embody it. We want to alter the arc of the change we're uniquely suited to implement. We accelerate changes. We are change. We become Change Wizards. We are a trenchant sword of progress, living on the cutting edge. We choose change. We let change choose us. We trust the unexpected change. We trust ourselves to make the change we feel in our hearts and see in our visions. We know change is constantly underway, and we are advocates for it. When people see us, they see change working. They are encouraged to make a change.

Open up to accepting inner change at the time the change will bear most fruit.

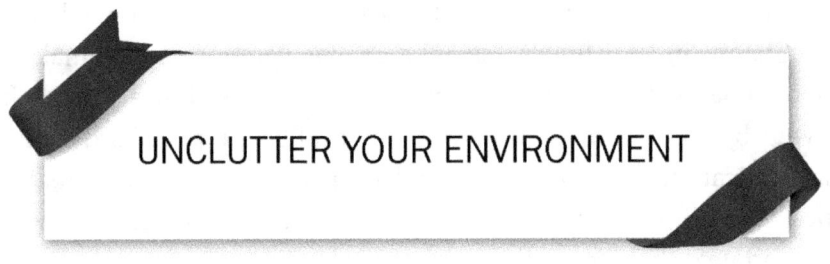

UNCLUTTER YOUR ENVIRONMENT

A hallmark of the ethos of change is belief in generosity.

Giving is the new acquiring.

We've moved from the glut of acquisition into the mode of scaling down to essentials, needs and must-haves. To be a lean, green change machine, one has to stay nimble in every way, able to move and make quick turns. To be nimble, one has to be streamlined.

Collecting stuff just to claim you have it doesn't work for anyone. Nor does defining oneself by one's possessions boost one's amplitude. It's who you are, and what you do—not what you have—that makes you, you. Nothing you buy can increase your worth. Your value is something that comes from within, not without, and you have to develop it. There's no shortcut through a pile of junk, no matter how expensive. No matter its label, pedigree or provenance. It's still just stuff. Stuff doesn't make you kinder, wiser, stronger, braver or one chuckle funnier. And the line between having a lot of stuff and clutter is a fuzzy one. Pack-ratting is passé.

A cluttered space reflects a cluttered mind. Mind clutter is not a plus. It's an obstacle to clear thinking. Your thoughts are creating your future, and they need an uncluttered path to it. Mind clutter constitutes cloudy judgment. That gets in the way of effective decision-making, efficient communication and other markers of progress. Good judgment is needed for every choice. To avoid disarray and malfunctioning, one must commit to be organized. Organization lends to efficiency. You don't have to be anal-retentive to succeed, but it does kind of help. And it goes without saying that leaders head organizations, not disorganizations. Leaders are good organizers. You want to lead, so be organized.

Unclutter your environment, and you find that you clean up your act.

When you're able to find what you need for a project, critical or trivial, you operate much faster, gain a feeling of effectiveness, and are more easily able to get things done with less exertion. Whereas, if you're on a deadline, and you have to relentlessly hunt through a pile of debris just to get to your scissors, stapler, pens, pads, notes or correspondence, you are probably not on a timeline that can lead to a timely achievement of goals.

If your home or office looks like a bomb exploded in it, something's off. Chances are you aren't thinking clearly, managing your affairs too well or fully committing to success. In clutter, there's a lot of waste. And much of it is time—time you can never, ever replace.

As writer Oscar Wilde once said, "Nothing exceeds like excess."

What a feeling of relief you get when you donate clothes that clogged your closet, pluck dust collectors off the shelves and sell them on the Internet, hold a garage sale, shred old files, or finally clean the junk drawer. How good it feels to reclaim that room that was storing unwanted paraphernalia you hadn't used in ages. When you get rid of clutter, you liberate space—in your physical atmosphere and mind—and you're free to move on to what's important. Clutter is baggage that isn't packed. It doesn't reflect who you are in the now. You're free. You deserve an unfettered life.

Think about clearing the following spaces, gifting or donating what you can:

- Closets
- Drawers
- Attics
- Basements
- Desks
- Kitchen Cabinets, Shelves and Pantries
- Filing Systems
- Bookshelves
- Storage Spaces
- Garages
- Yards and Patios

Think about people in your life. Start to review your friendships.

People come into our lives for a reason, a season or a lifetime. Not everyone we meet or strike up a friendship with is good for us, particularly over the long haul. Take stock of whether or not your friendships add to your quality of life or detract from it in unhelpful ways. Are there any who, rather than lift your spirits or bolster you with encouragement, seem to drain you, use you, put you down, break trust, or violate confidences? Does hanging out with certain friends feel good or try your patience? Only you can determine what's co-dependent, obligatory, loads of fun or a true connection built to last. If you find, when you're honest with yourself, a relationship needs to be put on hold or let go because it troubles you, it could be time to clear that space and make room for someone else. Someone who adds joy to your life. Someone who supports you. Somebody you can love, and who loves you in a more constructive way.

Write a list of things that burden you—people, places, spaces around your home or in your workplace—and decide how best to un-clutter them, making a schedule for how, and when, you'll get them off your mind and back. Leave empty, open space around the objects in your environment. Give yourself some breathing room. You'll be surprised how life unfolds when you lighten the load you're carrying. Sort out what's working from what is not, and your progress and the pace of change will accelerate at an amazing clip.

TRY NEW THINGS

Decide to do something new today. And do it. It can change your life.

You never see change if you keep on doing the same old things you've always done. Change comes from branching out. When you make a change, you shout to the universe, "Look, I'm here! I'm ready to go, to take the next step. I'm resolute. Use me to make more great things happen. I'm a ball of energy. I'm alive. I'm alert. I'm ready to go. I'm your Go-To Girl for new ideas. I'm free and open. Send me, World. No challenge is too big for me. I can take on any issue, solve world problems, sow peace everywhere. I can squeeze fun out of boring duties. Open the doors of life to me. I want to be where the action is!"

I personally have an adventurous spirit. When I try something new, something wonderful happens. I meet a great person that alters my life, learn something that propels me, or I'm able to give of my gifts in ways that change the lives of others. I update myself to my newest version all the time and love the feeling. You can update your operating system and your interface.

Trying new things is like crossing a bridge. You may not know what's on the other side, but you're certain you'll cross some terrain you couldn't cross any other way. Try a new thing, and you don't just experience something you've never done before. You build a bridge to future self. You invest in new possibilities. You affirm your openness to change, and to what a change can offer you. When you try something new, you experiment. New encounters stretch your comfort zone. You grow, because you participate with others in different scenarios. The broader your experience, the more good you are able to funnel through you. The more kinds of good you process through you, the more progress you initiate. The more you take on, the more capable you become as you reach farther than your grasp. Your grasp is stronger than you know.

What we do is linked to what we *can* do. Greatness hinges on willingness. When we're willing, we act with certainty. Certainty draws its matching energy as new abilities. New abilities make us more useful to the planet and its movement. Movements are building blocks of change.

No spot is designed to be permanent. Where you land is a function of how you take off.

Each choice is a snapshot or video playing, changing from frame to frame. You don't have to freeze frame anywhere. If a choice doesn't work, make another choice.

If you find yourself fearing to do something new, see if your fear is justified and rational or if it's outdated, outmoded or out of touch.

Race car driving can be dangerous, but learning a language, going out dancing, dating, or tasting a dish you've never eaten poses little threat. As do traveling, getting a new hairdo, moving to accept job, or taking a cooking or drawing class. You probably won't be arrested by the thought police if you change your mind about playing piano, joining a club, campaigning for local politicos or trying your hand at astronomy.

The quickest and easiest way to change is to do something different, shake things up. To grab the brass ring, you have to reach. Reach as high as possible. Everything is possible for those who are willing to take a chance. Think out of the box, don't live in one.

There's only one you. You should spread you around, paint the picture you want to see and be. You're part of a larger landscape waiting for you to expand your horizons.

WELCOME A NEW CHAPTER OF YOUR LIFE

Like all good stories, our lives unfold.

The story of your life is told in chapters. You are the author. Write your life. If you've been thinking the handwriting's on the wall and there's nowhere to go from here, you haven't been reading the signs. If your life is such that nothing's moving, turn the page now and begin the next chapter.

American baseball legend, Yogi Berra, once proclaimed, "It ain't over till it's over." You're breathing. You're reading. You're still in the game. Heck, you are the game.

If we sustain a major loss, we may feel the last chapter of our lives has come and gone against our will. This can be an awful shock. But there's a time for everything. Change is a chance to start again. It might come when we least suspect, in a guise that doesn't appeal to us at first, or be something we never wish for, but it's a chance at something wonderful. Beginnings can seem like the end, but the truth is, each change is a brand new start. If you're thinking your story is over, and your best days are behind you, think again. They've probably just begun. Avoid closing the book in the middle of the story. The hero can't be down and out. Quitting is not an alternative. The plot just started to thicken. You can encounter a plot twist anytime, even in the climax. Never give up—just opt for change.

When you're ready to make a transition into another phase of development, you will draw the resources you need to transform.

No two stories are the same, because we each make choices.

However much suspense, sci-fi or thrilling action there has been, you can write your way out of it anytime. A new chapter can mean a subtle shift in priorities, or a lifestyle change that hits every facet of your life. The scope of it is up to you. Go big with it. Go hard. Make sure you don't write a historical novel that chains your plotline to the past.

You are changing the world by example through the energy you radiate. There are those who are watching your story unfold from episode to episode, and their lives are being affected by it. You're the main character. Tell the tale. Say what you want to say. Make it good. Write a fable about your vision. Write only what will advance the plot and reveal the strength of your character. Make it a fairytale. Rhyme if you want to. Make it compelling, create red herrings, devise exciting passages. Make sure things turn out in the end. It's your life and others' futures.

Decide to start anew right now. Do you have an outline penciled in? A story has to start somewhere. Start now, and start off fresh. Give it a theme and a rip-roaring pace. Let your story be an open book, and be willing to turn every page. Start a new chapter, and when you do, be the brave hero you want to be by doing things you want to do, and being the change you want to be.

TRUE YOU

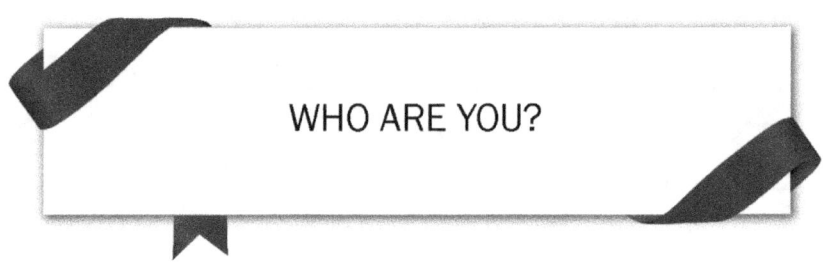

WHO ARE YOU?

Who are you? Do you know for sure? Have you taken stock of how you've changed?

Think. Do you know who you really are?

Do you like who you've become?

Sometimes, our self-perceptions can diverge from the person our acts reveal. We may see ourselves as being kind, when our thinking doesn't reflect that fact. We may feel like we're invisible, when everyone notices what we do, and our words are super-effective. We may perceive ourselves as weak, while the challenges we've overcome have made us stronger than we sense.

Because you assume so many roles, your personality is complex. You may be a capable businessperson, your co-workers' boss, your spouse's mate, your lover's friend, your children's parent, parents' kid, a runner, non-profit volunteer, designer, professor, public speaker, gardener, aspiring YouTube pro, amateur chef and other aspects of yourself—all of whom have different needs. They seek fulfillment in different ways, but all of them are comprising YOU. You're special and multi-faceted. All of you is beautiful. It's important to stay in sync.

We need to take time to go within, and examine how we're different than we used to be.

We change. We need to know whether the ways we've changed are working for us and others. We can only begin to improve our lot by understanding who we are and owning up to who we've been. If we're no different, we're not growing. Growth is essential to progress. If we've changed, we want it to be for the better. We want to make sure we're cognizant of how we're transforming and molding ourselves, if we're on the right track or have to shift gears. We must analyze our trajectory before we can change it in any way or resolve to keep our current course.

How radical must your inner change be to take on the role of a leader, for instance? To do what you see yourself doing, you must be the person for the job. Well, at least eventually. You're a work in progress. As every advancement starts somewhere, you have to know where yours begins. You must be honest with yourself. You can happily advocate for change by scrutinizing your own terrain before you take on the geography of the world with its complexities.

The good news is, whoever you are, you can change it up with just one thought. Your thoughts are the substance of what will be. You are now the result of your previous thoughts. Your thoughts have caused you to have certain feelings. Your feelings have caused you to do certain things. What you've done has accumulated skills, and you've taken on certain qualities.

You've listed your qualities and skills, so now you may want to determine how they've changed over time, and if that change is consistent with your dreams and goals. That is, whether the changes you've undergone are taking you in the direction you want and need to go. You're the architect of change, changing everything with thought—in yourself and in your reality. You don't have to sweat how you've changed to this point. You just need to be keenly aware of it, be grateful it has brought you here, acknowledge what's changed, and why, accept that as a simple fact, and be thankful for who you are right now, for who you are now is your starting point.

Now is what counts. It's all there is. You can, and will, change. It's the point of your life. If everything goes according to plan, who you are now will not be here tomorrow. Tomorrow, you'll be the Next-Gen you.

Start designing YOU now, with your very next thought. Draw images of you in your headspace. Begin molding the shape of your prototype. Come away from the world, if you need to, into the workshop of your eternal soul, and fabricate who you will become.

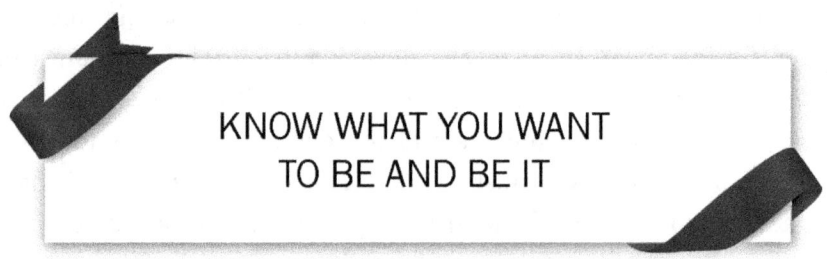

KNOW WHAT YOU WANT TO BE AND BE IT

It's important to make a decision now about who and what you want to be, because what you think, you will become.

Once you have delved into who you are, you're prepared to decide who you want to be.

Consider yourself a year from now, ten years from now, or twenty years.

How will you be remembered? Your legacy is the takeaway that lingers in people's memories. Not to be morbid or anything, but what would you like as your epitaph? If it's "drank everybody under the table", you might want to tweak that aspiration. Who will remember you, nearest and dearest, nobody, future generations? Do you want to linger in history books for centuries to come, inspiring quotes and biographies? How close are you to achieving that?

You can gauge your current legacy by how you appear to make others feel. You have an effect. That effect is profound. Do you have the effect you want to have?

Fate hasn't predetermined who you are, just who you can be.

You have determined who you are with the content of your thoughts.

You're meant to be a miracle, but you are self-determining.

Only a label that you adhere can stick to you. Remember that.

You don't want to wear any tag that's inappropriate or limiting. For example, labeling oneself as shy is a passive-aggressive method of abdicating responsibility. It's a cop-out. It's a ruse. It's a way to avoid making changes you know you can make, but refuse to. If you're shy, you're just an extrovert who doesn't take time to connect, that's all. It may take effort to change the thoughts and behaviors keeping you locked in self, but you could be more outgoing. You've just been declining to do the work.

Even if you were shy every second of life until this very moment, you can decide to change that trait. You could get help from a therapist, enter treatment with a psychiatrist or contact a licensed psychologist, sociologist or hypnotist. You can research those who once were shy and went on to be towering titans of industry, actors, singers or orators. You can strive to stop being reticent and open yourself to new social skills. You can start by smiling, shaking hands, and sparking conversations. You can do an open mic at a local club or restaurant. You can sign up with Toastmasters International, practice expressing your thoughts and feelings, or learn another language. You can join a debating team, host an event. You can take classes in eloquence. You don't have to be shy, because shy is a choice. You can be who you want to be.

We are who we decide to be. We are who we believe we are. We're who we've let ourselves become, and who we've trained ourselves to be. And yes, we may have tendencies from birth order, upbringing, prior events and the myth of societal constraint, but these aren't a life sentence.

I know you can be who you want to be. I feel it. I sense it. I believe. I know you can, and are, and will. We haven't yet met, but I know you aspire to highest self, to make a place in history, and to live a life that's meaningful. I know you're doing your best and you sometimes wish your best was better. I also believe your best is likely greater than you think it is.

You're a divine creation made for change and transformation.

You're perfectly you, and you're perfectly fine as you are, and you're bound to improve with time. I know your heart and mind are pure. I already love you for who you are. You radiate love so intensely, I can feel it where I am, over miles and borders and through the ether.

I'm committed to being your advocate. You are drawing me to your energy, which is good, and right, and healing. I see the whole universe in your eyes, as vast as all the galaxies. I am your friend, and I'm rooting for you. That's who I am, and I'm changing too, and I want to become a resident of a world where everyone is love, and love is given freely. Where every child is educated, everybody eats and drinks, and nobody ever goes hungry. Where peace permeates every interaction, every rock and every tree. Where everyone has shelter. Where music is more pervasive than noise, right action is a currency, and everyone creates according to their gifts and talents. I want to share this world with you—the you, you ardently wish to be.

I hope you'll give the world a chance to know the YOU you're meant to be.

Discern and accept who you are right now, and how you will turn into who you're meant to be when you're self-realized. Be confident you will become that you. You will, once you set your mind to it. That person already exists in you, alive, complete and viable, as visceral in its enlightenment as your blood or flesh and bone. She wants to be seen, felt, heard and known. She wants to make a difference. Get to know her, so all the rest of us can. Make her your superhero. She's able to lift and save the world, and she's working to manifest herself.

The more you move toward highest self, the more effective you'll become.

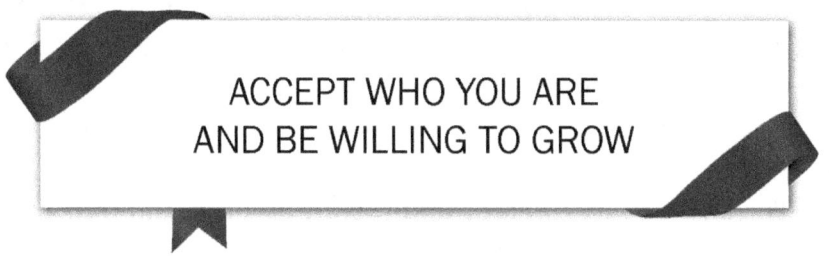

ACCEPT WHO YOU ARE AND BE WILLING TO GROW

Who you are now, and who you'll become, are living their parallel lives in peace. They are a team, though they may be diverse. Your thought patterns change as you progress. That's why you sometimes think, "What was I thinking?" As you look back at some choices you made, you may wonder why you did some things, though they might have seemed sensible at the time, maybe even your only alternative.

You may ponder why certain things happened. They happened because they reflected you. They represented who you were. They matched your energy back then. They manifested your beliefs. When you look back at an earlier you, before you knew all you know now, certain actions may even seem absurd, but you were the you, you were back then. You have more tools in your toolbox now, so you're able to make better choices. You've morphed into a wiser you, and that process continues unceasingly. You can't fault the you, you were. That former you did the best she could. Accept her, and love her for what she was. She was you, but she doesn't exist anymore. She is only a memory in your mind, and the minds of the people who knew you then. She is a former incarnation. She may not resonate with you now, but you have no resistance to her. She is only to be loved. She's in the rear-view mirror. One of the *you* personas that got you here.

Likewise, the current you is fleeting. You have lived, and learned, and loved in even the last half hour, and it's changed you in that span of time. Your thoughts are shifting subtly, and because of that, your feelings change. The change in your feelings is causing subtle shifts in your reality. These shifts should be happening consciously. Your feelings and thoughts are not hapless creatures confined to be buffeted this way and that, deflected by prevailing winds.

You're concocting your future as we speak, generating and spawning its new design.

The idea is to fully accept who you are as a gift, and to pour all your love into her as she aims to become a future you who's all that you desire to be. The vignette you are at this moment is just part of your progression. You're growing like that mighty oak, from the sweet little acorn you once were to a tree that can top Jack's beanstalk. You're willing and able to grow from here to a *you* who is hard to imagine now. A SuperYou of your own creation.

Pull out the stops. Decide to grow. Growth is a choice, just like everything else.

Accept who you are, and who you've been, envision the SuperYou you will become, be thrilled for the chance to consult and cavort with the angels of your higher nature, and open your mind to do what it takes to transform yourself. You're a butterfly. Show your true colors.

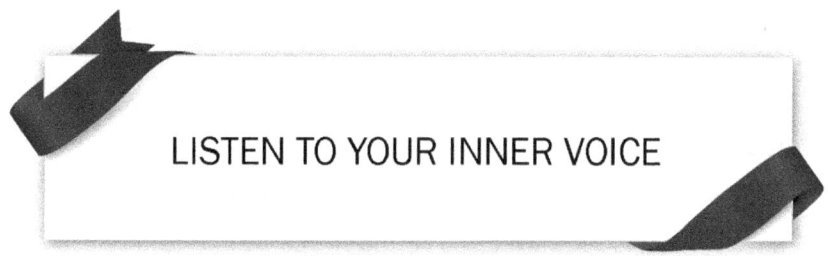

LISTEN TO YOUR INNER VOICE

Your instincts are impeccable. You must listen as they guide, protect and bless you with knowledge that nothing else can. Your inner voice keeps your best interests in mind and reveals what you are meant to do. When you cultivate your relationship with the still, small voice inside of you, it never lets you down. Ignore it, and you'll feel the pinch. Go against it for whatever reason, and you'll no doubt pay the price. Your instincts help you avoid missteps, have perfect timing, make connections, instruct you with all you need to know, and secure and safeguard your safety. Be confident your inner voice is always telling you the truth. Hear it over everyone, and heed it over everything. Others may give you sage advice, but no one and nothing knows what's best for you more than your instincts.

Through prayer, meditation, exercise and study, all will be revealed—the answer to every question and solution to every issue. Staying in touch with your Higher Power and its Universal Mind keeps you anchored in its good and its all-knowing omnipresence.

You're a Change Wizard. You work for change. Listening to your inner voice will always help you stand your ground while keeping you open and flexible.

Change may not come easily. Your point of view may not be popular. Your ideas and opinions may fall on deaf ears, but knowing they come from your gut will serve to keep you on your center. You may have to learn to say "no" to some things, and others might not want to hear it, but if *no* comes from your inner voice, there's a *yes* somewhere else, a better choice. A choice that puts your best interests first, preserving your values, schedule, health and pertinent interests.

There may be tasks to be run by committee whose multiple voices could drown out your own. You might be subject to criticism, prejudice, jealousy, second-guessing, a slew of unfair practices. Other parties may lack your work ethic, oppose your plans, try to fill you with doubts and fears you otherwise never would harbor yourself, but your inner voice is always true. It's like a North Star shining solely for you, always steering you in the right direction.

Follow your instincts. Stay in your lane. You may have to share and play nice with the class, but you don't have to compromise what you know intuitively for anyone—and you certainly don't have to subjugate your ethics or your values.

Listening to your inner voice is key to not only your success, but also your survival. There's no better way to sabotage or derail what could otherwise be a coup than to turn a deaf ear to your inner voice. It's the universe working to get your attention, deigning to whisper in your ear. It's your Higher Power loving you, feeding you through an umbilical cord. It's your purpose revealing itself to you. It's your angels reaching out their hands, your ancestors speaking encouragement. It's your mistakes and triumphs come to remind you of difficult lessons learned.

Intuition will give the perfect advice, as long as you respect it, and you're always on the lookout for communications from the source. You have to know how to read the signs, for your instincts speak in many ways. Learn to recognize them, for the more you do, the more they'll come. They will help you, and let you help others as well. However a message comes to you, believe, and follow the quiet voice, for it always leads to the righteous path.

STAND FIRM AND KNOW WHAT YOU STAND FOR

As the saying goes, if you don't stand for something, you will fall for anything.

Unless you stand up for your principles, you have no foundation, no platform, no moorings. Without any moorings informing your actions, you have no moral authority.

When you anchor your thoughts and energies in a principle or principles, it's a lightning rod, a hand to hold, a shelter against the storm. It's like leveling a magnifying glass between a sunray and the need for change. When you advocate for truth, equality, peace and the concept of justice, or you defend someone who's vulnerable, you train a white-hot light on what is right and conscientious. You animate solutions to the cause you work to champion. Lofty principles tend to have lives of their own. The more you assert them, the stronger they get. Such tenets are based on laws which govern how we get along. Ethics support the greater good. They're rooted in established rules of conduct everyone understands. Without principles, chaos reigns.

What do you stand for? Do you know? Maybe you stand for several things, yet unless there is a context, you are rarely compelled to assert your beliefs. Standing on a principle will tend to expose your character and highlight your priorities. Do you stand for freedom? Honesty? You know what you think, and you know how you feel. You know what you see that bothers you. You know what you like and would like more of. You have a sense of right and wrong and a penchant for common decency. If you bury your head in the sand and sit on the sidelines when bad behavior looms, rather than calling it out and acting affirmatively, change may occur, but it won't be for the better. Calling it like you see it may take courage and be perilous, but failure to do so runs the risk of diminishing returns. This is what sparks declines in civilization and civility.

To be the change you want to see requires that you take a stand. Therefore, you have to know what you stand for and be able to back it up. If you're looking for meaning in your life, you don't have to look very far. Even a couch potato can turn on TV and see a world of goodness itching to be supported, and problems caused by problematic people who need to be kept in check.

Act on the strength of your beliefs. Whatever your sensibilities, insights, impulses or instincts are, you must sense when it's time to take a stand, know what it is you stand for, and be ready to go to bat for it.

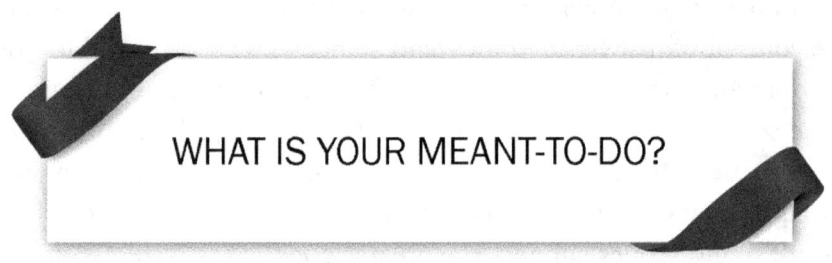

WHAT IS YOUR MEANT-TO-DO?

Going within and staying in touch with who you are, who you're meant to be and what you have to offer brings another ginormous benefit—doing what you're meant to do.

You, my friend, are a BIG IDEA.

The ultimate intelligence has formed you with a grand intent.

You're a showpiece by the Universal Mind, and you are on display. You're the universe showing its stuff through you, your Higher

Power's art exhibit. Only you aren't just for show, you're divinely utilitarian. You're useful as well as ornamental.

Each of us has a reason to be—a raison d'etre, the French phrase says. We are all born with a purpose in mind—that special gift that we alone contribute to humanity. We're each a distinct and inalienable piece of the puzzle completing the scheme of things. Our Meant-To-Do is more than just our profession, skill set, energy or persona we array. Our Meant-To-Do is our mission, the task or tasks we're assigned by the universal consciousness that gives us life. Our dreams, hopes, goals and instincts lead us to our higher calling. To discover our Meant-To-Do, and to live as the person meant to accomplish it, is to achieve self-realization.

It's as if you've been given a golden key that fits into a specific lock that only you can open. You are undergoing a mystical quest. The prize you hope to find is one that's placed inside of you. You are a complete, essential part of the greatest good that's yet to be, that already is, and always was.

The One Love is pure potential. It is, and will always be, determined to demonstrate through each of us its worthiness and majesty, to declare and affirm its love for us. We each represent the universe in a single, yet integrated, way. It's up to us to confirm this fact by actualizing higher self.

Your function is written on your soul. It's not hiding, it's calling out to you. You only have to ask for it to reveal its presence as your goal. It instills a restlessness in you, so you do not stroll along life's path, but take on your journey with spritely steps, aware of your principle aspiration. Life is not a mystery when you know why you are here. You're here to transcend the mundanity of your earthly illusion of stress and strain, and live as a higher energy form, a rising tide that lifts all boats. You're an essential plot point in an amazing course of history that knows no bounds and brooks no failure. You are a winning Lotto ticket. You are a touchstone, a shiny brass ring, the light that lights the world. You are who you, and everyone else, has been waiting for and searching out. You are no accidental tourist. You are a destination in yourself, an oasis for others who journey.

You've made an agreement to be who you are. You need to know what you're meant to do to uphold your end of the bargain. Believing who you're meant to be is the first step in your Meant-To-Do. Intention is your second step. Intending to learn your Meant-To-Do, act on it, make it the core of your life, and fulfill it as your mission is your route to total understanding.

In order to work to change the world, we must tap into the source of love, and be fully alive ambassadors of the good we each are meant to do, the reason for our being.

Your Meant-To-Do is a source of peace, emotional intelligence, hope, direction, human contact, abundance and eternal joy.

What higher priority could you have than reaching your full potential.

If you already know your Meant-To-Do, let your thoughts, words, deeds, intent and vision serve your mission dutifully. Live according to your commission.

If you're seeking your Meant-To-Do, it will most likely come through mindfulness, as you practice silent meditation, prayer, affirmations and health and wellness regimens with dedication. Study, and seek out teachers and spiritual guides to help your inquiry, though solely through plumbing your inner self and consulting with your Higher Power can you decipher your calling. Go within, and be one with the Universal Mind in its omnipresent love and limitless possibilities. Be grateful for everything that comes. Experiment. Do what brings you joy and allow yourself to be yourself.

When you find what you are meant to do, believe and conceive that it is yours. Persevere, and continue to act on it. Ask for the fortitude it takes. Ask for the dream that comes with it, and the goals and tasks you are meant to perform in order to make the dream come true. Be ready to receive the gifts that ultimately are a part of it—and just by affirming who you are, your energy will change the world.

YOUR BIG DREAM SCHEME

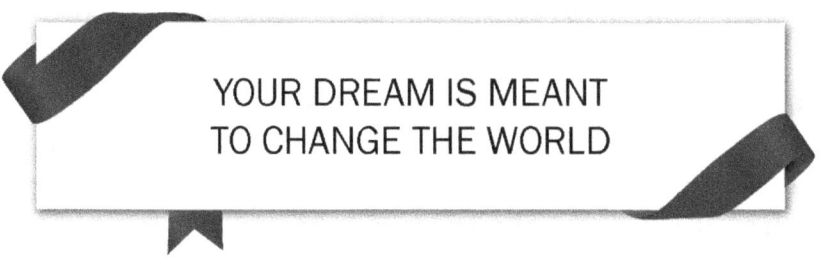

YOUR DREAM IS MEANT
TO CHANGE THE WORLD

Dream big, because if you dream at all, it only makes sense to aim high enough to make a difference in the world, and to change it for the better. Your dream is composed from the fierce field of energy from which all great notions come, and in which all greatness now resides. This energy lives in everything. Your dream belongs not just to you, but to everybody everywhere. To everything in the universe. Your dream isn't happening in a vacuum. All dreams are born of the same communal substance, which is the energy that produces light and love.

Your dream is bestowed by the universe, and unto it, it must return, as a fully realized miracle. The results of the work you do to achieve your dream are community property, so your dream should be massively conceived. Your dream has a life of its own, and once imagined, draws like energy the same way you draw your energy match. The more you believe you'll achieve your dream, the more energy you imbue it with, so the more resources it attracts, and the quicker and more easily it will transition from possibility into a tangible reality.

Dreams are born to inspire us to make something happen to levitate all beings to higher consciousness. Dreams are not merely for us to pursue in a longing to complete ourselves, they are meant to propel us to instigate the next phase of evolution. Your dream is a harbinger of the paradise we can bring into the here and now, a glimpse at a brighter future. A dream is a promise of ground-breaking things that already exist in the vast unseen, but have yet to be experienced.

Our job is to dream a great big dream, envision how all will profit from it, believe in its reality, and persist in the work required to breathe life into its fragile lungs. We're to nourish a dream and keep it safe until it becomes a full-blown mechanism in the world, a phenomenon that advances the cause, and changes the shape, of life itself. A dream like the wheel or the telephone. Like light bulbs. Like a song. Like penicillin. Cupcakes. Bras. Kiva. The United Nations.

Everything comes from a big idea someone asks for and believes in.

Your ideas are dramatic like everyone else's. Set your mind to dreaming. However you dream, from daydreams to nightmares, there are hints and clues in them. You have to tune in to their frequency in order to catch their drift.

Think of the energy Edison, Plato, Bill Gates and George Washington Carver had to radiate to attract the innovations we enjoy today. You have access to that now. The engineers and architects who built the pharaohs' pyramids certainly weren't thinking small. They tuned into the motherlode of ideas, and continued to mine it brilliantly. They caught the next big wave so well that hundreds and thousands of years beyond their efforts, we benefit from their endeavors.

You want to dream dreams big enough to reach across the centuries—so useful, extreme, jaw-dropping and forward thinking that they advance the refinement of civilization, bend the arc of history, stem the tide of pessimism, banish mediocrity, and proffer opportunities as strong as the Earth's gravitational pull. When you dream, you insist on reality, so why not demand a reality that presents a best case scenario. You want your dream to change the world by vaulting it forward by leaps and bounds. You don't want to limp timidly into a future. You want to provoke the next Big Bang. A movement as bold as a rocket launch. You don't want to come off like a lukewarm bath. You want to erupt like a fiery volcano. You're no half-stepper, you're a hurdler. You're a high jumper. You can fly. Your dream is as bright as a supernova, as fast as a meteor, vast as the sky, as volatile as a hurricane.

The bigger your dream, the more awesome the change you are destined to foster and bring about. Dream BIG, and the whole wide world will want to help your dream grow bigger. Dream BIG, and assets, ways and means will emerge to provide the wherewithal. Dream BIG, and you still can't begin to imagine how big your dream's outcome might be. Dream BIG, and you still couldn't dream any bigger than what the universe dreams for you. Stretch out. Look way beyond the horizon. Listen to your inner voice. Prospects will pop into view. Each occasion will be fortuitous. What seems like a fat chance now will spring up right before your eyes.

Your dream is the truth in advance, the face of reality smiling behind the veil. You must only be the thinker thinking thoughts of what can be. To win, you have to get in the game. In life, you have to shoot the shot, believe you can make the basket, and hustle to put points up on the scoreboard. When you conceive and believe, you achieve. Dream big, and you can only win.

Nothing can stop you from dreaming big. Obstacles can rise up, seas can swell, tornado winds can blow, but nothing can take big dreams away unless you let them go. Maintain a real tight grip on yours. You have the will, and there's always a way. Always. So, no matter what, avoid letting anyone tell you that your dream is too big to be possible, because every good thing is possible. Just because others can't see the sky, it doesn't mean the sun won't shine, or there isn't a canopy of blue, or the moon isn't willing to light the night. It just means the naysayers ain't looking up. Bless them, let them go their way, and keep both eyes on the sparrow. Even if dark clouds should appear, they're only passing in front of the sun, eclipsing it temporarily. The sun shines even through the rain.

Your dream is bigger than any worry, doubt or fear can ever grow, more vivid than any past event whose memory ought to fade. A big dream is your life force ready and willing to go to whatever lengths it must to make the world a better place.

Think BIG. Dream BIG.

Ask, believe, and receive.

You are a giant. Your dream should be too. For the bigger the dream, the more good it can do, and the more ways that it can come true.

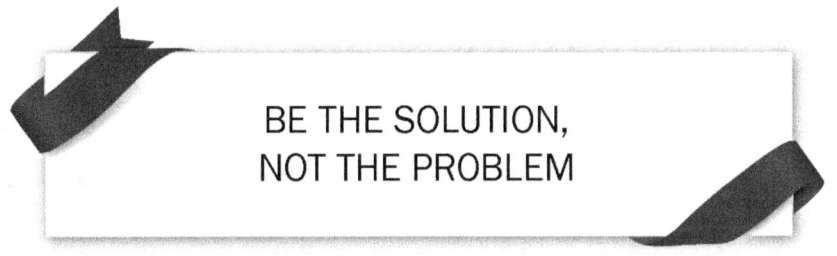

BE THE SOLUTION, NOT THE PROBLEM

Look for what works, and you'll find it. Concentrate on solutions, not problems. Change comes from a *yes*, not a *no*, state of mind. Be on the lookout for YES, and be a *yes* person. Yes is faith that a solution stands in readiness. Regulating your thoughts and emotions, stepping out of ego mode, and upholding an optimistic approach will not only keep you from being a problem, it'll make sure you implement solutions when they're needed. Positivity draws its energy match, helping you regulate what comes, and doesn't come, into your world. Take care to keep yourself in check, and avoid any negativity. Creativity is your stock in trade. Creativity is change food.

Be what works, and know what works.

Making a difference in the world is really as simple as 1-2-3.

1. Identify A Need And Fill It
2. Recognize A Problem And Solve It
3. Create, Innovate, Revolutionize

These precepts overlap. They're really just three different ways of approaching how to urge change in your everyday life—change that's commensurate with your vision, skills, the challenges you may face, your interests and the different arenas in which you may have to operate in order to achieve your dream.

How your mind works will determine how you go about prepping your life for change, diagnosing what change is needed, being an incubator for such change, and staying connected to your impetus for making change. Pretense won't bring authentic change. Have motivation that's sincere, pronounced, upright and genuine. Motivation is the desire to do. People always have motives for what they do. It's best to be sure of yours. When you know why you want to do something, it's much easier to keep at it. When you know why you're doing what you're doing and what outcome you may gain, you have a mighty force driving you, something bigger than yourself. When you know you're solving a problem or filling a need, your motive is just. Change originates in the heart, with a feeling something isn't right. You can begin to set it straight.

Let's take a look at the first concept: Identify a need and fill it. This is straightforward and very effective. This is how businesses get going, how they find customers and clients, and how they are able to keep them. They search to find something people need. They comprehend what they personally need or observe what those around them need, and they work to devise a product or a service to address it. People earn change by making change, by finding new ways to fulfill a persistent deficiency. People will do almost anything to get what they feel they need.

Needs not only drive businesses, they're also how non-profits form. Kind people see others without enough food, and they open food banks, organize food drives, cook and deliver hot, healthy meals, and help others learn to plant and grow and irrigate land available to help them feed themselves. People of conscience build missions to counter the homeless epidemic. Doctors, researchers and scientists often devote their entire lives to finding cures to thwart grave illnesses and diseases that are taking lives or diminishing quality of life. Politicians go about solving cross-sections of problems plaguing society. That is, if they aren't a problem themselves. People raise money and pose ideas to solve environmental issues, cruelty, aging, education, poverty, even fashion woes. They know one of the most efficient ways to foster what can be lasting change is to peg an existing, pressing need, develop a passion for filling it, map out a plan for a practical solution, determine a starting point, commit, and persistently implement.

However big or small a solution may seem, it's a step in the right direction.

Every step counts in the process of change.

Intent alone won't lead to change, but the process of implementing change and making incremental changes leads to bigger accomplishments. You can beget a significant snowball effect beyond your initial reach and bring about exponential change. You can start small on a great big dream, and it can balloon into something magnificent, significantly more far-reaching than your original expectation. The universe wants to work perfectly. It will help you work things out. Identify a need, then fill it in every way you can think of, and eventually it will start filling itself.

The second method for bringing change is a sticky situation—recognizing a problem and solving it. Problems are issues involving difficulty and raising doubt.

Recognizing a problem is one thing. Solving a problem is another.

People tend to struggle with problems. Instead of cooperating, they may wrangle, making matters worse. Many haggle over messes that wouldn't be problems if they didn't drum them up.

Problems can be entirely unnecessary and manmade.

There's a difference between addressing needs like food, shelter, clothing and water, which are pressing and can be life-threatening, and engaging in problem-solving. Needs are basic to human existence. Problems may suddenly arise. Problems more likely than not can worsen. Needs are consistent, persistent, raw. When you try to solve a problem, especially if it's for a greater good—whether family, office or worldwide concern—you're stepping into trouble. Whereas change to satisfy human needs is essential to survival, change to accommodate human desires for comfort, advancement, convenience or entertainment, though it may be an advance, often involves conflicting aims.

Many problems flare up out of conflict. That's why an issue becomes a problem. People perceive an issue as a problem and blow it out of proportion. Then somebody has to bring change to bear to reestablish balance. The best way to solve a problem is, first, to not be one yourself. To not be even a part of a problem. You're either a solution or part of a problem if one exists. You have to decide which you will be. Hint: Being a solution is like being chocolate candy.

Avoid regarding resolvable affairs as "problems" in the first place. Reconceiving the notion of "problem" opens the door to possibilities. A problem can be an inquiry, something to note, a point of interest. These references wring the emotion out of an issue, cut back on drama, remove the stigma of controversy, and lessen the chance of dividing people into separate camps.

A problem is only a question that hasn't been adequately answered yet.

Answer the question from the perspective of love and higher consciousness, and the problem is already starting to solve. Reinterpret a "problem" + be a solution = welcome change.

This is what brings us to Door Number Three: Create, Innovate, Revolutionize!

In my view, this is the most fun way to change up anything you want.

I am an artist. I'm a creative. That's just me. I think up stuff and bring it into being. I love it. I create characters, situations, romance, trouble, other worlds and fantastic scenarios, both as an actress and a writer. I choose to bring change through writing, acting, speaking, designing, visual arts and other artistic modes of expression. It's who I am, what I'm meant to do and how I motivate myself—by creating, enlightening and entertaining. It's what makes my heart beat faster, makes me grin, and lets me hop out of bed each day before the sun begins to shine.

Artists have historically stood at the vanguard of society, saying what others shy away from saying, and in creative ways that make truths seem more palatable.

Whatever you do, why not think of yourself as encouraging a renaissance—creating, innovating and revolutionizing how things work in your field or present environment. You don't have to be an artist to approach your work artistically.

Creativity applies to every industry and all activities. The tech sector—a scientific field—has, in recent decades, imagined a broad landscape for how we enjoy technologies. Audio-video toys and gadgets top most people's lists of what they want to purchase next. Everyone craves the latest appliance, equipment or machine. Updated versions of cell phones, laptops, tablets, storage devices and televisions unite us more each day. They enhance communication, spreading ideas and information around the globe with lightning speed. The pace at which technology moves is enough to boggle the mind. Engineers use their artistic flair to create, innovate, and revolutionize almost everything we do—from chatting, to writing, to learning, to reading, to shopping, to even romancing each other, and playing all kinds of games. Inventors see people struggling to open jars, and come up with lid openers. Packaging changes all the time, as do nonstick coatings for cooking surfaces, self-driving cars and GPS. Brands of makeup jam the shelves with potions and lotions to beat back the signs of aging. Folks wear Spanx and silicone booties, blow-up bras, hair weaves and copper socks. Nothing is out of reach on the branches of modern ingenuity.

We've come so far in so little time that the Technological Age is giving way to an Age of Change. In part due to the way we communicate, we've entered an age of enlightenment, an era when mindfulness and transformation is seen as what is to come. Because pain thrusts us into change, the profusion of lower energies such as the hate and fear that lead to war is causing mankind to develop a cognizance of the basic fact that we create the world with thoughts, and that we must care for each other and the planet as never before.

Create, Innovate, Revolutionize! is the currency of the Age of Change. Unconditional love is its credo. Light is its trademark, and peace is its brand.

The Age of Change beckons, for it is our destiny. Change what you will, only change for the better. Change can be your calling card. Find change you're uniquely suited for by seeing a need and fulfilling it, or by finding a problem and solving it by tactics you originate. Create. Innovate. Revolutionize. Wherever you are, in whatever field, speak positive words emphatically and let them affirm your identity. Be the change by seeing a vision big enough for all of us.

Your big dream can change the world.

The above are just three ways to consider going for the change you crave—traditional ways to stimulate your thoughts and get you moving. You might concoct a mixture of all three, or devise your own technique or routine, and sharing it, change the way all change is conceived for years to come—change that enriches your life and exists to enrich the lives of others.

Change isn't rooted in sacrifice, though it may demand great sacrifice, and often does, and might from you. Change is, at its essence, love and joy in evolution—revolution, if that's what it takes. Not the kind where people take up arms, but spiritual revolution. In which people of goodwill envision a world inclusive of every other being and join to exert mind power to materialize their vision. Author Rhonda Byrne (*The Secret*) quotes author and motivational speaker, Jack Canfield (*Chicken Soup For The Soul*) as saying, ". . . when people start focusing on what they want, what they don't want falls away, and what they want expands, and the other part disappears." This is the shape of things to come, of the movement that heralds the Age of Change which is currently emerging.

BE WILLING TO DO ANY GOOD THING TO ACHIEVE YOUR GREAT DREAM

Since willingness undergirds your passion and what you attract in energy, people, places and things, be willing to do whatever good thing it takes to accomplish the change you seek.

Any *good* thing means just that. It doesn't mean to be ruthless or callous, cut corners, sleep your way to the top, or believe any end justifies any means. It means to go that extra mile to stretch yourself and reach for things outside your comfort zone. That's what it takes to win at what no one has ever done before. It takes willingness to sacrifice, surrendering to other-orientation, valuing compassion. It may take extreme measures morality dictates. It takes being brave and unflinching in the face of dire consequence. It means, once committed, you cannot shrink from the duty to complete your task. You cannot abdicate leadership, abandon principles, self-defeat, or retreat because of an obstacle or due to unpopularity, inconvenience or fatigue. It means mining the strength to continue when confronting overwhelming odds. It means willingness to serve in a field of agape love without reserve—to do your Higher Power's will and be its hand on earth.

Think of willingness as a commodity, an asset you can trade for peace, and love and the oneness of everything. You're willing, right? Your willingness to try new things, to be all you can be, and do all you can do is a fungible product. Patent it. Manufacture your willingness all the time, on a basis that cannot run out. You are the factory, vendor, supplier, distributor of your willingness. Being willing rests with you alone. You are the one who is willing to engage your heart's desire, and to magnetize the tools for change. You don't want to be recalcitrant.

Commit right now to be willing, and the universe gives you what's required to reach your goals, fulfill your dreams, and make change that is positive. At school. At work. In your city or state, profession or community. Wherever change is needed. Decide to be willingness itself, for the Universal Mind is pumping out good, and you have to be ready for it. Willingness paves the road to great success in all you undertake. The heart that's filled with willingness is the beating heart of change.

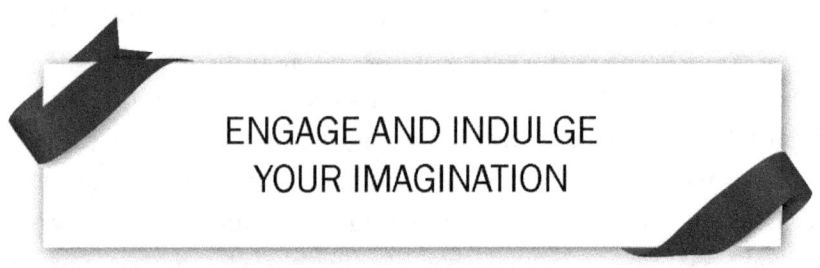

ENGAGE AND INDULGE YOUR IMAGINATION

What if anything good were possible? What if you could only win? What if, if you just persisted, you could achieve your biggest dream? Well, guess what? That's reality. It is, and you can. It's a fact of life.

Most people don't achieve their dreams, because: (a) They never imagine a dream, or; (b) They don't ask the universe to help them make the dream come true, or; (c) They don't envision the dream coming true, far less achieving it through their own concerted efforts, or; (d) They envision, but never plan, or; (e) They plan, but don't act on their plan for whatever unknown reason, or; (f) They act inconsistently or without enough positive energy, or; (g) Having acted, they don't persist, and lacking persistence, they fail to see the infinite possibilities to pivot from what doesn't work to what can make their dream come true, or ; (h) They give up, stop believing in their dream, quit believing in themselves, and then it's—game, set, match—they can't receive, because they've blocked their good, because they're not receptive. This is not your paradigm.

All you have to do is engage and indulge your imagination. *Poof!* That's it. And then keep moving. What you imagine begins to be real the minute you imagine it.

Everything starts with imagination. Everything starts with the BIG IDEA—including you, and everyone. You are the One Love's dream come true. You are a reality in the process of being self-actualized. You started by being imagined. You live in the Universal Mind that imagined you. It lives in you. Your imagination is fertile ground—Ground Zero of the Dream Machine that cranks out creativity. You can access it at any time. Imagine infinite potential, and it will be your legacy. The realm of possibilities is stored in your imagination, ready to shape the world you imagine. Your belief this is true is what gives you your magic power of manifestation.

Understand you have the power to achieve whatever your mind conceives. Imagination makes this work. Believe you have everything you envision, and if you should need something up the line that isn't contained in your bag of tricks, imagine it being delivered. Imagine a shipment of good on its way to you when you need it most. Good streams from your imagination constantly, creating dreams, storing them on the cloud of your mind, ready to download at your will. Your energy matches what you imagine. You imagine your dream for a reason, because you're custom-made to live it. You're part of the dream. It's part of you. You imagine the change you want to see, and you are the changer changing change with your imagination. You imagine a change in concert with the universe, Your Higher Power and every Universal Law.

Never mind what the odds appear to be, or the chitter chatter on TV, or the videogames where the world is doomed or the fear in other people's minds. Your imagination is for real. It's an antidote to all of that. It's a place where fairies can fly free, where giants roam, where kisses speak, where every broken toy is fixed, where even fatal wounds are healed, where love prevails, and peace is air, and you can tiptoe on a star.

Nothing outdoes your imagination. Nothing. Nothing's beyond its reach. It's vibrating so fast, it's a wonder it doesn't emit a sonic boom. It's a luxuriant cosmic phenomenon, no less of a force than radiation, ionization, electromagnetics or lightning hitting a rod. It's so captivating an energy field that by calling upon it to visualize, it can crystallize whatever thought and make it a reality. Your faculty of imagining can conjure up most anything. Use the alchemy of your imagination for good, for it is sacrosanct. You can pull heaven right out of your hat. Work your magic for the greater good.

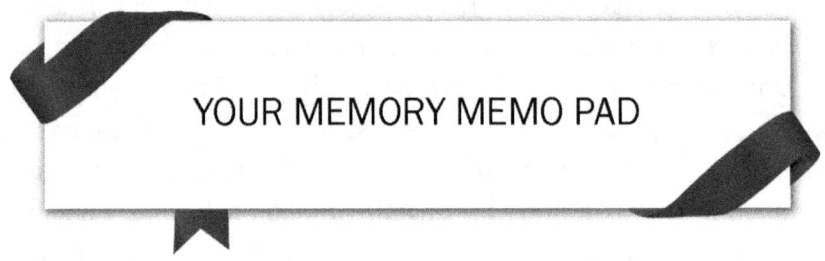

YOUR MEMORY MEMO PAD

As we discussed, visualizing your life creates it with the power of thought. As you feel joy in imagining a future, you draw it to you proportionately. When you see where you're living, what you're doing, who's in the future with you, vividly picturing each detail, you are actually making your dream come true. You easily switch from past-life view into live-in-the-now and see-the-future. This is how you create what's yet to come in a purposeful manner.

Since we tend to believe we can't create our memories even though we do, it's important we comprehend the link between recalling and creating, how it affects us, and how we can use it to make constructive change.

Some of us only recall the bad things. Some of us mostly recall the good. Some churn memories over and over, unforgiving, unrepentant, unable to drop them and move on, unwilling to change perspective. Even witnesses to a crime recall particular details differently. We recall according to point of view, so when our viewpoint changes, memories take on different meanings. We can use the morphing of memories to our benefit, morphing them consciously.

Repetitive thoughts recalling the past are in our control, and yet they loop. It's important not to let them loop. The more the past loops unconsciously, the less power we use to imagine a blissful future. This is wasteful. We can reverse this unhelpful trend by using a Memory Memo Pad, as I call it, to preserve what serves and routinely discard detritus.

Making peace with the past is the healthy choice. As we let memories recede, we adapt and are thankful for what we have now. We make room for change within ourselves, instead of trying to change what cannot be altered—aka the past. When we learn lessons memories teach and live in the now with enthusiasm, we shed any hold old memories have, and free up more space in our future. We become grateful for where we are, and even more so for what's to come.

We can't alter what's passed, only how we perceive it, and therefore how it affects us. We can work to come to terms with it and live in the present moment. We can alter perspective by cherry-picking only empowering memories, selecting recollections to reinforce goals, release old pain, and renew former feelings of success that remind us we can achieve our dreams.

This is a wonderful aspect of thought—it's absolutely malleable. You can mold how and what you choose to think. Every passing thought is one more chance for you to learn and grow. Every time you think new thoughts, update an outdated point of view, or modernize outmoded memories to embrace fresh methodologies, you change, and the world you imagine shifts.

If it seems some memories won't let go, it's untrue. Memories can't come back unbidden, unless we place them in a queue, press the play button, then sit back and watch.

We're the Rememberer *doing* remembering. Remember that. We can remember what we want. Or forget what we want. And we do this well. Memories are thoughts we actively think. We're not their victims or their shills, and we don't have to be their accomplices when they hog up space inside our psyche, ripping off time and energy we could better use to forge ahead.

Barring memory disabilities like Alzheimer's or dementia, or traumatic memories best dispatched with help from a professional, we filter data all the time and file it into memory, reworking, reshaping, reorganizing what we will choose to recollect, and how we will choose to recollect it as a function of our will. We weed out what we would rather forget, consciously or unconsciously, and store the remainder on mental hard drives, emotional flash drives, backup drives and .mp3 players that play playlists according to our mood. We let memories determine our mood and mindset, going so far as to dig up clips we're keeping in deep memory. We add special effects like reverb. Then we play them on big screens in our minds. We amend, re-write, and edit scripts to cast ourselves as victims or as heroes we can live with.

No one else on the planet dare hazard a guess as to what we recall at a given time. We tend to let memories do their thing, so we hardly even know ourselves what thoughts will crop up when we least expect, and how we'll allow them to make us feel. It isn't our only alternative, but we make ourselves believe it is, thus shedding responsibility for the gremlins we neglect to ban. The truth is, we can transmigrate memories, and we often do, moving and resurrecting them.

YOU CAN CHANGE THE WORLD

We don't remember the things we forget. Well, that's obvious, but it bears pointing out that we can forget most anything. We forget faces, places, names. And yet we remember minute details of events that happened long ago. This would suggest—no, it confirms—that our memories are selective. So, if we're remembering what we want, in the way we want to remember it, isn't it best to make up our minds to let disabling memories fade, and remember what enables us. If you're playing a loop, play something good. Here's an easy way to do it.

You can use your Memory Memo Pad to log in memories you should keep as touchstones for your reference—successes, feelings of joy and passion, accomplishments, connections.

Instead of meandering down Memory Lane with no mandate, function or constraint, you can consciously ask your memory to rerun what you want to see, to replay helpful memories. You can re-think thoughts that encourage you, flashbacks of triumph, peace and success—only those worth remembering because they can move you to action, soothe your soul, or remind you of how you are when you're at your best and doing well. Rerun classic storylines. Store upbeat memories as they come, and read from your Memory Memo Pad to bolster, not undermine, you.

Log into your favorite storylines populated with characters you respect. Use a Memory Memo Pad to recall the set you want to live in, costumes you still want to wear. Choose images that delight you. Hang Hollywood lights that illuminate your future. Hear the score you want, the music that makes you want to dance. You're the director, the writer-producer, the showrunner for the video of memories playing in your mind. You can retain the best things you've done, and use them like clip-art to illustrate your thoughts, dreams and the change you crave. Tag your best ones with 5-star reviews and watch them like a Facebook friend, Twitter follower, Instagram fan.

Changing the world isn't retroactive, yet it's a cumulative enterprise. It may require all you have, and every useful memory, but you don't want to be bogged down by memories that no longer serve you. You want to let go and be free to change. Changing the world is forward-thinking. No sense looking back unless it moves you forward in some way. Use your Memory Memo Pad to draw from the past and present a perfect picture of your perfect life. Let your good memories live and last and breathe in you as recall. More are developing. Brain-record them as icons, memes and emojis. Picture them as neon billboards lighting up buildings in Times Square, or as landmarks seen from outer space.

Picture a perfect world, and your world will turn out to be picture perfect.

CREATE A DREAM BOARD

Speaking of pictures . . . *Cool segue, huh?* One of the best ways to focus your view of what your future world will look like is to construct a Dream Board.

A dream board is a pastiche of images—usually on a cork board, foam board, large cardboard or poster board—that collectively represent what you hope to lure into your environment. Things that contribute to health and wellness, happiness and motivation. Create a dream board to inspire you, to out-picture what you're visioning.

So, say, if you're dreaming of a house, and you're working to find, finance, or fix one up, you might want to focus on pictures of houses that look like the one you want. When I did it, it worked like a charm for me, though I wasn't remotely aware of its power when I dreamed it up. I did so strictly on hope and faith. I believe that's what made it effective. If you're hatching a goal for, say, your career, a romantic life you've been yearning for, or you want to lose weight, gain a circle of friends, attract a new job, or a skill, or do a wildly successful project launch, think about what it might look like. Round up photos, drawings or artwork illustrating your desires.

If you want to attract a new car, go get a bunch of car dealer brochures, take cell phone pictures, print them out. Pick up some auto magazines. Obtain a slick pamphlet of the make and model of the car you want, and paste a great picture of you inside it, waving from the driver's seat. Maybe tape it to the ceiling over your bed, so it starts and ends your day. If you dream of a gig as a fashion designer, snag colorful fabric swatches, photos of top designer studios, workrooms, drafting tables, photos of supermodels wearing sketches of your own couture. If you're an actor, find pictures of Emmy's, Oscars, flicks of sets from shows, costumes you will love to wear.

You get the idea. Create a headspace. Support the vision in your head with physical pictures of what you want to attract, so you can look at them as manifested in the world.

Once you've collected your images, sit down at a table or on the floor, and begin to cut them out. Trim around actual shapes or cut the backgrounds into different shapes depending on your aesthetic sense. Position them on the board any way you imagine them. Work from top to bottom, left to right or inside out. Place them in concentric circles, group them in sections according to topic, or drop them in, in random order. Do it how it best suits what your concept of your future is, prioritizing as you go. If career comes first, put those clips front and center. If finding a mate is most important, place a dream date at the top with descriptive words to drive that home—kind, smart, bold, hilarious. Whatever. It's your dream board. Go for it. Get it like you like it. Move stuff around till you're satisfied. Overlap. Scribble captions. Use stickers, hot colors, trinkets, whatever speaks to you. When you have all your bits where you want them, use a glue stick to adhere them.

Have fun. You're being clairvoyant now. You're seeing into the future. You're creating in pre-school arts and crafts mode, playing in your playhouse. You're finger painting, making mud pies, drawing smileys with your chalk. Enjoy it. Have a blast. Let your inner critic take time off. It's recess, make your move. You're sculpting the shape of things to come.

When it's done, your board should look like LOVE. It should scream unbridled passion. It should look like you want to hug and kiss it. Do so, and look at it often. Your Dream Board is an action tool. It's showing the universe what you want and how you plan to change the world.

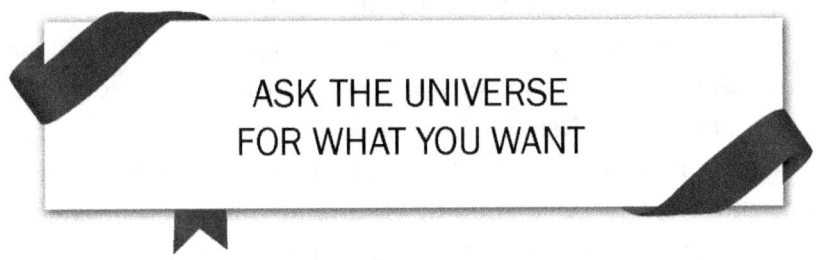

ASK THE UNIVERSE FOR WHAT YOU WANT

Asking for what you want is chief to obtaining anything in life. If you don't ask, you rarely get. You can't even get an answer to a question you don't ask. Asking puts desire in action. It's the first phase of commitment. It's as simple as what the Bible says—ask, and it shall be given to you. Seek, and ye shall find. Once you summon the gumption to ask, your wish becomes a purpose statement. You're stating that something you see in your mind is consistent with your being. That you think, feel, and have certainty that a thing that seems outside yourself belongs in the prototype of the change magician you're becoming.

Ask the universe for what you want, for it is what provides your needs and quenches your desires. You can ask in many ways, so ask in every way you can. Ask vocally for what you want. Meditate on it. Visualize. Take time in silent vigil to examine what it means to you, and feel the emotions it evokes. Assemble your dream board. Let it ask. Pray. Make a plan. Set goals, and work. Be consistent in your actions. Your energy will radiate and draw the object you desire.

To be a Change Wizard, *act as if.*

You definitely want to act as if you already have the thing you want. You do, it just hasn't materialized as yours in your reality. Acting as if is a sign of belief. If you want that new house, buy the chair you'll read in, sit in it, stash it on layaway. Envision it in situ. Scout paint colors, gather samples. Go house-hunting every chance you get. Whip your credit report into tiptop shape. Save every penny you can to make a sizeable down payment. Start selling and giving away the stuff you won't need when you move in. In turn, the universe will move to shake the atoms of your house, and re-position everything you need to get you into it.

If you want a new job overseas, buy a ticket. Go there. Look around. Meet people. Soak in the atmosphere. Traveling there is an act of faith that signals you're ready, it's where you belong. Traveling there is a form of asking. You will be acting as if it's yours. If you want to run a marathon, go out and meet runners who already race. Go for a run every morning or evening. Buy some snazzy jogging togs. Google what marathoners do, and the marathons taking place near you. Ask the universe for stamina, and the strength you'll need to reach your goal.

If you're an artist who wants to exhibit, analyze your portfolio. Make sure your best paintings are set to go when opportunity knocks. Create opportunities for yourself, so collectors can see and buy your work. Whip your contacts into shape. Attend local gallery openings. Put your face in the place, your ear to the ground and your shoulder to the wheel. Post your artwork up online, and announce you're preparing for a show. Even if you have to rent a loft yourself as a makeshift gallery, you'll be telling the truth in advance and advancing your budding art career.

Ask for the changes you want in life, and expect you will hear a resounding "YES!"

THE ROLE OF YOUR GOALS

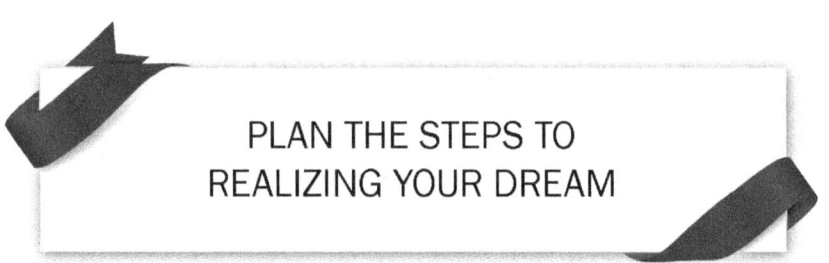

PLAN THE STEPS TO REALIZING YOUR DREAM

Now that your dream is firm in mind, you've already begun to experience it. But, to close the gap in time and space between who are now, and who you will be when you're fully inside that reality, you need a set of goals and tasks. Your goals are the steps to achieving your dream, so now it's time to set some goals consistent with achievement.

A dream is a picture of what can emerge, an idea, a possibility. A goal is an objective, or an aim you set in your head and heart that, once accomplished, moves you closer to the dream you're dreaming. Goals pave the path to your Meant-To-Do, and push you nearer your

Meant-To-Be. Goals are essential to progress, because they act to reverse engineer your dream, breaking it down into parts and pieces and letting you assemble them. In other words, goals are steps to dreams, and since you dream big, goals eat your elephant one bite at a time.

When you set a goal, establish a time in which you will accomplish it, for an open-ended goal amounts to essentially none at all. Without a deadline, projects lag. Other distractions may come along, dissuade you, shift your focus, sap your motivation, take up time, or cause you to abandon what you once thought to be crucial. Setting deadlines for your goals will keep them preeminent in your mind, and prompt you to make arrangements in your schedule to pursue them. A cut-off date gives you a timeline, too. It plots a roadmap you can follow, planting signposts along the way, making achievement imminent, substantial and more real. Your goal is no longer undefined, not a nebulous, wannabe, pie-in-the-sky prediction. It's a priority, a way of life. Your goals are connected to sense of self, so you want to see benchmarks of success, concrete evidence that your efforts will eventually make headway. Every goal reached gives you confidence that each successive victory will build upon the last. Your goals are promises to yourself, to follow your passion, trust your gut, and reach self-realization.

Ponder what it will take to build your dream, invest in the goals you set, and start on them immediately. Define your first goal and the time to complete it, take the first step, and go from there. By working on a goal each day, you are certain to complete it. The goal is a tangible thing in itself, and as you continue to act upon it, doors begin to open. A goal has vibrant energy. It will pull you along at a faster clip than if you proceed without one. Pretty soon, the timeline of your goal, and the timing of all your goal entails, will align, and that's called kismet—luck meeting your preparation in the arrival of opportunities. Synchronicity and perfect timing will be watchwords on your quest. With these, you can pursue more goals, and then the ball is rolling.

By plumbing the Internet, libraries, mentors, social networks, professional associations and personal contacts, you can efficiently educate yourself as to what it will take to launch any sort of project, business, enterprise, production, assignment or calling.

Work at your goal to become the very inspirational energy that originally inspired you. Be intrepid and resourceful. You can do it. You have whatever it takes, or can get it, because it is meant for you. Set goals so big, they embolden you and strike you with a sense of awe. Goals that excite more impetus to get fired up and make sparks fly, to galvanize a following. Goals as buoyant as holiday Macy's Parade floats soaring above the crowd.

No goal is too big or unwieldy for you. Huge is just right. It's how you roll.

Your dream deserves the goals you pursue to assure it becomes a reality.

Get out a notebook, sheet of scrap paper, journal, back of a sales receipt, a pad or even a restaurant napkin. Jot down the first goal you'll undertake to invoke your next adventure.

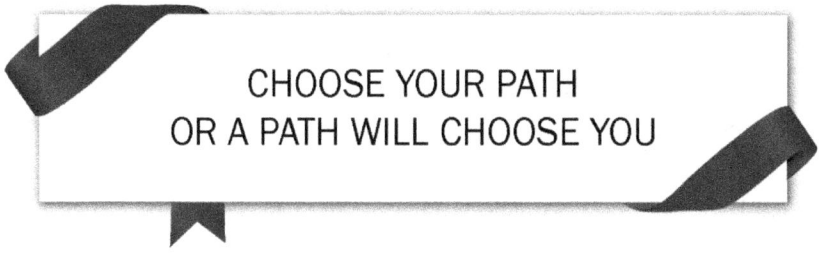

CHOOSE YOUR PATH OR A PATH WILL CHOOSE YOU

Knowing you'll meet your goal is half the battle. Then there's *how*. You don't have to know how, you just have to believe, make a plan, and take positive action. You can be gifted with sudden bursts of speed, meet goals in unusual ways, get unanticipated help, and leap from the pits of uncertainty into a done deal overnight.

Change is like a newborn baby's process of development.

The path to transformation can be long and winding, short and sweet, obscure or defined by its clarity. One must be willing to travel the path, be it through dark woods, up steep inclines, driving a side road, rocketing into the depths of space, or trekking a more familiar route. We can choose the path we take, whether we wish to accept that or not. Our path is laid out from choice to choice. Whatever happens along the way, we choose what to believe, who to live our lives with, where we go from day to day, what activities we engage in, words we say and every thought we think. These are flagstones on our path. We determine how we traverse it.

We can go it alone. We can marry, have kids. We can pour all our energies into career, a sport, our health or charities. We can build a life around our friends, care for elderly relatives, travel and opt to see the world. Our choices influence who we become. The nomad, leader, loner, intellectual, philanthropist, caregiver, sage or parasite. The scientist or composer.

To choose your path is beneficial. To purposely act accordingly can deliver you into a state of grace. To pave a new path is ingenious. It allows you to orchestrate a life in concert with your values, and to live a life that's tranquil, yet momentous, fierce, impactful and worthwhile beyond your own pursuits.

To evolve your self-concept to change the world is the pinnacle of change wizardry.

Each individual's journey matters. All our lives are consequential.

Your passage may be mysterious. You can't predict each twist and turn, and you needn't preoccupy yourself with every port you journey to, for some may be placid and some warlike. You choose to make the journey more fortuitous and amicable or fraught with peril and distress.

You are a spirit with free will. Be proactive. Choose your path. If you don't, a path may well choose you. If you aren't on a trajectory of your choosing, any wind that blows can sweep you into uncharted territories you may not withstand. You aren't riding in a caboose that hasn't pulled out of the station yet, you're the engineer of a train that's speeding along and needs to stay on track. Avoid rambling about as if you aren't piloting a mothership.

Choose a route and make it work.

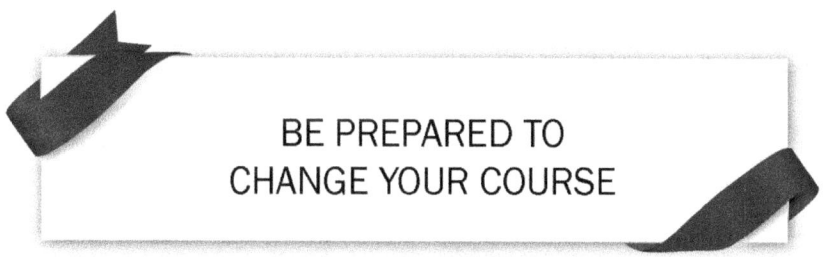

BE PREPARED TO CHANGE YOUR COURSE

You have a dream. You see it clearly. You're prepared to meet some goals. You set off on a path. There's a fork in the road. You have to elect to go right or left. You aren't sure which way to turn. You might even elect to hook a U-ey, travel on some unpaved road, or venture down an alleyway. It's dark and cold. You feel alone.

You have to believe you're still on your path, no matter what terrain you cross or how your course may vary. Changing your course is par for the course. You might have to pivot at any point. You might have to take a detour. You have to stay nimble. You have to be quick. You may have to jump over a candlestick.

Flexibility is your hashtag when you're working toward your dreams and goals. The tree that can bend is less likely to break. This is not to suggest that you turn into Jell-O, wobble like a Weeble, or channel Gumby every time you hit a snag, but being rigid rarely works. Intractability, though it's the flip side of steadiness, can be dull and dangerous. Not everything goes the way you plan. Your game plan may not turn out to be as sound as you anticipate. Stuff happens. Deal with what comes up. The universe proffers the ultimate plan. It is perfection, and always wins.

Decide on the course you want to take, and be ready and willing to make the adjustments needed as you go along. Conditions are dynamic, so even a practical plan may have to shift. Each response you consider and change you make contributes to your growth. These reveal and reinforce character, like irritation in an oyster shell will make a gorgeous pearl. The changes you have to undergo cut the facets of the gem you are. The sterling nature of your soul and spirit shines each time you rise to meet another challenge. Trust the process. Do what works.

You don't have to fall every time you trip. But you do have to rise every time you fall. Again and again, if you have to. Over and over. As much as it takes. That's the nature of keeping it moving, and keeping it moving is your nature. Keeping it moving is your tagline, website banner, theme song. Fly, run, walk, crawl, inch along or levitate telekinetically—as long as you keep it moving in the direction of improvement. That's how your Meant-To-Do gets done.

If, for some reason, you're tipped off-balance, find your center instantly. Be humble if you trip or fall, rise smiling, dust yourself off. Be eager to regain your stride. Hold your head up, keep your dignity. You're learning. You will overcome. The surer you are, the less likely you'll fall, so focus on being decisive, deft, quick-witted and fast on your feet.

Assess when you need to course correct, do so swiftly, and be on your way. Dragging your feet in indecision only wastes time, and you value your time, because your time is valuable.

When you stay ready, you don't have to get ready. Stay ready to make change readily, and be prepared to alter course. Every change is a gift keeping you in the present.

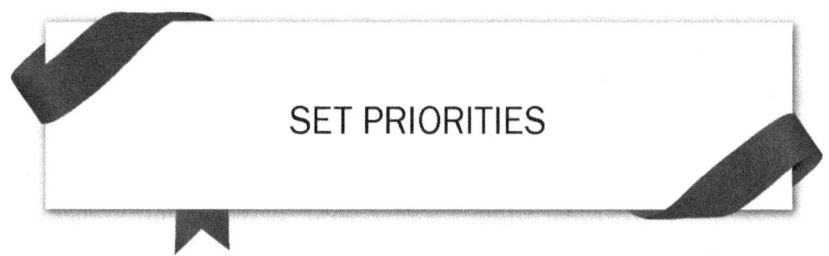

SET PRIORITIES

Declare your priorities off the bat—your lineup of what matters most.

Priorities are the structure of what's important in your life. Priorities help you organize. They increase your effectiveness. The hierarchy in which you place things dictates how you deal with them, the time you decide to devote to them, and the order in which you work. Appropriate prioritization focuses your energies, allows suitable application of resources, and avoids delays. It highlights what is vital, weeding out the unimportant stuff, and relegating the trivial to the bottom of the pile. Urgent matters can be attended to with efficiency and precedence when you label them as such. You no longer confuse activity with accomplishment or waste your time. You evade exhaustion, misdirection, draining people, places and things, and the feeling that the more you work, the less you're getting done. Without a list of priorities that reflect your dreams, goals, plans, work ethic, moral imperatives and ideas, the wrong tasks can get done in haste, and the right tasks can get thrust aside, forgotten, or neglected.

Once you know your Meant-To-Do, it's essential to make best use of what you have to make it happen. You want to avoid any squandering of effort, thought or capital. Armed with your priorities, you're effective, and you command respect, which allows you to take on the mantle of authority and leadership. As a leader, you're able to build a team to which you can delegate some tasks.

Determine your priorities, and write them down in order of the highest to the lowest.

Make priorities for your day, your week, your year—as far as your eye can see. Refer to them to stay on track, to help avoid distractions.

For instance, realize your laundry should wait till tomorrow, so you can get e-mails off to those clients you're trying to woo. The ones you networked with last night. They asked for your materials. They have a big project coming up, for which you totally fill the bill. Their submission deadline is today, so you have to apply by the time they get to the office to look over candidates. Your college roommate vouched for you—the one you haven't seen for years—so they're likely to take you seriously. It's an amazing opportunity. It should be Priority Number One. Make sure you know it's #1. Otherwise, when you see your laundry crowding the hamper, it could beckon you, make you worry about whether your skinny jeans with the cute little pockets are going to be clean by the next time you step out with friends, and *bam!* You might delay that cover letter containing those links you intend to send. If it's late, that great job could wash away in the washing machine with your dirty clothes. The momentum you built with that airtight referral could spin right down the drain.

You can't let that happen, right? You're not going to let it happen. You're on it. You have priorities. Your work is in order. You have a plan. You're in a competitive marketplace. Your business is built from the ground up. You lost clients in the economy crash, but you're not going down without a fight. You're not going down at all. You're powering off your music, and you're booting up your e-mail app. You're making progress toward your goals. The laundry has to wait. No doorbell, podcast, breaking news, or singing cat video someone sent can derail your mission to get that job. Your neighbor's breakup, though it's sad, can't draw you into chit-chat. You're acutely aware of priorities. Your Number One Priority is pending. You don't procrastinate. Your butt is on the case. And hey, now that you think of it, after you get e-mails sent, you'll put in some time on the new website, make a couple of calls, check your PayPal account, and by dinnertime, cut through a mile-long list of carefully set priorities.

That's what priorities do for you—allow you to focus on matters that count. You can't change the world with idleness, inanity or useless chores. You have to move some mountains. You make the right moves, the moves that count, the moves in an order that makes some sense.

Right now, your first priority is to order your priorities as if your life depends on it. Why? Because it does. The quality of your days on earth and the meaning your life takes on from here in relation to the greater good is weighing in the balance. So, know what's significant. Act on it. Move the most far-reaching thing you can do to the top of your list and keep it there until it gets done. Prioritize.

A way to be truly exceptional is to attack your most momentous tasks—which are often your most difficult—before you do anything else. Do the hard stuff first. Be brave about it. You know what is paramount. Do it now. Proceed with imperatives. Concentrate on the most salient tasks and refuse to take no for an answer from anyone. This isn't the time to be unfocused, scattered, or hit the easy button. That won't amount to anything.

This is your time to organize, prioritize, and finalize. Shore up your plan, leave no loose ends, and adhere to a set of priorities. There is no higher priority than to act to change the world.

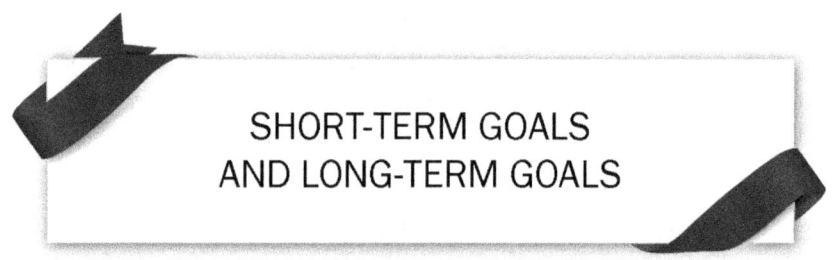

SHORT-TERM GOALS AND LONG-TERM GOALS

Your goals inform your priorities, and your priorities inform your goals.

Rather than sweat the goal thing, make it fun. After all, it's about your bliss.

Imagine doing what you want because you've structured your life that way. Your Want-To-Do is your Meant-To-Do. You let go of the should-do's haunting you, because life is now congruent. What you should do, want to do, must do, and do are one in the same, and they bring you joy.

Joy can't be imposed by guilt, prevailing opinions, societal norms, peer pressure or other impinging outside forces trying to run your life, including your finances. Your should-do's are ingrained in you. You'll do them as second nature as long as your goals translate into positive steps along your chosen path. Trust yourself to choose goals wisely. Let them arise from your inclinations, as you decide what to strive for next.

When you set a goal, you express belief in yourself and your abilities. You challenge yourself to reach for something. That something should be momentous enough to resonate with others and to help your fellow man. Goals constitute promises to yourself. They impact your pact with your Higher Power to strive for the best that you can be. They assert your availability to take the next step to receive more good and reveal more goodness in the world.

Though you may be pleased with the way things are, you know you can do much better. You know you're meant for greatness, that you have a place in history, and now's the time to claim it. You know there's a reason you're alive in the ripeness of this moment. You have a cause, a mission, a reason to be. You have a Meant-To-Be that's itching to be fulfilled.

What you're reaching for, and what makes you happy, should always be synonymous. Allow passion to urge you to make big goals that let you live in joy. Feel yourself living in the harmony between your goals and what you love. They should be in sync.

For example, if you want to be a gourmet chef, vegging out on the couch playing videogames all day is not your move. Unless you want to program games, or be a world class gamer, playing games shouldn't be a priority. It's a pastime. You don't want to pass time, you want to make the most of it. Time is a thing you can't get more of. If you want to be a chef, you have to cook. You have to learn to cook in ways that make your meals exceptional. This will be one of your goals. It will be top priority. And perhaps finding work in a restaurant, with a caterer, or privately. Or maybe running a mobile food truck, opening a restaurant of your own, teaching other budding chefs, writing a cookbook or cooking blog, or producing gourmet videos.

Set goals that can be long-term goals. Others can be short-term.

For starters, as a short-term goal, you could begin today to cook every meal you eat. That's doable now. That way, you can stockpile recipes for fresh and healthy offerings. Another possible short-term goal could be volunteering at Meals On Wheels, a soup kitchen or food pantry. Such a goal would have immediate impact. Feeding the hungry or homeless would be a way to put your skills to use in service to others that need your care. You could do this while you write your first cookbook. That goal could be set for a longer term—finishing your first draft in, say, the next six months. Wouldn't that be great? Or maybe a year is more realistic, seeing as taking photos of your dishes will be critical. Meanwhile, shooting videos you'll post up on the Internet could change your life in other ways, including increasing your following. Imagine becoming a YouTube sensation and then a celebrity chef. One goal to the next can get you there.

What you want to do, you're meant to do. It's here for the taking. Set the goal. Make it fun, and do it now. Believe it will happen, and when it does, it will bring a world of joy. It will make a contribution to a world that longs to receive your gift. This is no dress rehearsal. This is your life. Pursue your calling. To answer your calling simply means to do the things that call to you, setting goals to complete them step by step. This is what goals can do for you.

Your dream is a confection made of mysterious, tasty ingredients. Start whipping it up by setting goals and adding them to your daily life. Turn up the heat by setting a timer for each goal. Prioritize. Do the work. This is an award-winning recipe. Follow it. You can change the world.

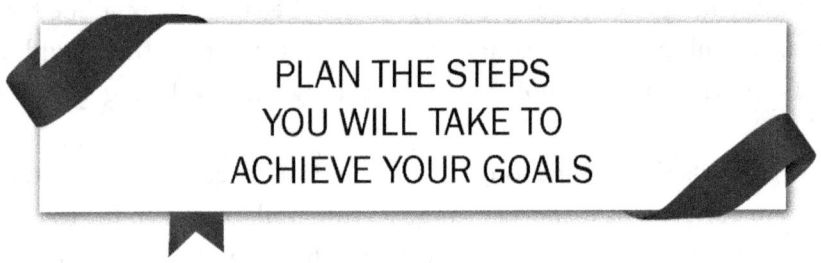

PLAN THE STEPS YOU WILL TAKE TO ACHIEVE YOUR GOALS

You will find that each goal has a series of steps you will need to complete to reach it.

It may take perseverance on your part to take each step with grace. Phone calls could require that you make your way past talking bots, listening to elevator music while you wait in endless queues. You might have to stand in lines sometimes, or wait for some assistance. You might have to apply for a loan that requires piles and miles of paperwork. You'll have to figure out clever ways to build your brand, streamline your services, differentiate your product. You may have to cajole gate-keepers such as assistants, agents, managers. You might have to follow up several times before you are able to score an appointment. The angle of your learning curve could be quite steep, so be prepared. You have to take these things in stride.

Keeping your ultimate goal in mind—recalling why you're doing what you're doing, and for whom—is your entrance fee. Accept that fact. You're entering into the next step of your evolution. Go with it. You'll never run out of things to laugh about, or people to meet and love. No matter how many steps it takes, you'll eventually do what you have to do. As long as you take it step by step, you're bound to hit your stride. The future belongs to those who persist.

Nothing lasts forever. Everything comes to pass, the Bible says. Things always change, so no matter what happens, know that it will pass. Enjoy what feels good for as long as it lasts, and know that whatever is difficult can be gone as abruptly as it came. Everything's a process.

Change is the only thing that doesn't.

Realize it's vital to welcome change, and to let it improve your game.

Be privileged to change yourself as changes occur that you cannot control.

Be an example of what can be done.

Love what you have to do, and do it. Do what you have to do when you have to do it. Timing is of the essence. Pat yourself on the back for accomplishing every step you take with such aplomb. You're a person of action. You have a plan, and your plan is in constant motion, expanding like the many stars and orbiting like the planets. Think of it as an adventure, because it is an adventure. A great adventure. The great adventure of being you. Every challenge you face is building a greater destiny ahead of you.

Learn what completing your goal will take. Take action. Act relentlessly.

You're not a couch potato, you're a whole farm of inventive ideas. You're a field of wildflowers, a national park, a rain forest, wetlands, mountain ranges. Every seed you plant is a possibility longing to come to fruition. So what if you have to plow a little, irrigate or fertilize. Look at the crop you're going to raise. Keep going. Keep growing. Keep making moves.

Examine the steps your goals require, and educate yourself about them. Learn what you have to do, where you have to go, who you have to contact. Cling to your vision. Steel yourself to possibly encounter the unforeseen and unforeseeable. Organize your steps, resources, methods and priorities. Recognize what you have going for you. This will give you confidence, help you avoid mistakes and missteps, recover, pivot, take a stand, and keep ahead of the game.

Here is a checklist of what you can do to start off on the right foot out of the gate, and make swift and steady progress:

- ☑ Rejoice In The Oneness Of All Beings
- ☑ Stay Connected To Your Higher Power
- ☑ Absorb How You Are Meant For Greatness
- ☑ Dream BIG!
- ☑ Strive Toward A Vision Larger Than Self
- ☑ Visualize Your Dream Come True And Feel What It's Like To Experience It
- ☑ Commit To Making Your Dream Come True
- ☑ Stand Tall In Who You're Meant To Be
- ☑ Know What You Are Meant To Do
- ☑ Monitor Your Thoughts, Words, Deeds
- ☑ Realize Your Thoughts Create Your Life And Always Keep Them Positive
- ☑ Understand That Your Energy Draws Its Match

- ☑ Recognize Your Emotions Magnetize And Manifest Like Energies
- ☑ Follow Your Passion, Joy and Bliss
- ☑ Ask The Universe For What You Want And Believe You Can Do Anything
- ☑ Be Open To Receiving Limitless Good And Act Like You Already Have It
- ☑ Set Long-Term And Short-Term Goals To Manifest Your Vision
- ☑ Create A Plan You'll Follow In Your Quest To Change The World
- ☑ Establish The Tasks Involved In Goals And What It Will Take To Accomplish Them
- ☑ Set A Deadline To Complete Each Goal And Plot Target Dates On A Timeline
- ☑ Take Persistent Action Every Day In Order To Achieve Your Goals
- ☑ Be Increasingly Open, Flexible And Adept At Handling Situations
- ☑ Keep Moving Forward No Matter What And Trust Your Instincts
- ☑ Reward Yourself For Accomplishments Of Any Size Or Magnitude
- ☑ Know You Are Changing The World Right Now And Accept That Responsibility
- ☑ Be Grateful And Thankful For Everything.

ELEVEN

BUILD YOUR TEAM TO PICK UP STEAM

NETWORK ONLINE AND ONE-ON-ONE

Many sports are structured in teams for a reason. Work groups tend to get things done.

The great football coach, Vince Lombardi, said, "Individual commitment to a group effort—that is what makes a team work, a company work, a society work, a civilization work."

Though your vision is given to you alone, to achieve at the highest level, it helps to team up with like-minded people. It's hard to do everything alone. A team can increase functionality. Industrialist Andrew Carnegie opined, "Teamwork is the ability to work together toward a common vision ... the fuel that allows common people to attain uncommon results." None of us is common, but we do have much *in* common. We're all special, so when we work together to do something special, that combination is added bling that can make an endeavor sparkle.

Of course, changing the world, in particular, is not something you can do alone. It goes without saying that the world includes everybody in it. The world has 7.4 billion people. That's a lot of hearts, souls, minds, potentials, bodies, spirits. A lot of opinions, emotions and thoughts.

"None of us is as smart as all of us," author Ken Blanchard (*The One Minute Manager*) points out. That's why you want an eclectic team composed of different intellects. You don't need a bunch of mini-me's that parrot everything you say. You want people with varied sets of skills, ideas, backgrounds and temperaments, and methods of tackling complex tasks. Folks with experiences you don't have, perspectives from contrasting angles. Seek fascinating people who will do intriguing things. You want every link in a chain of thought to be as strong as it can be, so the intellect of the whole is off the charts, and can accomplish feats no one individual could pull off.

You want a team that's a microcosm of the world as it should be—cooperative, loving, supportive, creative, collaborative, focused, visionary, kind, fundamentally good. A team that is willing to live to give and give to live, that sees beauty and possibility everywhere, in everything. A team that's multifaceted, yet its members complement each other, having similar motivations, fine intentions and beliefs. You want people with healthy minds and bodies, egos that are well in check, and one-for-all mentalities. Your team needs a great work ethic too, and a hopeful outlook, positive energy, peace and unrelenting drive. Tall order? Maybe so. Such rapport may be challenging to find. Loneliness is prevalent, but it doesn't have to be your lot.

You may feel like you're out here oh solo mio, but nothing is further from the truth.

We are never alone in the world, for as long as we live, and that's a fact. We are always aligned with our Higher Power, having some common experience, helping others, being helped. We are loved by many more people than we can imagine, and we're a part of things that happen, have happened, are currently happening, and haven't yet begun. We contribute to things unknown to us, and influence folks we'll never meet.

A new friend, acquaintance or partnership is only a handshake or smile away.

We are only alone if we wish to be. Even then, it takes a lot of work. It's not healthful or helpful to isolate ourselves, even if we feel adrift. We are more effective when we reach out into humanity and strive to make connections last.

We need each other, crave affection, long to be touched, and to touch, one another deeply and with a lasting effect. We want to give love and be loved, and we want to have meetings of the mind. Few are the tasks we can do by ourselves, if we're honest, when it boils down to it, when the rubber really meets the road. It's more fun when we work together rather than going it alone. If we labor in obscurity, try our hardest to handle everything, or worse, push everyone away, we are likely to get overwhelmed and experience burnout, stress, depression, substance abuse, poor health, compromised immune systems or other unwanted side effects.

The bigger your dreams and goals, the more room there is for more to join your cause.

When many stand to benefit, many ought to be involved.

If what you're doing is worthwhile, it ought not to be very difficult to build a team to get it done. It ought not, but it sometimes is.

To build a team, inspire people. When you inspire people, they're likely to come aboard with what you do. They'll want to be a part of it, because they sense it will turn out well, they're likely to enjoy the ride, and working with you feels so good. And mostly, they don't want what you sell, they want you and all that comes with you.

They see who you are and like it, so they invest in who you're meant to be. You make your vision clear enough that they see it as you do. They want to buy into it as well. You're a seductive hand to hold, and people crave camaraderie.

People respect you when you respect them.

The easiest way to build a team is to be a terrific leader. Build something that people can rally around, and you will attract good, eager people with a variety of talents, strengths and skills to complement your own. You're focused and able to organize a group that is cohesive.

People will want to work with you because you're a wonderful person. People want to work with people they want to work with—and that's you. You have the kind of passion that inspires people with your dream. You listen. You are attentive and brave. You're open to new ideas. You're a fun and creative collaborator. You have clear goals you communicate effectively and readily. You have brains and social skills. You're hardworking, focused, energized and prepared to take on challenges. You exude confidence, class and style, and you model strong ethics and moral imperatives that can be hard to find elsewhere. Everyone wants to join forces with you. The energy you radiate draws workers with amazing vibes.

Granted, with more chefs in a kitchen, more opinions come to bear. More communication styles, work habits, personality quirks and hidden goals can lead to misunderstandings, conflicts, clashes and other blips and bloopers. Add to that, that some folks may refuse to blend no matter what the group dynamic seems to be. More moving parts mean that more can go wrong. But, on the other hand, more can go right.

As my late grandmother used to say, "Two heads are better than one . . . even if one is a cabbage head." And you know what? She was right. We all might know some cabbage heads, but even a broken clock is right twice a day, so everyone is worthwhile in one way or another. Your task as a Change Wizard is, in part, to look for the best in everyone, and to bring it to bear for a common cause. Nobody can, or should be, written off, because everyone you meet is a work in progress, just like you. We all deserve respect.

With respect, we can do most anything together. We just have to make the effort.

When people are given a chance, they can surprise and successfully motivate with stimulating management. They can come up with off-beat fixes no one else can offer. People can drop insecurities at the most propitious intervals to become team players on the spot if they realize how much you value them. They can stop being bossy, scheming, know-it-all or contradictory, and display their vulnerability for the sake of productivity.

Every meeting you have is advantageous, if you let it be. Each interchange is meaningful, when you enter it with that intent. It's you who make relationships rewarding and constructive. You, who bring out the best in folks. That's why your network grows. Yet it's rare to have folks knock down your door to get to you. You may be swell, but you still have to go where the action is. You have to get out to meet and greet. Fortunately, there are so many ways to network in this day and age, that you almost have to live in a cave on a desert island not to bond. People want to be helpful by and large, and they're looking for others. If you walk out the door, you will come across personalities who'll love the chance to work and play and dream with you. You just have to be willing, imaginative and unafraid to take a chance to expand beyond your inner circle. Accept the invite. Make that call. Take the next opportunity. It's likely you'll be glad you did.

You can meet interesting people one-on-one on many occasions. Business meetings. Parties. Mixers. Private clubs and country clubs (if you're able to afford the dues and like the amenities they offer). You can meet people through sports activities. There are alumni groups to join. Classes. Speeches. Seminars. Neighborhood watches. Union conclaves. You can find people in bookstores, libraries, churches, coffee galleries. Smile. Be happy. Break the ice. Go where you're unknown, and socialize. Introduce yourself. Swap business cards. Nobody's going to bite you. Well, somebody might, but you'll survive. More likely, you'll make friends.

You could play it a little safer, and start by renewing old acquaintances. Friends you might have lost touch with, past colleagues, former classmates, roommates—anyone in your field or a related field that you might tempt to team up with you on a project, enterprise or business deal. Get to know your neighbors, too. You might find a kindred spirit.

You can seek out interest groups—folks you have something in common with, like, say, environmental groups, or book clubs, knitting circles, small investment groups, the Elks Club or the Rotary Club, ardent animal lovers, vegans. Whatever grabs your interest and is consistent with your brand, your dream, your vision and your goals. You want a wide span of relationships that can open up new vistas if you want to court the influence that helps one change the world.

You'll need to network online, too. Online, you can build a worldwide team.

Select a few social network sites you think will work out best for you, and consistently use your phone, laptop or tablet to gain contacts and communicate with ease. Lately, a shooting star in pajamas can influence what many people wear, where they live, what they eat and what they think. Not to mention where, and how, they spend their time or waste their money. Power is found in the oddest places. Make a plan to build a team by using your power strategically. The internet is a megaphone. You can build a platform anywhere you like with just some clicks.

Strive to make deep and lasting connections. Form a team of exceptional individuals that can work together like fingers on a hand. Building a team is essential to living happily, spreading your heartening message, implementing your brilliant plan, and making the world a better place.

FORM A CORE GROUP WITH WHOM YOU WORK WELL

Your team might consist of a large group. However, your core group is more intimate. A core group of friends who are there no matter what is a major blessing. Do whatever you can to maintain true friendships. Relationships can be frail, because it is trust which binds us together. Trust is a backbone easily broken. Once broken, trust can be hard to mend. Impossible, in some instances. Developing trustworthiness, therefore, should be uppermost in your mind.

Choose a core group you can work and play with. Commit to them being in your life, and to being a blessing in theirs. Always behave in an ethical, moral manner they can rely upon. You're an integral part of their bustling lives, and you want to help uplift them.

Be focused on who your friends are, and be forgiving of the things they do that might be unconstructive. Know each pal is a beam of light to illuminate your path to growth and help you to formulate change within. Keep in touch. Make time to socialize. Find ways to get together. Let your pals into your inner sanctum, no matter how much you may feel you've been hurt in the past. The past is gone. They're here now, so be grateful for them. Cherish the people with whom you can build the future, keeping in mind the fact that every change begins with love.

MENTOR MOJO

The centerpiece of your team can be a mentor. Do you have one?

Whatever your vision, there is a mentor with whom you can find simpatico—someone who's lived a parallel life, who can teach you, guide you, lend support. Someone whose wisdom lights your path, because they're farther up the road and are able to see things you cannot. A person who lives the kind of life you'd like to live, has values similar to your own, and is practiced in ways that you are not. This is a priceless gift and valued friend to make and keep.

A mentor can lend a different perspective, help you determine what you need, share their process, critique your plan, hook you up with influencers, and maybe invest in your dream. They might be able to show you how to tackle various daunting tasks, answer questions, find solutions, hip you to strategies they applied as they struggled toward their own success, or just be a source of encouragement or a sounding board to bounce things off. You can learn from their experience, and they can be a hand to hold or a shoulder to lean on in tough times.

You may wonder who'd want to mentor you, but you're likely to find it incredible how many wonderful people would love to share their insights with you, give you that boost you're hoping for, facilitate progress, show you the ropes, and make it easier for you to live your dream. It's their way of giving back. Someone will gladly take you under their wing when they see you working hard to achieve a worthy goal. Not everyone will have the time, but most will have the inclination and the genuine desire to help you achieve as they've achieved.

People love to help people who help themselves.

To find a mentor, make a list of people in your community—be it local or professional—whose actions you admire and would be happy to emulate. Think of people for whom you have high regard, and whose reputations you respect. Maybe they aren't local, they can be anywhere you can e-mail, phone, contact through a third party, social network, or the contact page of their website. You could possibly contact a manager, agent, publicist or publisher, if they happen to have such an entourage. Facebook has found that the six degrees of separation once connecting you to anyone you wished to meet has shrunk, through modern technology, to three and a half. That's an eye-opener. You're three point five people away from even the president of the United States—the most powerful person in the world. So you really have access to anyone. You might know someone, who knows someone, that's the cousin to the next-door neighbor of your ideal mentor. Literally, no one is out of your reach.

Connecting with a mentor can mean the difference between you schlepping a long hard slog or suddenly making a quantum leap. It could be the difference between somebody snapping their fingers to open a heavy door, and you struggling to learn the door exists.

A leg up is nothing to sneeze at when you consider the impact it can have, and how, as soon as the tables turn, you plan to pay it forward.

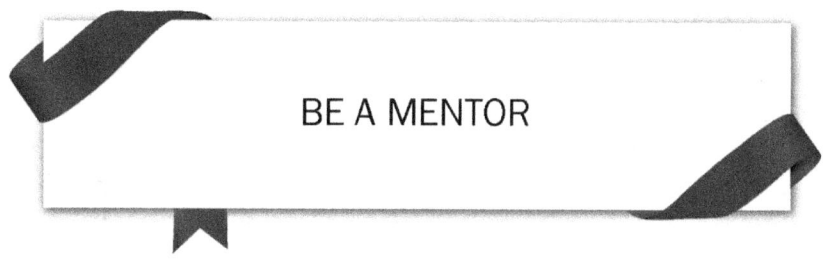

BE A MENTOR

Just as you can receive from a mentor, you can be a mentor, too. You might not conceive of yourself as one, but lots of people may need your help. You listed what you're good at, right? You have it all down in black and white. You have experience. You have a skill set. You have a degree of education, formal or self-taught. You're a source of inspiration. You have an interesting story to tell. You have ideas. You're informative. Teach someone what you know.

Mentoring is a form of teaching. Whether it's been you're intention, or not, to this point, you've taught a lot of things. You may have shown how to use a software program, change a flat tire, tie a tie, exhibit proper etiquette, or bookkeep like a math pro. You may know about farming, flipping houses, styling hair, applying makeup, pitching projects, interviewing, writing a killer grant application. You have techniques for many things a younger person needs to know. You can show someone the way to go.

When you mentor, you will learn as well. You'll learn to become a better teacher, learn from the mentee you're instructing, learn a lot more about yourself.

When you help someone succeed, their success is partly yours. You change the world.

PIONEER AS A VOLUNTEER

You don't have to look far to find a need you can volunteer to fill. Even if volunteering isn't convenient for you at the moment, you can find a way to make the time to change the world. Waiting until the perfect time doesn't ever quite work for anything. The only perfect time is now. There are tons of opportunities to help turn lives around. Health clinics can give you a chance to serve. You can teach people how to read, read audiobooks for the Braille Institute, collect and donate children's books for kids without their own. You can clean beaches, or plant some trees to help save the environment. You can rescue animals, deliver meals to hungry seniors, help build houses, clothe the homeless, donate goods or services. You can even start a charity of your own for a cause that inspires you.

Instead of binge-watching reality shows or playing another round of golf, you can go out this weekend to change the world, and have it really count. You don't ever have to be bored or contemplate the meaning of your life. You can *give* meaning to your life, and feel the intense satisfaction of making inroads where they're needed. If you feel disconnected, don't. We're cells of one body, the family of man. We're meant to recirculate good and put our gratitude to use.

Must you really store another pair of shoes you hardly wear? Or could you forego those heels to buy work shoes for someone else. The latter could change somebody's world. Work shoes could even save their life, and who knows, they could cure cancer with a decent pair of shoes to wear to work or to try to find a job. Nobody knows what good can come from a single selfless act. We just know that good is exponential. Good multiplies at a rapid rate and always circulates. When you volunteer to help others, baked in the cake is some good cycling back to you. You don't volunteer for that reason, you go into it to give, not get. But the benefits to you of generosity and altruism go beyond the temporal. Yeah, you're hyper-busy these days—overworked, underpaid in the main, and probably stretched out way too far—but you're going to spend your time somehow, and doing for others will change the world in wild, capricious ways.

On the other hand, you might start at home. You might need to take care of a loved one for some reason—because they're elderly, infirmed, addicted, mentally impaired, bereaved, or otherwise challenged to care for themselves effectively. Instead of warehousing an older relative, you could take them in. You might want to raise your grandkids, nieces, nephews or a godchild.

The old World War I adage doesn't apply when it comes to volunteering now. Back in the 1920's, would-be soldiers were cautioned against volunteering, warned off with the warning, "Keep your bowels open, your mouth shut, and never volunteer." In the 1950's redux of this basically cynical advice, that got shortened to "Never volunteer for anything," a stern rebuke to those inclined to throw their hat into the ring. The underlying premise is that no good deed will go unpunished if you volunteer for jobs that no one wants to do. You might bite off more than you can chew. But you can chew anything on your plate. You live in hope. You know you're entirely capable. You can bet what you freely give is going to pay off in dividends. Volunteering is an act of trust, and trusting can only bring much more to you that you can trust.

When you give of your time and energy, you give what's irreplaceable. You are investing your life force, feeding energy into something outside yourself, and that is powerful. You are using your gifts for the common good. That's why they're called gifts—they're bestowed upon you to help you give to others. When you volunteer, you give of self. You give what only you can give. In so doing, you change your life and prove how you can change the world.

BE A GREAT COMMUNICATOR

You have a mission, so you have a message. You want to get your message out, because that is what your message is—something you're meant to communicate. Communication leads to understanding, which brings more peace and love. That's worth speaking out about. When you speak, you want to be understood. You want your message to be clear, and you want to evoke emotion, because through emotion, you open hearts and minds.

You want to be able to articulate ideas, tell stories, relay who you are, and be willing to forcefully address the pressing issues of the day. You have to know how to make your point concisely and to great effect. You want to expand your vocabulary, picking up words from various sources, retaining their meanings, getting to love words, effortlessly spinning clever yarns. Through words, you can freely express yourself, so choose your words carefully, never say careless words, know words can equally wound or heal, relay or obfuscate the truth.

Denotations and connotations of words may be different, and you can work with that.

Denotations of words are their literal meanings. Connotations of words are what they have come to imply contemporarily. You want to speak with passion, because it matters what you have to say, and it matters more with every day, because, as your influence amplifies, more people will be listening. Be glad that your words are compelling. Trust that you'll speak as you're meant to speak, no matter the size of your audience. You are a flume for divine intervention, a pipeline for mystical messages that stream through you at will. You are the voice of the unseen as it acts to convert bad into good, and good into what is best for all. You're open to incoming messages, and you deliver them with clarity. You are an aqueduct for every righteous word and turn of phrase.

Not only must you speak well, but you will wish to become a fine listener, too. Focus on hearing the meaning behind words just as you hear the words themselves, because others might speak in unartful ways though their content may be significant. Be ready to hear a truth however it comes to you, and champion it. Recognize truth, and continue to speak it, not varnishing it in any way. Understand truth when it comes to you, and assimilate it easily, accepting it into your paradigm and passing it along. Truth is so beautiful on its own that you need not gild its lily.

Refrain from using the truth as a weapon. The truth is a gentle breeze that blows away all of the stench of dishonesty, like the quickening breath of a happy child. Carry the truth like a newborn baby, delivering it with gentility, sensitivity, warmth and compassion. Be soothing in your vocal tone, and poetic with your every phrase. Be commanding when you need to. This is the duty of leadership.

Be patient enough to decipher the genuine meaning behind what people say, giving the benefit of the doubt. Filter out the negative, and always consider the source. And for heaven's sake, look folks in the eye. See through their curtained windows to the soul to what lives and breathes beyond. Make yourself understood, and be understanding. Know when someone needs to talk, or be talked to, so they feel they matter. Relent when it's best to back off from interchanges that go sour, and be ready to give a compliment when you sense it can uplift. Shun any urges to gossip, carry rumors, or violate confidences that others place into your care. Relay how you feel when it's necessary, not when it might be burdensome. Prepare your phraseology as if someone's world depended on it, for you may not know when it actually does. Think before you speak. A cruel word can be a final straw, or a kind word can open a long-locked door to the secret of great oracles.

Above all, listen. Listen closely. Hear what people have to say, and what they don't say, equally. Serve your attention like a meal, to nourish someone's being. Listen with your ears and eyes. Discern with all your senses. Body language is eloquent, but look beyond the physical.

Open your "third eye"—your canny sixth sense. You are a wholly sentient being. You are not limited in your scope. You can expand your awareness to include the metaphysical. Attune yourself to detect with extrasensory perception. Your ability to comprehend is unconstrained by time and space or this plane of existence.

Once you accustom yourself to ingesting more than what you can see with your eyes, hear with your ears, taste, touch or smell, you can begin to receive and transmit in the highest realm of human consciousness. Information can come from beyond the veil, and anywhere in the universe. Facts are available outside the earthly. Nothing is incomprehensible. Avoid limiting what you are able to fathom. Your ability to relate, inform, reveal, interact, connect, educate and enlighten is all-encompassing. You can see into the future if you look to it, and train yourself to see through your third eye. Through it, you can see realities you otherwise wouldn't recognize or be able to communicate. You can connect with ease and grace to auras and other phenomena, and peer into other beings' souls.

You are a great communicator. Use the power of spoken and written words for the sake of the multitudes crying out for a balm of peace and love.

Know who you're meant to be, what your message is, and what you're meant to do, and strive to reach all of the 7.5 billion people with you on the Earth—for this is how you'll change the world.

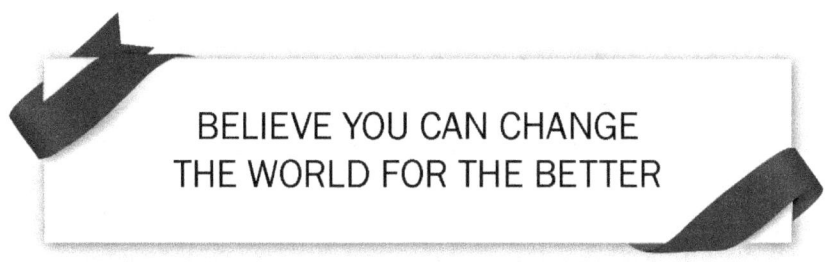

BELIEVE YOU CAN CHANGE THE WORLD FOR THE BETTER

Believe.

Belief is everything.

The difference in those who change the world, and those who never even try, is belief. Belief can move a mountain, catch a star, and part the seas. When you believe in a thing that's yet unseen, it will start to materialize simply because you believe in it.

The world is a ball of energy. And we, after all, are energy. We are energy moving, and morphing, and rearranging even as you read, and as I write my words of love. We are changing the world for the better every moment we radiate energy that's filled with hope and gratitude.

That energy travels around the globe and out into the universe, restructuring what it touches.

Believe that you can change the world for the better, and atoms start to shift.

The architecture of your dream is being erected with building blocks the instant you see it taking shape. Others begin to see it, too.

We change the world through the act of believing we can, and will, and have already started, knowing it is up to us. We are the ones turning hate into love by loving more than we've ever loved. We are the ones turning war into peace, putting down weapons and picking up the sword of justice in their stead. We are the ones converting inequality into the Oneness of all—everyone accounted for, all being nourished, housed, and taken care of as to need. We are the kindness replacing the cruelty. We are the civil eschewing the rude, the crude and the casually arrogant. We are the generous counteracting the greediest in our midst. We are the creativity churning out beauty to conquer the ugliness that creeps into the discourse as discord in our society. We are the sterling excellence outshining mediocrity. We are the outstretched hand instead of the closed fist primed to strike a blow of medieval, monstrous acts that harshly seek regression. We're the broad-minded openness to face down xenophobia. We are the calm that spreads throughout the land, the belief to silence doubt, change that moves forward, never turns back, and is transformative.

Believe that you can change the world, and you will do everything it takes.

Your dream is already happening. It believes it's supposed to come true through you.

Your personal power comes from the infinite source, and, as such, is unconquerable, exact and inexhaustible, no matter how exhausted you may sometimes feel from day to day.

Let go of the fear behind disbelief, and believe what you are destined for. Believe your Meant-To-Do will happen once you commit your will to it. It is flourishing in the wellspring of the invisible, eager to emerge.

Just because you can't see it, doesn't mean it doesn't exist.

Potential for everything exists as a forthcoming possibility. Because anything is possible, reality can span many spheres. Reality is all-inclusive. Reality is what we make of it. Reality is what it makes of us. Believe in one, and it exists if only in your mind. Once it exists in your mind, it exists as an idea that can become a dream. Once it's a dream, it can turn into goals. Once it is goals, it's achieved by tasks. Once it converts into tasks, it will spring into action. Your actions will make it more real, advanced, and palpable to all. Others will climb on board with it, and help you make it materialize—making it into a thing they can see, feel, taste, touch, smell, and believe in. They believe, because you believed, and you kept on believing until it caught on.

You must BELIEVE, because when you believe, you create what you believe in.

You must believe in yourself. In life. In the One Love that exists in you. In the One Love in which we all exist. In the world. In your fellow souls and spirits. Your faith and belief will give you strength. Faith and belief will empower you. Faith and belief will free you from the bonds of skepticism. Faith and belief will show you vistas you have never seen before. Faith and belief will dissolve your past and crystallize your future.

Believe that you can change the world, and you are an authority. Your vision becomes the rose-colored glasses through which others see a brighter day. You are the go-to girl or guy that is plowing the field and tilling the fertile soil of a visionary landscape. Believe you're a genius, and you're aligned with intellect, talent, inspiration, vision and inventiveness. New ideas are unveiled and revealed to you. As you're steeped in possibility, you're an engine of ingenuity. You attract everything you need to you, and all you want is in your hands. Enthusiasm follows you. People are keen to adopt your procedures, products, methodologies. You believe, so you're a meeting hall for all who want to say, *me too!*

Belief is the password admitting you to the private club of miracles.

Believe you can change the world, and you can, and you will. It is already happening.

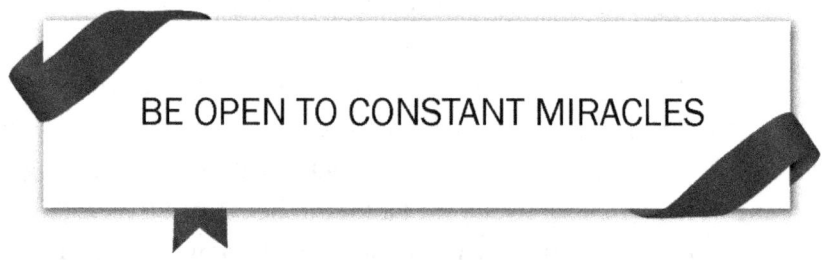

BE OPEN TO CONSTANT MIRACLES

Every miracle needs a place to land. Your shoulders are the perfect spot. Why you? Well, why not you. You're kind. You're good. You're ready and willing, right? You see miracles everywhere you look. You're breathing. That's a miracle. Your heart is beating. That's one too. You woke up this morning from your slumber. That's a miracle, for sure. You were born. That's a yowza miracle. Babies are being born right now, from the ether into this space and time where there really is no space or time, except that we've agreed there is. Getting the world to agree on anything is a giant miracle. Spirits are assuming flesh and blood at the rate of two hundred fifty five babies per minute. Miraculous. Miracles happen all the time, from a place beyond our reckoning. The sky is a miracle. Oceans, too. Grass grows. That's a miracle. Trees that provide us with food are a miracle. Miracles are more plentiful than human beings are on earth. And you deliver miracles. What you contribute to others' lives may often be seen as a miracle. You are a healing energy. You're unleashing a string of miracles that stretches clear across your life.

If miracles happen all the time, then miracles can come to you. In a flash, one can change your entire life. Just as not-good stuff happens, and you accept that, so can a miracle strike like lightning, lighting up your world. Miracles are as numerous as stars in the sky and grains of sand on the beaches of eternity. Miracles are the natural order. The next miracle is due along in a trice, pronto, at once, any second now, more often than any train or plane. It is set to transport you so much farther than you've ever been before.

Expect and court your miracles with faith, belief, and action, and they'll line up like the Georgia font print in the pages of the New York Times. You never know when your next miracle will arrive, or how it will change your life, but you know it'll come from a universe that wants to surprise the world through you, and has every desire to realize your dreams and fondest wishes.

Miracles are yours to the same degree as you're expecting them—and more are on their way right now.

BELIEVE YOU'LL RECEIVE WHAT YOU ASK FOR

You may believe in many things, but you must believe you'll receive what you want.

Believe your dreams are already real, and also right and good.

Be specific in what you ask for, as specific as what you would like to receive. If you want a pink rosebush, it will not do to simply ask for flowers. If you do, you could get a bunch of weeds, which might be lovely in themselves, but not precisely what you want. If you want a pink rosebush, ask for that and believe you will receive it. See pink roses in your mind. Smell their lovely fragrance. Feel what it feels like to stand in your garden admiring their petals as well as their thorns. Draw strength from the fact that they're delicate, and yet able to protect themselves and grow more abundant every year. Think about how you would like to personify qualities the pink rose has. Pink roses will be drawn to you the minute you believe they will, and they'll start to show up in your world. When you take pictures with your cell phone of pink roses you come across, realize you believed you'd spot some, and because you believed, it is coming about.

Write down the things you want to attract as though you were writing a shopping list. When you're going to the grocery store, you believe the items on your list will be in your cart, then kitchen, soon. You look for them with certainty. You believe they are already yours. You've already assembled a recipe in your mind that's made from what you bought. You can see it, smell it cooking, taste it. That's how it should be with hopes and dreams. You have to believe.

But be certain you want to attract them first, so the power they hold is not misplaced. You can tell yourself you want a thing, and yet not really think about what it will mean. You don't want that to happen. Know why you want what you want in your life. That knowledge informs your belief system.

If you're asking for twelve million six hundred thousand forty two dollars and seventeen cents, why do you want it? To save it? Horde it? See what it looks like? Give it away? To buy your Mom and Dad a house and educate your siblings? Do you want to jet off on a permanent vacation, hike the Himalayas? Or would you rather get right to work on that project you've been saving for? Is it power and influence you're after? What will you do with your influence? Will you wallow in throwing your weight around, or use it to advance a cause? Consider exactly what you want. What kind of lifestyle will it afford you? Will that make you happier? Won't you be happy, no matter what? Really. Think about it. Try on possibilities, and be certain you want the things you thought you wanted, way before you ask.

You can ask for anything you desire, and by asking, put it in motion. Make sure it's a current desire and not a thing you wanted way back when that doesn't suit you now. Maybe you've always wanted a wedding, but now you no longer want to be married. Maybe you wanted to travel the world, but what you want now is hearth and home, and a family to love and be loved by. Maybe you wanted adventure, but all you want now is to write about derring-do.

Try on your new life in your mind, so you can be sure it's what you want.

When you ask for what you want, believe you'll get it based on your belief. Ask and believe, and whatever you get will be for the best in any event, because you believe. Belief can animate anything, and anchor it inside your life. Your belief is a barometer that's measuring atmospheric pressure, indicating there'll be change. Change for the better is what you want, so be as fully invested in your belief as you are in your current reality. Belief turns longing into assurance. Belief can turn hope into gratitude. If you don't believe in your dream, who will?

Believe in your dreams, and believe you will see them come true, because that will capture them and make them real for everyone. Belief is the fuel on which dreams fly.

I'm pumping energy into your dreams, and I'm rooting for you to achieve your goals. I believe other readers will do the same, which means you're believing for all of us. Your belief churns my belief, and my belief churns more. Believe in the change you want to experience so much that you experience it long before it's realized. Ask for the things you believe in with the belief your belief is creating them.

Be thankful for all you have right now, and believe this includes the dreams you can now see only in your mind.

RECEIVE AND REMAIN UNATTACHED TO OUTCOME

Openness to receiving unattached to any specific outcome prepares you to receive your best. When you ask and believe this way, you're accessible. More than you asked for can appear.

If you're receptive, what you receive may be so much more than you ever dreamed.

But if you hitch your wagon to one star, you may limit yourself to it, and resist the entire rest of a cosmos chock full of stars in billions of galaxies. Why do that, when incredible gifts are no doubt available outside your view. Be prepared to receive outcomes commensurate with this expanding universe of ours. It's all but incomprehensible to us humans here on Earth. We occupy a single planet in a single solar system in the innumerable solar systems that may exist beyond our scope.

Your life and your dreams are made of the very same stuff as all of the universe, and the outcome of your asking and believing expands at its awesome rate, unless you pigeonhole your dreams. You might be able to fly without a plane. Who knows, it's possible. Everything is possible. Your dreams are carved out of a universe of limitless possibilities, where anything can happen. As you dream, you snatch possibilities out of the air and into your life. If you ask for only a plane, you may be blocking yourself from receiving anything more than that plane. You might preclude be granted flight without one, or getting your own set of wings. That may seem an absurd analogy, but in the realm of possibility, there is no absurdity, nothing restricted, no obstruction, no constraint. Once, an airplane seemed absurd, and yet planes are pretty much old hat now. It's time for teleportation. Keep your options open. Let the cosmos do its thing.

Be sure to let outcomes sort themselves, because your hypotheticals are only a fraction of what can turn up. Remain unattached to what you envision, for it may be short-sighted in relation to all that can appear—and what can appear are the miracles you were created to facilitate, which constitute your Meant-To-Do. Be prepared to receive more than what you conceive.

Dreams have power all their own, and lives as real as yours or mine. What can transpire is awesomeness superior to your range of sight, so believe and receive with no holds barred.

CHANGE YOUR RANGE

LEARN TO LIVE AND LIVE TO LEARN

In order to be exceptional, or to do anything exceptionally, you have to learn to do it well in the first place, then apply it. You will have to learn a lot of things in order to achieve a dream. You have to learn facts and information, sure, and a whole lot of other things. You will have to learn patience and fortitude. You will probably have to unlearn, and relearn, many things you thought you knew. Because the world is changing, what you know could be largely irrelevant.

Learn from the best, and learn quickly, too. A steep learning curve moves you faster. Timing is everything nowadays. In fact, it always was. Opportunities don't tend to wait on those who aren't up to speed. Do you? I don't. I go with the ready Mr. or Ms., the one who knows their stuff.

Fortunately, there's no excuse for being unprepared these days. You can learn all you need to know by Googling. Classes—in person or online—can radically sharpen up your game. Many community colleges offer courses over several weeks that can land a certificate in a given field with little expenditure. They're a minimum investment for the knowledge they provide. An adult class at a community college may last a day, a weekend, or a few weeks of your time. They are often taught by professionals in the field you want to learn about. Meeting a pro in a class they teach can get you a mentor, a friend, or a colleague to work with, which is a major plus. And they'll typically share a traditional education plus practical elements of the trade, craft, art or business you are endeavoring to plow forward in.

A plethora of seminars is available from private teachers, tutors, motivational speakers, coaches, Internet videos, eBooks, live-streams, CD disks and podcasts. You can sign up for free tutorials, haunt your library for printed books, newspapers stored on microfiche, audiobooks and mp3's, and all kinds of films and movies.

There's nothing like a good book, though. And reading is essential if you want to expand your knowledge base. Reading is fun, it really is. It isn't the arduous task some people make it out to be. And the library is a free resource—an inexhaustible research mine. You can read fiction, escape to another world, walk in somebody else's shoes. You can read biographies, and learn from another's mistakes, or be inspired by their success. You can peruse how-to books that are designed for beginners and break things down. And for those who want to learn to write, reading the writing of others can help you develop a style all your own.

To be labeled an expert in a field, you have to know how to create content. Books, ad copy, magazine articles, newspaper editorials, letters to the editor, employee manuals, business materials, proposals, graphic novels, pitches, grant applications, speeches, poems, e-mails, bios, websites, blogs and other essential professional texts can lend you credibility. So, reading is required. You will not write well if you don't read. If it hasn't seemed to you that way, be sure to heed that takeaway. It'll stand you in good stead. Reading advances your know-how, intellectual prowess, grasp of facts, depth of knowledge, comprehension, understanding of history, personal philosophy, and ever-expanding vocabulary.

No one can't afford to read, and no one can afford not to.

Not reading is a leading cause of ignorance, and that's no joke. Ignorance is no one's friend. Ignorance causes incompetence and leads to unwise acts. Pick up a book and choose to read. Buy a newspaper or magazine. Listen to audiobooks in the car. Educate yourself. You can't blame another soul for not making the most of your brilliant brain and for failing to do it justice.

If you know how to read, exercise the gift to advance your awareness, mindfulness and the breadth of your cognitive learning skills. Reading leads to expertise, good judgment, and proficiency. It contributes to enlightenment and improves your muscle memory. It will expand your paradigm beyond your own experience. It'll give you *aha!* moments, breakthroughs, big ideas, epiphanies, and while curling up with a good book, you may discover you love to learn.

If you aren't able to read just yet, there's a wondrous treat in store for you. You have many other skills. You can also learn to read. No matter what anyone has said, you only have to believe you can, and commit to learning how. No matter how difficult it's been to learn to read, I know you can. I believe in the vastness of your mind. I have faith in your abilities. I know your will is stronger than a learning disability, or the situations you've been in that caused you not to read. Reading can melt away stress, encourage empathy and amend life goals. Reading will open new worlds to you, no matter your current age, or sex, or where you live, your schooling, or your lack of it. It doesn't matter. Not knowing how to read is in the past the moment you put it there by picking up a book and getting help to read its contents. What you read can change your world.

Find, and attend, a reading class. Ask a friend to teach you. They'll be delighted to share the journey with you, happy to see you grow. And in the process, they'll grow too. You could also learn from videos, buy a reading learning program, hire a tutor to teach you in privacy, or get into a reading group. Avoid allowing pride to stop you. There is no shame in not knowing what we don't know—just in not finding out. When you read, you connect to a conversation.

The only ignorant question is the question you don't ask.

Questions are patiently waiting for answers. You have to ask about many things when you plan to change the world. You have to reach farther than your grasp. But that's how grasps get stronger. If you fail to ask, you deny yourself opportunities to change and grow. That is the tragedy in life. When you ask, you learn, and your question marks turn into exclamation points.

Read, and keep reading. Learn, and keep learning. Knowledge is a high-wattage light that illuminates possibilities. Develop a thirst for knowledge that can never be quenched or satiated. Intellectual curiosity is a VIP all-access pass—and there's one that has your name on it.

A "PROBLEM" IS ONLY A QUESTION THAT HASN'T BEEN ADEQUATELY ANSWERED YET

We approached solving "problems" before in the context of changing the world in different ways. Now, we come at it from the perspective of learning how to be self-taught.

Often, when issues arise, we react immediately, showing feelings of anger, frustration, resentment or pain. This is counter-productive. More than likely, this serves to inflame instead of ameliorate a situation. It may form another intractable, crusty layer on top of the circumstance that originally irked us. It's like having an issue, and, rather than solving it, choosing to drink or do drugs to escape it. This only results in compulsive behavior becoming a far more disastrous issue. The underlying cause remains. Acting out only makes things worse. Yet, in the heat of dilemmas arising, solutions may elude us.

A "problem" is only a problem if we label it as such. Avoid letting unanswered questions fester. Don't make mountains out of molehills. Identify the question behind the predicament you may be facing, and uncover a suitable answer to correct it by informing yourself regarding your alternatives. Problems will fade, and you will advance, when you strive to educate yourself.

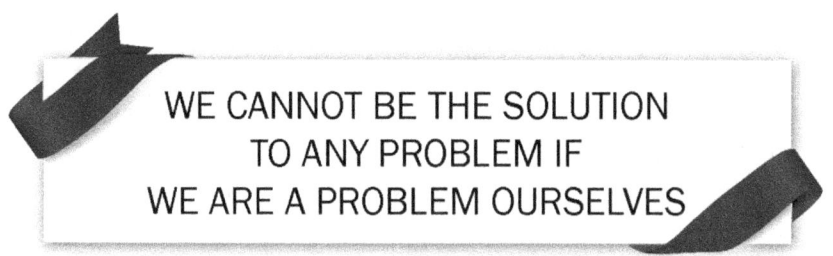

WE CANNOT BE THE SOLUTION TO ANY PROBLEM IF WE ARE A PROBLEM OURSELVES

We know that less helpful than seeing a problem is *being* a problem. That's a conundrum. The good news is, we can stop this cycle before it begins if we check ourselves.

If things aren't working properly, and you don't see the boondoggle, hey, let's face it, the boondoggle's you. That's not the disaster it may seem. Fortunately, you can change you.

There's a cycle—change happens, we react. A reaction is rarely positive. Responses are more helpful. We can develop a learned response. Stuff happens, there's no doubt of that. But we create what happens next. We either choose to flow with the shifting tide or elect to struggle. We can teach ourselves to be the change. This is a better alternative. We know everything has an upside, we can train ourselves to roll with that. Since everything is a two-sided coin, even being the object of discrimination due to our gender, race, religion or creed can lead to something good—if only exposing the wrong that's done. Counting everything as a blessing can render more change than a Vegas slot machine. We just have to learn to accept this fact.

Train your mind to see a reality where there are no problems plaguing you, and life will be disencumbered of any needless stress or strain. Learning change is good lets any movement in or around your environment propel you forward willingly. Learn to let go. Learn to let things be.

When we learn that the universe buttresses us, and everything works together for good, we can accept any swing or sway, and embrace the gifts it brings to us. When we do so, we are a healing balm instead of another problem. If we resist and cling or judge, regaling ourselves about life's travails, we need only stop, use self-discipline, stand back, and upshift into gratitude. Gratitude for what we have, and what we may stand to gain from what's transpiring in our favor.

Nothing that happens can hurt us unless we allow it through our perceptions.

Nothing can stress us unless we agree to process it as stressful. Stressing can make us problematic. What if we process a "stressful" event as exciting, interesting, stimulating. Doesn't that change the dynamic? What if we simply refuse to acknowledge it's happening on a level that affects us in a significant way? What if we call it unimportant, irrelevant, undue, acknowledging its existence, but not taking it on as a cross to bear. How quickly this can shift energy from deleterious to benign. What would our response be now? Barely a blip on the screen, perhaps. We are no problem. We have no problem. Ergo, no problem exists.

Seeing the upside of all that occurs will undoubtedly change the nature of it. Learning how to cope will, too. We Change Wizards change the world for the better, we don't let the world change us for the worse. We make change within to make change without, maintaining our vision of who we are individually and as a global society.

We learn to be a solution, because in the process, we can change the world.

SPREAD PEACE EVERYWHERE YOU GO

Since viewing anything in a positive light not only changes the nature of what might otherwise bring harm to you, but changes your own nature too, ushering peace into the world is a matter of contemplation. Where there is peace, there is no separation. Where there is peace, there is justice, too. Where there is peace, there is understanding, calm, respect and dignity. We know like attracts like, and that works for us. Peace-lovers attract the atmosphere of peace, so peace is native to us. Lovers attract other loving spirits. Love itself makes all things right. Therefore, we are filled with love, and peace can rule unfettered.

On the other hand, if we go out in the day worked up about some perceived unfairness, this would attract much more to be angry about throughout the day. The next thing would be an argument, or waiting forever in the slowest line, missing the bus or elevator. Catching a spritz from an errant sprinkler. Getting a run in new pantyhose. Staining a tie or breaking a heel. Being pulled over by a cop. Other pissed off people cropping up. One warlike daymare to the next.

The vibration of peace solicits right people, places and opportunities to change yourself and change the world.

One human like Gandhi can stop a war. So, be at peace and pass it on.

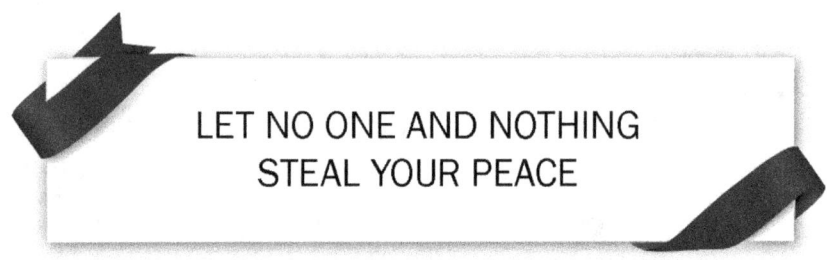

LET NO ONE AND NOTHING STEAL YOUR PEACE

Your peace of mind is your domain. Your every breath can breathe in peace. If others behave in a way that seems not to consider you, change the game. Go within your place of peace. Play by your rules. Be a person of peace. They may mow their lawn at 5:00 a.m., vacuum when you're on a deadline, race to you wanting to bicker and fight, or refuse to hear it's not the time to burden you with foolishness. You may not know why they're consumed by dilemmas, and though you are sensitive to them, you definitely are aware of what's important in your world, what's unimportant or trivial, and why interacting with conflict is unadvisable. Remain at peace.

You deserve peace. And to live in peace, you have to regulate the thoughts that enter into your consciousness and deal with them constructively. Tune out distractions, remove yourself, or find peace with the fact that your quiet repose is disturbed for a limited period, and will return as soon as you deal with the circumstance that's disturbing the peace. Whatever your choice, what cannot occur is any loss of peace of mind. Stay in your peaceful quietude.

Your peace of mind is a sacred thing. You must guard it with avid vigilance. To let anyone cause you to strike out in anger or compromise your inner stillness is to relinquish your freedom. You don't have to let that be. Nothing anyone does can cause your emotions to scatter, or lurch from up to down. You are the thinker of your thoughts, and your thoughts control your emotions. If you choose to think someone is trying to harm you if they're being thoughtless, you could get angry, sad, frustrated, hurt, or even blow your top. If you stop and think how everyone shares the same space—traffic, home or work—you realize they are just being themselves, which might fall short of enlightenment but certainly isn't a crime. Be calm. Be who you're meant to be. Respond to a challenge instead of react, and be a peacemaker where none exists.

The only one who can steal your peace from you, is you, so let things go. Be committed to keeping it Zen, and then, when static comes in on the airwaves from external sources, stay in place. Remain in the recesses of your mind, impervious to pain and strife. Go within if a force would threaten peace. Refuse to allow your serenity to be wrenched away by anything. Situations and circumstances don't control you. You control yourself. There is whatever is happening, and there's you in your resolve. You, in your tranquility. No one can take your harmonious cool away without your permission. Neither can they bestow the same. Only you can command your inner peace. So, soothe yourself and remain undisturbed through every condition and gust that blows, be it hot or freezing cold. Others will do, and be, what comes to them, and nature has its ways. But you, regardless of any of it, are centered in your evolved repose.

When you are unruffled no matter what comes, peace is your nature, your calling card, and the vibe you bring to a stressed-out world that can seem to be besieged. You are a place of peace, a dove amidst division, discord and the senseless animus that sometimes mars or destroys the unity of teams, communities, countries, faiths and organizations around the world, not to mention the nuclear family. Your peace is a source of agape love that radiates outward from within, permeating your environment and distributing peace to everyone. Let go of the petty, trivial, irksome energy drains that filter through. Let lower energies pass in peace. Allow them to be transmuted. Go within. Tap into unshakeable peace. Infectious peace will change the world.

THE MAGIC OF REBOOTING

Whatever your notion of success is, you might not notice what it costs as you go about pursuing it. If you're in it to win it or please someone, or you're acting the way you think you should, or worse yet, acting out of fear, you might be living out others' dreams, such as your parents might have dreamed or planned for themselves in their younger years.

Everyone does what they feel is right. Most people just do what they think will work. We go with the judgment we have at a given time, and learn from experience. We know what we know when we know it, and the more we learn, the better we do. Everyone's trying to do their best. Of course, there are those that are unconcerned about how their actions impact others, those who find joy, for some reason, out of causing chaos, hurting feelings, and fomenting needless drama. Those are few and far between. At least, that is my hope. It is my estimation, too, that as we strive to do our best, it depends on who we are at a given stage of development. Our personal development is dynamic, and varies from person to person depending on how we evolve.

Everyone can change the world, and anyone can change things for the better in some form or fashion. We all have that capacity. We only need to have the will, a plan, determination to, and the positive thoughts, words, deeds and interactions that can make change for the better rather than the worse. Knowing our strengths and weaknesses, what we bring to the table, what we want, and how we think the world should be, we set goals for what we do, how and when we like to do it, and we strive to act on these. But we may or may not remain cognizant of who we are as we race toward goals, how the ensuing process morphs us, or what the pursuit of the goal is currently doing to our lives. This can forestall our happiness.

We want to be happy, healthy, free, but some of us tether our happiness to circumstances, situations, people who tend to come and go, and other shifting factors. Happiness is a state of mind. Happiness is a choice we make. We can sometimes have goals or priorities that undermine our happiness, so when we set goals, we need to be mindful of what they entail, the tasks they involve, how they impact how we live our lives, with whom, and what we might encounter.

What do I really want in life? That's a question you need to continually ask, because your wants and needs do change, and you don't want to come up empty. As you set a goal, commit to it, and work for it with all your might, you could be determining years to come—work hours and other activities, the people populating them, and places you might find yourself—not completely realizing that that's what you're doing at the time. You might not always get it right. You could wind up in Is-That-All-There-Is Land, disliking your job, your friends, your mate, yourself and everything else. If you do, though, you don't have to stay that way. Instead, you can think and reboot. Restart. Just like a computer. You have that power. It's your life. You can always turn your life around, and head in another direction.

It is critical that you take time to reboot, restart, refresh, and renew yourself. You can power down at any time, unplug when you need to, and start again. Resist plowing ahead to go nowhere or running on automatic. Avoid thinking what you've chosen is the only thing that you can choose, that it's written in stone on a Flintstone's tablet, and you can't get out of it. How can you change the entire world if you can't even change your own. The answer is, you can, and will—so know if you happen to need to.

Since change is the only thing that doesn't, you always have a way to change. You might not see the how or what, but you can get a second chance. You're never stuck. You're never trapped. You're never in a dungeon. To change, you have to look for ways. You have to go on believing in changing yourself and changing the world. You have to end-run fears and doubts, and focus on possibilities. You have to stop clinging to what is familiar, plunge into uncharted waters, and perhaps go swimming in the dark.

You might have to leave some people behind, leave places and find new ones. You may have to take some risks. No, scratch that, you *will* have to take some risks. Big risks bring big rewards. You may have to drop your entire way of thinking, and come out of self—or rather, delve deeper into self instead of sacrificing for persons and principles that no longer serve you.

When you reboot, you can look around and see where you belong. You might not belong where you are anymore. Where you are may not even exist anymore outside your imagination.

You might have been living on automatic, not realizing your world has changed and now you have to change as well. But you are meant to reinvent.

Rebooting gives you a fresh, new start. Change your mind, and you change your reality. The latitude of your attitude can change your positioning in a wink. Your thoughts are becoming things right now. You become who you think you are at the moment you think it. You created the person you presently are, and you can recreate yourself according to your specs. Reinvent. Go within, and see who's there, and learn who's waiting to come out—a being that's even more beautiful, thoughtful, kind, creative, brave and true—who wants to show up in the world as you. Reboot. Download a new operating system. Update apps and get bug fixes. You can start again.

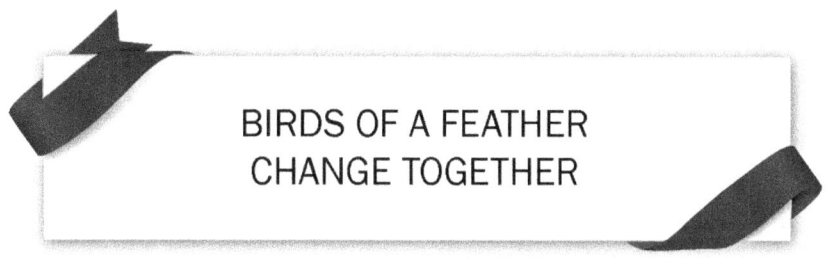

BIRDS OF A FEATHER CHANGE TOGETHER

You have a team, a core group and supporters, but are you cool with Number One? You have to be self-sustaining. Self-reliance is important to your well-being and mental health. It is also a shield against loneliness. When you love your own company, solitude works. You know that whoever comes and goes, your relationships to yourself and your Higher Power are intact. You want to feel at peace alone. Many find that difficult. Estimates state that a third of people are lonely. That's a lot. Plus, one in five Americans experience chronic loneliness. That is, loneliness that's not temporary. This occurs for several reasons. The quality, not quantity, of relationships is one. Another is the loss of someone close. Another is missing someone to chat with, hang with, or do nothing with. Loneliness is complex.

If you feel alone, you don't have to feel lonely. You are connected to everything, and everything is connected to you. This isn't mumbo-jumbo. Since you are made of the very same substance as the planets, sun and stars, you are constructed from stardust that erupted in the Big Bang, when the universe exploded from a tiny singularity into the world as we know it now. You are a star child, just like the Earth and everything that inhabits it. Your makeup connects you to all that exists as closely as your DNA connects you to your family.

Plus, you have your spiritual connection to all things within the one consciousness, the Universal Mind. You are never alone. You are integral. You are always loved and supported.

This is why you can feel compassion for people you do not know, and never will. They are your brothers and sisters, experiencing earthly life as you are. They feel the same emotions. They have similar hopes and dreams. Like you, they are spirits manifested into flesh and bone. You are connected to ancestors also, and to all who have traversed this life and now exist in the firmament. You're connected to every creature, thing and being, and they are connected to you.

Loneliness is merely a tale we tell ourselves repeatedly in the absence of inner peace. It's a scary story we make up to cloister ourselves in troubled times. In the story, we're the victim. In this guise, we feel sorry for ourselves when we don't draw comfort from gratitude for all we are and have. But if we're not careful, the story seems real, and the sad, lonely tale we tell ourselves can become a constant companion. It can paint everything sad and blue, keep us from reaching out to others by stealing our trust. Loneliness is a sneaky thing. It's a crummy excuse to not care or help, and to cherish isolation. It can make us selfish, too, because it can feel more real than love, which is present and available to give and receive abundantly.

To feel lonely is to misuse our imagination to sense we exist in a void or vacuum. That's a cruel mirage. We live in a world of eternal light, an intertwined community. To feel lonely, we disassociate and refuse to participate. This is counterproductive not only to how we relate to other people, but to the healthful progress of our lives and advancement to our higher selves. Loneliness is just a lie, for we are not alone. We are all part of humanity, of all creatures, of the One Love. We need only look around at the human and animal personalities, flowers, trees, plants, seas and sky, and all that's alive in the universe, to understand we're part of something grander than ourselves. Something to which we're responsible, and to which we are inextricably linked. We are more similar than we are different, and we are meant to evolve together.

Aloneness is not loneliness. It is an incubation period. It is a time to become more yourself. Use your alone time to meditate, think deeply, educate yourself, pray, and listen to the silence. Use it to commune with nature and swim in your reservoir of peace. There is infinite love for you everywhere. It's meant to help you change and grow. Ask for it. Believe it's there. Be grateful it is in endless supply, and you will, even in solitude, exchange pure love abundantly.

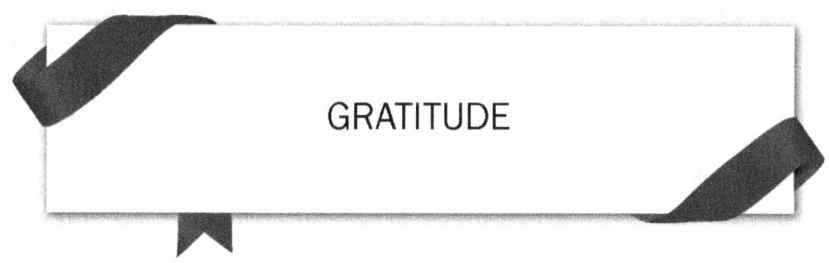

GRATITUDE

Gratitude is an elixir. It can change more than metal into gold. It can change wishes into phenomena, shape the nebulous, lift the downtrodden, and make speculations tangible.

Gratefulness for what you have will magically summon more of it. Thankfulness invites multitudes of other gifts you can be grateful for. Gratitude conjures up good in your life, as it raises your vibration to the high level on which happiness, health, creativity and abundance flourish. The realm in which synchronicity and miracles of all kinds vibrate. In short, where you want to hang out. Miracles happen where energies collide and find their ideal match. Pollyanna and Gloomy Gus don't roll on the same wavelength. There's no energy match. They don't oscillate in sync. Energy aspires to the highest level it can reach. That's where gratitude lives.

We know we are forms of energy, and all matter is pure energy. Matter is composed of atoms. Atoms are made of a certain number of protons, neutrons and electrons particular to the chemical element in which they exist. The center of an atom—its nucleus—is composed of protons and neutrons. Electrons orbit this nucleus in energy levels that range on a scale that we measure from low to high. An atom of gold, for instance, contains six powerful levels of energy. The oxygen we breathe has two, and sodium—a component of salt—has three. Amazing, isn't it? Think of the identities of the energy possibilities. The above are only three of the one hundred eighteen chemical elements in the Periodic Table. All of their energies whirl around in search of the perfect energy match. We humans have much more sophisticated energies, and we control them. In addition to our physical bodies, which, though they look solid, are energies, we have thought and emotion energies vibrating on various levels. These, too, seek and draw their match.

Fear has low energy. Faith has high, as do love and creativity. That's why fear and faith cannot exist simultaneously in the intricacies of your ever-evolving consciousness. They cannot contemporaneously cohabitate in your psyche. You have to choose one or the other, and when you choose, corresponding energies will be drawn to you as experiences. You can either have faith that all is well, or fear that it is not. It's your choice. Whichever you think and believe will pop up in your life. Love will not draw indifference, but rather high level energies such as joy.

It is easy to understand, then, why if you choose to feel absence or shortage of something rather than hope and gratitude, and you act as if from deficit, loss or imagined insufficiency, you can't attract abundance. Abundance vibrates on the level of gratitude. They have matching energies. Thus, if you're grounded in gratitude at the center of your emotional life, thinking thoughts of what you're thankful for, you magnetize energies that will invoke more changes for the better. When you are grateful, you actively ask for more miracles with your vibration.

Positive auras, by their existence, positively change the world.

Think about it. If you were the universe, wouldn't you hand out goodies to those who were already happy with what they were and what they had at hand? Wouldn't you help those who helped themselves, and had their hearts set on a better world and a better life for all? That would only make good sense. You'd want, as all we mortals do, to sow your seeds in fertile soil, to make sure your energies and resources got built upon rather than laid to waste.

Gratitude creates.

Gratitude equals plentitude. It doesn't exist in fits and starts. It's like happiness. It's an identity. It's part of who you are. It's part of who you're meant to be and what you're meant to do. It isn't about being thankful for this or that gift or condition—a new job, car, house, mate, gadget, toy or whatever strikes your fancy. Having your gratitude hinge on something you feel you may want or need is not a genuine spirit of thankfulness, it's a tit for tat reaction to random, desirable stimuli. Gratitude is not seasonal. It is a state of being in the world that acknowledges and affirms the ultimate goodness of life itself. It generates not from exterior sources that wax and wane, but from within. Gratitude begets itself, and draws more to be grateful for.

Individually and collectively, our gratitude is assembling our tomorrow. As surely as atoms circle a nucleus, gratitude changes our world for the better. No matter how things may appear, there is always more to be grateful for than not. Change your outlook from lack to abundance, selfishness to generosity, and acquisition to contentment. In order to bring about change, you must focus on blessings rather than disadvantage, disapproval, blight, ill will, criticism or complaint. Unconditional gratitude transforms. Be grateful, and see what unfolds. Switch focus from that which you don't have to all you do have, and you are the soul of change.

GIVE TO LIVE AND LIVE TO GIVE

When we hear the name Scrooge, it's a bummer, right? But Santa Clause, he's the man. That's a guy you want to see. So, which are you? The reindeer guy with the jam-packed sleigh, or Grinch the green-eyed monster? There's a pretty easy way to tell. Do faces light up when you approach? Or do people clam up and run away? I'll venture to hazard a guess that the response you elicit from others is in direct proportion to how your presence makes them *feel*. Does that ring a bell or strike a chord? People love you because of who you are, what you do, and what you give to them because it is your nature. That can be support or money, laughter, pain, respect or slight. Generosity, like gratitude, makes us a lightning rod for positive people, places and things. When we give, we circulate giving, and that energy returns to us. We're positioned to receive.

Many believe the act of giving depletes their resources and lessens them, but we know the opposite is true. When we commit to giving as an aspect of our Meant-To-Do, the universe sees us giving and responds by providing more to give. More love. More happiness. More ideas. More wisdom and insights to pass along. More money to give, donate and loan. More material goods to use and share. More ways in which to serve. The aim of giving is not to receive. Receiving is a by-product. Giving is its own reward. This is why it feels so good to give.

Giving makes more of who we are, because it stretches us outside our needs and wants into the greater good. It makes our lives expansive. When someone has needs we can fulfill, giving is the natural order.

Generosity sustains our culture. Systems cannot survive without any energy circulation. Lacking replenishment, systems fail. Your body needs food. Your car needs gas. Governments run on taxes. Other than the universe itself, nothing can give perpetually without some measure of receiving. When you give, you circulate energy as it's meant to be circulated. All the energy in the universe is moving all the time. We all need to give and receive to keep moving forward.

Your generosity is helping the ecosystem run.

The law of conservation of mass says energy can neither be created nor destroyed. It can only be transformed. Therefore, you can never sustain a loss. What may appear to be gone from you exists in another form. For every erg of energy given, recycling naturally takes place. A new thing is created. Knowing this, you can give as a way of life. The better world you hope for is dependent on your giving. That world is here and now, but you may have to sacrifice to see it.

Trust in the generosity of the universe, and rely on it. Be willing to give and be sustained. A paradigm shift toward your higher nature as giver comes quite easily when you're confident in the belief that all your needs are always met. Knowing this, you can give without fear of loss. You can be generous willingly—without resentment, reservation, revulsion or reluctance.

You organically elevate when you give to live and live to give.

NO RESISTANCE + NO JUDGMENT = NO PAIN

Resistance. What's the point of it? I mean, think of the things you've resisted. Think of the things you are resisting now. Does resisting anything ever really get you anywhere? Doesn't being *for* the thing you want have tons more power than resisting what you don't want? Why, sure it does. When you go after what you want rather than being resistant to its opposite, you have a goal. You're on a crusade. You can make a change. So, why take the time to resist at all? Resisting is a negative. It's using your thoughts, words, deeds and creative energy to fight something defined by someone or something else. It's a negative, not an affirmative position. It's a defense, not an offense. It's a counter-punch. It's pushing against a force that might not survive but for your resistance.

Half of what we resist is stuff that hasn't even happened yet, and might not ever happen, except for the energy we afford it through resistance. What's the point in that? It doesn't make any sense at all to empower what we oppose. We might do better, before we resist any concept, person, place or thing, to consider why we're resisting it, and what our resistance is liable to net, what it will get us and what it will not. Will resistance make a difference or result in significant change? Consider how resistance makes us feel, which isn't very good.

What we resist most of all is change, and change is the only thing that doesn't. Change, I mean. Change doesn't change. Except to become some other form of change, which, in itself, is change. We are not going to unchange change by simply resisting the concept of it.

Change is occurring consistently. What in the world would the world be like if we had resisted every change that's happened up till now? This book wouldn't be an eBook or an audiobook, for one thing, that's for sure. Neither format would exist. If we resist every change that comes at us, we'll never be productive. If we were only half as persistent as change we resist from day to day, we could accomplish anything. We can, but accomplishment is change. Change is going to happen, face it. Change is a constant we can't change. Change is relentless. Change endures. Change changes. We can't alter change.

We can change the quality of a change, but can't change, change itself. Change is changing all the time—itself, and us, and everything. Change is completely self-altering. It rolls on like a snowball down a hill, creating bigger changes. Trying to stop change will just put you through changes. Choosing to go up against change is like two million rounds in the ring with Muhammad Ali. You're gonna get beat real bad. It's like running into a raging fire, my friend. You will get burned. So, c'mon, let's team up with change. Let's court that sucker, call it forth. Let's change the linen in the guest room for it, make it a cake, and call it our bestie, forgive, forget, and un-resist. Let's make change our BFF.

And speaking of BFF's, change isn't the only thing we resist. We resist people for all kinds of reasons. Maybe because we're convinced we're unappealing or unacceptable, that others won't like us the way we are when they really get to know us. Who knows what the world might think of us. Like the wizard in *The Wizard of Oz*, we might rather no one paid attention to the man behind the curtain. Or perhaps we feel we might get hurt if we let anybody come into our inner sanctum, into our heart and mind, and try to take up residence. Or maybe one someone will harm us in ways we're afraid we won't survive. And what will we do if that happens, huh?

We might resist if we feel we're too busy working hard and chasing dreams, or trying to survive. Or maybe it's that we'll need to reinvent ourselves if we open up. We might feel we're not good enough to negotiate change successfully. We may feel undeserving, put-upon, or have trust issues. Trauma lingering since our childhood could cause some intransigence. Or what if a change is burdensome in a way we don't expect. These beliefs become self-fulfilling prophecies if we let them.

Our resistance doesn't change others, though our presence with them might. Resistance might well change us, though. Resistance, by definition, is opposition, hostility, combat and antagonism. That's not us. We're into peace and harmony. Resistance can only pull us apart as a people, make us smaller, slow our evolution, shrink us. Resistance only prolongs the magnificent process of becoming "us". The us we're meant to be—the thriving, thrilling tribe of man.

Most of the people and things we resist, we resist because we judge them. In our minds, we label them as bad, or at least, as bad for us. Many of these judgments, we make with minimum information, compassion, proper perspective, insight or understanding—without so much as a test drive first. We make up our minds with a blindfold on, oblivious to the up and downside of the thing or person we prejudge. This is not prudent. Neither is it fair or just.

Pre-judgment is another word for prejudice. Everyone knows that word. All of us know how it warps our world. And not in a good way, that's for sure. It starts with, you're African American. I don't like you. You can't rent this place. Or you're Jewish, I can't trust you. You women are the weaker sex, and I don't hire weaklings, toots. You're Muslim, you must blow stuff up. You're rural, you must be a hick. From the City, you're a slickster. You're fat, you're a glutton. Old, that's useless. Short, and I don't like short dudes. Mexican, you're an illegal, right? Asians make me nervous. You're bald. A bald guy robbed my house. You're beautiful, you're dumb. And children should be seen, not heard. Prejudice is a dirty deal.

Resistance plus judgment equals pain.

Judgments don't just hurt the judged, they harm the mind that judges.

We aren't meant to judge ourselves, far less to pass judgment on other folks. We need to lighten up. Without judgment, we can be ourselves. Without judgment, we can free ourselves. We can look at the world with open eyes, and respect the people in it. We aren't perfect. No one is. So, let go of resistance to things resistance won't and cannot ever change.

We can't change what we can't change, but we can change what we can. What we can change is our state of mind as we encounter changes. We can flow with changes cropping up. We can't see around corners, but what we can do is trust that the universe evolves in perfect order when we let it, and that when changes occur, they're meant to be and work for us.

Each change brings a solution and a better way to be.

Every change can bring enlightenment to a spirit open to being enlightened.

No resistance. No judgment. No more pain. Just moving in the flow of life, and letting others be themselves. Allowing good to happen. Because good is always going to happen when we're determined to *be* the good. We are a terrific *us*. Each of us is a fantastic person when we give ourselves a chance, when we avoid resisting change that makes us more of who we are. Everyone's special and one-of-a-kind, and each of us holds a precious gift, but when we resist connecting with other people, we withhold our gift. If we resist new people in our lives, or the folks who are already there, we sell ourselves and others short. We change the whole world by subtracting us from the sum of its equation.

If we resist experiences, people, places, situations, moving our location and the like, we resist new ways of being that can change our lives and change the world. If we resist a new job, we resist new skills, success, abundance and the happiness that these can bring.

No resistance. No judgment. No more pain.

When we're pain-free, we don't cause pain.

We're examples of happy transformation. This is how we change the world.

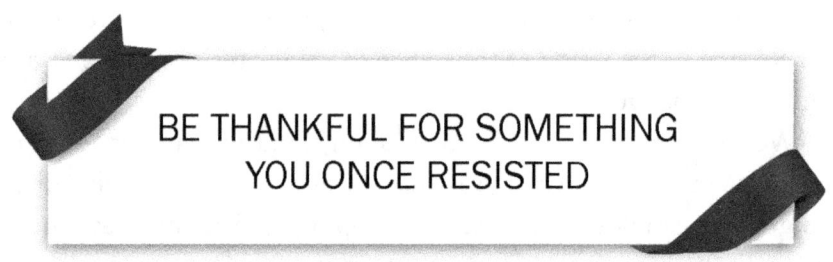

BE THANKFUL FOR SOMETHING YOU ONCE RESISTED

Sometimes, we choose to resist a condition, and because we resist, we draw more of it. We suffer the very consequence we originally wished to avoid. As resistance is negative energy that draws its energy match, when we place our attention on issues rather than what we hope will happen, we are strengthening adverse energies, lending more power to them than our goal. As energy flows where attention goes, irrespective of its negative or positive polarity, when we shift focus, our energy shifts. That's why we say we're "paying attention" when we're investing our energy into a thing, for better or worse. What we pay attention to is costing us or paying off. What we want is to pay attention to the positive, and only that, for this creates positive change in us and changes in our world.

When we resist or fail to embrace, accept, or incorporate a condition, we can make it worse. Anger and other emotions that aren't upbeat can start creeping in, because if we felt good about the condition, we wouldn't resist it. We only resist what we don't feel good about, or fear we won't feel good. The emotions attached to not feeling good are low energy vibes, so they match the bad vibes we anticipate coming our way. When we don't feel good, we attract much more to not feel good about. So, now we've not only resisted, we have souped up the unwanted thing with funky emotions like being pissed off. Stop. Wait. Hold on. Back up. Turn.

The good news is, we have a choice. We can change any prior choice by consciously making a better one. All we think, we think by choice. All we do, we do by choice. No matter what happens, we can respond in a myriad of ways. The best response is foregoing resistance in favor of being proactive.

When something painful hits us, like a heartbreak, we can choose to process heartbreak or relief that we've been rescued from a mate who wasn't right for us. We can choose to move on without giving our errant ex another thought, or we can resist getting dumped altogether and beg our ex to take us back. We can try to determine what went wrong, so our next relationship works out, or turn to drugs and alcohol. We can choose to immerse ourselves in work, or tears, regrets and recriminations. We can become a fixture at the gym, or let ourselves go. We can take up a new hobby or plot revenge, lose hope or Internet date. We can tell ourselves we have no choices, even though we know we do. We just need to make more good ones.

Which is why I now introduce to you, *tada!* The joy of re-choosing.

Even if you made a poor choice before, when you realize it, reverse your course, veer right, turn left, go under or over, freeze in place, or abandon your position. It's your freedom of choice to re-choose or un-choose anything you've chosen. Nobody can prove it's not. The beauty of it is, it works for thoughts, words, actions, anything. So, rather than placing responsibility for choices that are rightfully yours on the shoulders of any other party—which can lead to blame or shame, ill will and, let's say, a rocky road—accept responsibility and, wait for it . . . re-choose.

What is the best re-choice, you ask. Well, here's my personal favorite. It's a beauty. It rids you of negatives and gets you where you want to go. Ready? Here it is.

Be grateful for something you previously resisted. Works like a charm. When gratitude replaces resistance, gratitude becomes your springboard out of the angst of resisting, and before you know it, all of the pain of resisting is gone. And believe me, that's a relief. It might seem resisting was helping you out of a bad situation, but oh no. You have better alternatives than resisting what you want to change than stubbornly opposing what exists as your reality.

Mother Teresa, The Saint of Calcutta, is quoted as saying, "I will never attend an anti-war rally; if you have a peace rally, invite me." It's a great point. Be for, not against. She championed the poor.

Opposing is negative energy. Gratitude moves at a higher vibration, supplying more to be grateful for. Resistance yields to gratitude, which presents more options.

Gratitude and resistance, like fear and faith, can't occupy the same space simultaneously. Resistance condemns. Gratitude upholds. They are polar opposites. This is why you cannot at the same time both be grateful and ungrateful to the point of opposition.

Here are your choices in the nutshell. *The Oxford Dictionary* defines gratitude as "The quality of being thankful; readiness to show appreciation for and to return kindness". Well, that's certainly clear enough. Thankfulness and kindness are very positive states of being, likely to lead to positive outcomes. Resistance, on the contrary, defined by *The Merriam-Webster Dictionary* is the "refusal to accept something new or different; effort to stop or fight against someone or something; the ability to prevent something from having an effect". Refusing, preventing and fighting are negative stances rooted in strife, and worse, they can spawn incoming resistance to your own plans, goals and endeavors. Hmm . . . which seems like the better choice?

Even if you have to protest something due to its harmful or unjust nature, there is a positive position to advocate, one that is more likely to ultimately bring about change.

When we let gratitude help us let go of resistance to occurrences and conditions that pass through our lives, we open our arms to welcome change.

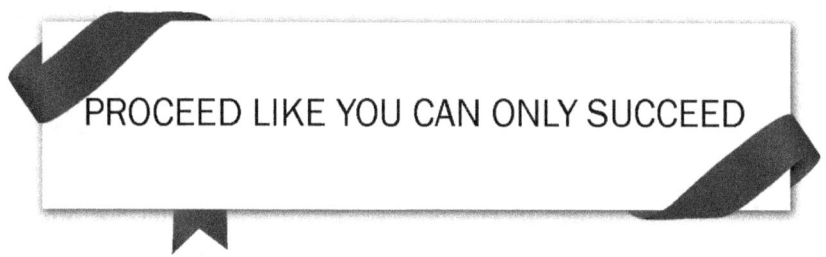

PROCEED LIKE YOU CAN ONLY SUCCEED

The universe wants you to succeed. This is truth. This is your reality. The universe has already created your Meant-To-Be and Meant-To-Do, and it's helping you bring them into the realm of materiality. The universe is on your side. There is no opposition. The universe is all, and it is good, and it is for you. The substance of it is love for you. The universe roots for every good thing to come about, persist, and grow. Everything is created to net the highest good it can. That includes you. Especially you. You operate and have your being in upward cosmic mobility. It is only for you to realize this, believe it, receive it, and let it be.

The only thing that can come between you and success is you. So go for it.

Get out of your way if you're standing in it. Success is in your hands.

There it is—the simple, cold, hard fact. Simple, because it is understandable. Cold, because there's no one else to blame for any mistakes, missteps or misunderstandings that might have previously kept you from success. And hard, because there might be mistakes still causing consequences you may need to rectify with answers you may not yet have. But hold on, shoppers. Wait, there's more. If you order right now, we'll include this truth:

The key to your success is love.

Love comes with a lifetime guarantee. You have all the love there is. Not an allotment, infinite love. You can give love anytime you want, as much as you want, forever. And when you proceed with love as your mandate, one way or another, you succeed. You can also receive all the love in the world. Without an extended warrantee. You don't need a credit card, and you won't even get a monthly bill. Love never runs out. It's always there. And with love in your pocket, you succeed.

Now, you may need to tweak your definition of success. Success means different things to different people. What's your concept? Of course, it's entirely possible you've never had one. That's okay. Many of us have a vague idea that needs to be fleshed out.

Success for some may be oo-goo-gobs of cash, a luxury car, the house with a white picket fence, an impressive job. This is materialistic success, and it could be what you're after. It could be what you already have, so you already feel successful. Others may determine success to be anything north of happiness and health, a red-hot date or mate, or kids that are well brought up. Others, like moi, hope to change the world for the better. We feel this is our Meant-To-Be. But even this outsized definition of success can be interpreted in many ways.

A little league team of happy kids certainly changes the world for the better, and this is what some of us see as success. Others want to play in the major leagues ourselves, and success is shaped like that. Others want to be a world leader, a religious leader or business guru. Others want to invent the next tech breakthrough that changes the way we achieve objectives. Others construe success as curing cancer, diabetes or heart disease. Others can change the world with a speech, a design, a film, a joke, the right word at the right time or a cookie.

Whatever your definition of success is, learn it, seek it, study it, write it down, take it into the core of your being, and above all, know that success is already yours. You just have to claim it. This is your truth. The vision you see was put in your head to come true, be realized, manifest, and change the world for the better—through you.

When one tiny thing in one corner of the world makes a change, the whole universe shifts with it. Every shift is born from a ripple that drips from one cloud to the oceans, seas and rivers, and flows out into the cosmos.

Your every thought, word and deed is already changing the world. Remember that. So, take responsibility for this now. Right now. This moment. Whoever you are, whatever you do, you are changing the world every time you have a single thought. That thought is traveling around the world, and being relayed through the cosmos. It exists in the Universal Mind, way beyond the sphere of influence you perceive as your domain.

That little league team of happy kids will eventually cause exponential changes in the way the world evolves. What you do will have an effect on them. What they do will have an effect on others. What those others do will have effects that will grow increasingly numerous. Those numbers will rise and expand. One needn't be president of a world power in order to bring significant change on a level that touches everyone. Some bring change by delivering mail.

Know your definition of success, and live your life accordingly.

You can succeed by believing you can, and accepting nothing less than what you see in your dreams and know in your heart is how you're meant to change the world.

YE SHALL OVERCOME

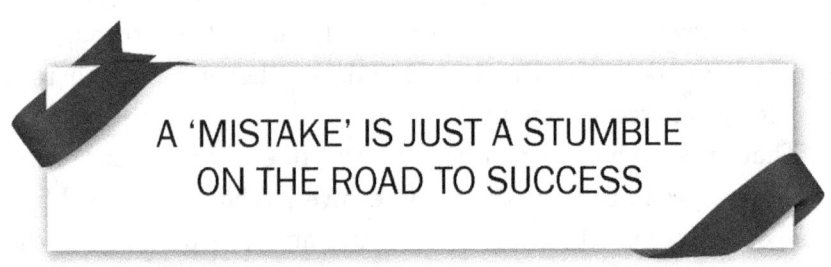

A 'MISTAKE' IS JUST A STUMBLE ON THE ROAD TO SUCCESS

One reason why living in the past doesn't work—aside from the fact that we only have now—is that, when we distract ourselves with the preoccupation of looking back at what was instead of enjoying what's happening now, we tend to focus on what we call 'mistakes' or 'failures' in the past, rather than successes. Even when we learn from our mistakes, we can sometimes dwell on them, dooming ourselves to repeat them in a cycle we can't seem to break. This can slow our progress.

When we decide to live in the now, we are more apt to take things in stride, because the next now comes along quite quickly, highlighting possibilities and renewing our sense of direction. We can move on with hope and speed.

Living in the past is like driving a car with your eyes on the rear view mirror. You're bound to have an accident. Perhaps repeated accidents, making the same mistakes again. It's better to look through the windshield at where you're going. That's all you can change. In life, there are no accidents. Everything happens for a reason. That reason is your best good.

There is a gate to your future in every wall that springs up in front of you. Just as pain serves to warn you of physical issues, mistakes can signal something in your behavior that's amiss. A mistake is a teaching moment, and each lesson is a gift to you. You are meant to learn at the point of discovering mistakes, not relive them for eons to come. If you learn lessons when they're taught, you don't punish yourself unduly, and you don't repeat mistakes. Your learning curve improves in direct proportion to your willingness to learn, and to forgive yourself. A mistake doesn't happen as an excuse to belabor a point, self-ridicule, or turn back the timeline on your goals. And it certainly doesn't occur to derail you or give you an excuse to quit. A mistake is a chance to course correct. Besides, there are no real mistakes. There is only what happens, what you learn, and what you do about it. Consider that what you've perceived as an error is just one more step on the road to success.

Keep going. No matter how costly the detour, its price will be kept to a minimum if you act to cut your losses. If you let any dark clouds pass you by without raining on your parade. A river doesn't suddenly stop when it reaches the edge of a cliff. It flows, and turns into a waterfall, picking up speed and power. The river doesn't look back at the cliff, wishing it could turn back time and never encounter the cliff at all. Nor does it refuse to bend with the winding landscape at its banks. It keeps bubbling and gurgling over rocks, swelling with each passing storm, and refreshing us with water. It freezes when the world goes cold, and turns to a gas when the heat is on. It transforms itself with the terrain. It does what it must, and in doing so, it changes itself and its environs. So should we, by being present, accept responsibility, look closely at the path ahead, use our instincts to avoid obstacles, seize new possibilities, and learn to make better choices.

Any obstacles, such as perceived mistakes, exist outside your attention and emotions. Don't incorporate them, other than absorbing the lessons they teach. Avoid condemning them, letting them define you, or denying they happened in your life. Bless them. Let them go in peace.

Anyone can make mistakes. Not everyone recovers well. We can't let any slip-up shift our focus, undermine our confidence, subvert our intentions, play havoc with our feelings, or act to waylay our next steps. No random occurrence, person, place or thing is allowed to buffet us about or thwart our accomplishments. A mistake is not a failure, it is only proof we tried.

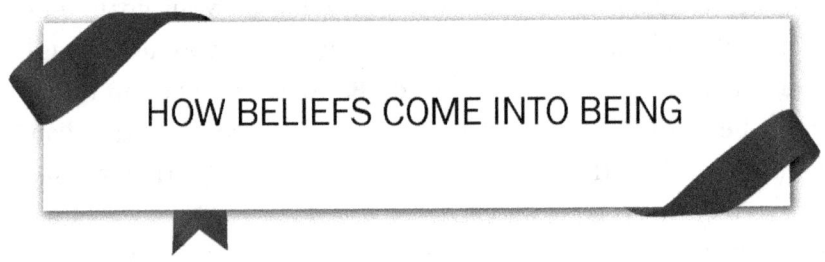

HOW BELIEFS COME INTO BEING

Empower yourself with the firm belief that anything and everything is within your reach and can be done. You are created with all of the characteristics, tools and abilities to accomplish anything you dream, for your dream was given to you to do.

You don't have to know every means to the end. You just have to know what the end looks like, and start with good intent. You need not see all that comes between where you are and where you want to go. That's set to unfurl itself in time. You need only believe that it exists, and see it in your mind. Your thoughts affirm your beliefs to yourself, and to your Higher Power. Speak your beliefs into your ears and into the minds of others. Your words convey your mission, so develop a voice that effectively communicates your beliefs.

When I told myself I could write this book and give it as a gift to you, nothing but time and space could come between the first word and the words "The End". That's what I believed, and believe more now. And obviously, I completed this book. I intend to write several others. I cannot know who will read this book, yet I'm speaking to you on the words of this page, and you're hopefully being inspired to change the world for the better by what I say.

I know you're out there reading as sure as I know you're in my heart. I believe I can, and am, and will complete my mission, see my vision and live my dreams come true. Believe I can, or believe I can't. Either way, I'm write . . . uh, right. I'm writing now what you'll read later.

I believed, and now you're reading. As you read, you will know that I believed. This will hopefully increase your belief that you can do your Meant-To-Do. Keep moving. It will happen.

I might have had moments of quiet exhaustion, but I didn't have moments of doubt. This was harder than I thought it'd be, but I always knew I'd get it done. I had something I needed to share with you. I may have chosen to walk at the beach, or cook, or tweet, or create pretty things, binge-watch a trending TV show, chat up a sick friend, shop online, dance to my favorite jam in my jammies, or cut my Mom's hair when I could have been writing at times, but I got this gift to you. I might not have had the best desk to write at, or my dream computer. But, guess what? I do have them now. I got them the week I finished this book. Because I believed and kept believing, they came to me out of the blue. I might have busted my ankle, too, and been grieving my former spouse as well, and still hearing from him from heaven. I might have been seriously overworked, but that's another story. What matters is that you're reading this, that I got these truths to you because I believed it was what I was meant to do, and that I'd become more of who I'm meant to be in the course of recording these thoughts about making change and being changed.

Even cooler than that is that now you know my belief was so strong, it encouraged you to believe in this book and pick it up. Of course, you only know that now—which for me, as I am penning this, is a *then* that's in my future. See what I mean? Thoughts and words create. Beliefs come into being.

Believe in yourself. Believe in your life. Believe in who you're meant to be, and what you're meant to do. Tell yourself that you believe, and how much you believe. Keep believing more and more. Believe in the power of your dreams, and that now is the time they are meant to come true. Now is the time, where you are is the place, your dream is the thing, and you are the person. It may take some doing, as you'll find out, but it's already getting done.

Take time to remember viscerally all the instances when you believed, and because you believed, you accomplished things. Be fortified by these memories—and importantly, by the great feelings they invoke whenever you think of them. Wrap up in them as you would a warm coat. Repeatedly do this throughout the day. Concentrate, and focus. This will fuel your belief in the possibility, probability and absolute fact that achieving your goals is inevitable. Visualize your dream in detail, and be clear that it's a reality in advance of manifestation.

Meditate on an idyllic world, and avoid becoming distracted. Let go of people, places or things inconsistent with your vision. Believe, and stick to your principals, your faith in yourself and your Higher Power, and all you're meant to be and do. Be, as Mahatma Gandhi, the peace-loving Indian leader urged you to be, "the change that you wish to see in the world".

Your life is not something that's happening to you. It is a living, breathing entity no less than your physical body. You are the one who can dedicate and consecrate it for the good. Take command and exert control. Only you can surrender it into the care and will of the universal force, and thence direct your energies into action for the greater good. This is not to be entered into lightly. It is a task for daily living. It'll result in self-actualization, fulfillment and optimum health. It is not just an option. It is *the* option—to take responsibility for the meaning of your life.

Every life matters. For better or worse, everyone will change the world. The question is how, to what extent, and for the negative or positive.

You're a world-changer. You changed it today. You smiled or frowned, you gave or took. You bummed people out or exalted them. There's no getting around your profound effect, so do what you're doing consciously, deliberately, and benevolently. You are leaving footprints.

There may be some needles you can't move right now, but there are plenty that you can, so concentrate on those. There's no time like the present to do what you have in mind. Get going now. Waiting for somebody else to do it doesn't cut the mustard. Nor does feeling powerless affect the things that need to change or the lives of the people craving change.

Move forward on your project now. Prioritize your goals. Be disciplined and motivated to go beyond the workplace, family fun or obligations, chatting up clients, hanging with friends, texting your acquaintances, barbecuing with neighbors, attending events, commiserating with co-workers, social networking, hobbies, concerts, sports, vacationing and all the stuff that crowds your days as time flies by. Dive into that commitment that's been tugging at your heartstrings.

It may require later nights or earlier mornings than you're accustomed to. You might have to work bone tired, or have to push past some constraints, but your mission will fill you with light and love, and, once begun, compel you. And like the smiles of those you love, it will make you jump up in the morning looking forward to the day ahead. It will drive you past fatigue, doubt, worry, fear and bouts of uncertainty, and, before long, take on a life of its own. It will draw you and others into its spell, because it is bigger than any one person. You will realize all that went before prepared and pushed you to do it now, because you believe in a better world.

While pursuing your dream, you will need every lesson you learned from every mistake you made, every bit of your education. Avoid comparing your own progress to that of anybody else. Show respect for the dreams and goals of others, help all you can along the way, and deploy your work ethic to do what you must. Move to the beat of your inner drummer. Move at your own pace, keeping it quick. Your beliefs want to come into being.

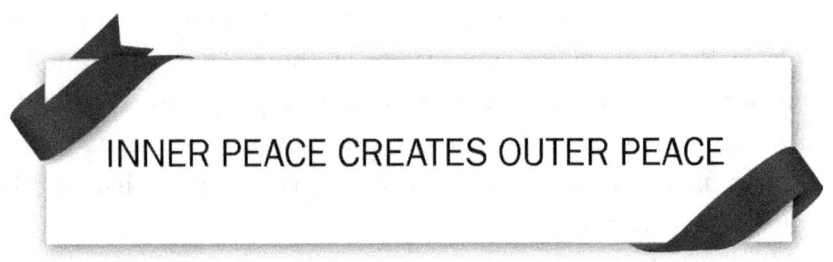

INNER PEACE CREATES OUTER PEACE

For most of us, peace may top the list of how we see a perfect world.

Peace may seem an amorphous concept. Some of us think of it purely as the absence of war, but it's more than that. Division, hatred, misunderstanding, tension, strife and anarchy so coarsely pollute our media and our collective consciousness, that we sometimes forget that peace is the natural order of things, yet it is.

Prophetic peace advocate, the Reverend Dr. Martin Luther King, Jr., defined peace as social responsibility, opining, "True peace is not merely the absence of tension: it is the presence of justice."

Without justice for all, there is no peace—neither for those who find justice denied, nor for those who so cruelly deny it. In the face of what is unjust for some, there can be no peace in the Zeitgeist. Injustice mirrors society. Society cannot harbor injustice and claim to be at peace.

Though peace encompasses justice, it supersedes it, as justice comes from man, and true peace derives from a higher source. Justice is only an outward reflection of presence or lack of inner peace in individuals. Peace is an inner resource we reflect in our thoughts, words, deeds and how we treat each other in society. Individual energies draw their match, and, as a result, we experience greater alienation or greater peace as a whole.

Peace within brings peace without. The moment each being finds and establishes peace within is the instant the world will be at peace. If all human beings achieved inner peace, world peace would break out and burgeon until the aura of peace was the substance of the universe, irremovable from any corner of the cosmos. There would be no place on the Earth or on any other star or planet where a fight could take place or injustice prevail. All nations would be one.

Since peace is the natural order of things, conflicts are unnatural. They destroy the threads of inner peace individuals may find for themselves, and tear at the fiber of international peace that fails to coalesce. This needn't be, and has to change. We all realize we have to do something about it, but as special interests come into play, and money and power undermine the process of achieving peace, the family of man is destabilized.

Nuclear families live with love as the basis of peace in relationships, but even they hold great divides. And when we examine workplaces, organizations, social networks and politics, lack of peace abounds. Neighborhoods and communities thrive when governance is equitable, but when inequality rears its ugly head as oppression, injustice, socio-economic imbalance and cruelty, broad microcosmic fissures in the realm of reality known as peace can cause tumultuous rending in the macro world. This can stunt our growth. Lack of peace can suppress creativity and generate other counterproductive outcomes we can do without.

Peace is not something that we, by nature, have to strive for in the world. Peace is instilled and ingrained in us. We are made to live in peace, and peace is made to live in us. The absence of peace is a mutation, like a virus in a sci-fi flick, or a nightmare or delirium mankind has yet to awaken from. We are created in peace, and meant to live in a peaceful reality, as one, for we are born in love. Ubiquitous love gives birth to peace. And yet somehow, we tend to find ourselves reaching outside ourselves to grope for peace—yearning for it, praying for it, begging for peace, and yet thinking, saying and doing things that undermine our search for it.

We are proponents of peace, and there is a simple solution in each of us to bring world peace about, to break down barriers to world peace that appear to exist, but really don't. World peace is a thoroughly doable aim, as it hinges on individual peace. We're each an ambassador for world peace as long as we declare we are. When we consciously nurture the peace within, and become so broad a channel for peace that we're its angelic conduit, worldwide peace will rule the day. Love and justice match the Earth's vibration, and they will take hold.

Imagine for a moment pure love breaking out all over. Wouldn't that be enchanting? Imagine the whole world loving you, and you loving everything in it. That's how it is now, if you see it that way. See your love as infectious, taking over the entire world. Claim and command your inner peace, and this is how the world will look if each of us does the same. No straining, struggling, or stressing out is necessary for the job. Just connect to the universal peace beyond yourself that works through you. Since peace within is peace without, be in your inner peace with such resolve that your personal peace is a lasting source of outer peace.

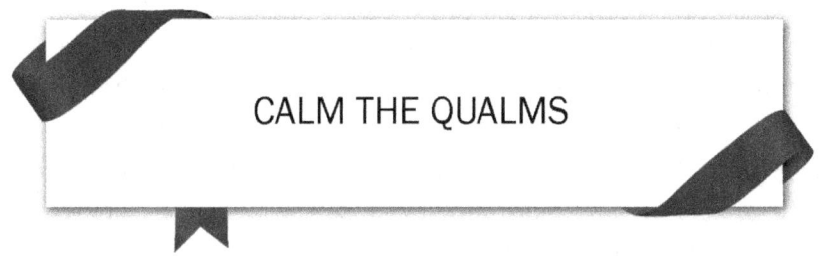

CALM THE QUALMS

When you go about your daily life with a portable place of inner peace, and you have a quiet center, your peace translates to others as a feeling of well-being. Whatever issues might arise are more likely to resolve themselves in the presence of accord. Accord results from inner calm informing communication. Calm can make you a soothing center others draw upon.

Think about your commute, for instance. Some drivers freak out at the first red light, and even a bit of roadside trash can make them go berserk. They may chase after the car ahead to avenge themselves for the merest slight, glare at the driver, speed up, brake, or holler a stream of invectives. They're sure other drivers are after them, that every commuter on the street has the make and model of their ride, their license plate number, itinerary, routes by which they come and go, and employ these to make them miserable. They're sure they won't find a parking spot, and that every wild animal in the woods looms in the dark on deserted byways, waiting to pounce out in their path. And they're right. They see their beliefs. Once they have that attitude, every poor driver on the road is drawn to their car to cut them off, rear-end them, tailgate, flip them a birdie, run a stop sign, fail to signal, stop short, honk a blaring horn, and do them and their car some damage. Lacking inner peace, they court outer chaos, danger and calamity.

Other drivers, on the other hand, are calm enough to share the road. They see other drivers as a plus. They don't balk and take it personally every time some other traveler cuts them off or makes a sudden turn, eats or reads, or swerves a bit while chatting on a cell phone. They don't like these behaviors, but they adjust. Drivers who maintain their cool get honked at just like anyone, but they're content to coexist and let the traffic flow. They decline to get overexcited and throw their own vibe out of whack. They know what they can change and can't, and don't confuse the two. They know their inner calm maintains a balance in their dealings. They believe things will work out well no matter what occurs. They believe any traffic pattern honors perfect timing. And since they come and go in peace, things tend to fall in place for them.

People are who they are. They do what they do, as they are who they are, and they draw their match in energy. Do what you do from highest self, and whatever anyone does, you're fine.

One cannot give what one doesn't have.

When others are not calm themselves, they're unable to be calm with you. That needn't dissuade you from being calm. When you realize others are doing their thing at the level and the way they can, if you're calm, you adjust your expectations to accept their way of doing things as merely that, the way they are. They're just being them. They're not trying to do anything to you. You might not enter their mind. In your place of peace, you realize this, and conflict is avoided. You avoid trying to get what they don't have to give, which is unattainable no matter how hard others try, how angry they get or how frustrated they become.

Givers give, and takers take. And it's useful to note this carefully, because nine times out of ten, when we're facing a negative input in our lives, it's because we've had expectations beyond what others could give. That doesn't work. Give, because that's who you are, and avoid letting takers drain you. Do what you do from your peaceful reserve, and let others evolve in the ways they can with your love to help them along.

IF IT'S LOOMING, JUST UN-LOOM IT!

You have to go hard at stuff you dread. There. I said it. Flat-out. Deal. You have to blow past whatever might stand in the way of what you're meant to do. O'erleaping fears and obstacles and heroically banishing dastardly foes is part of your Change Wizard job description. It's part of who you're meant to be, or you wouldn't have to do it. It's how you do your Meant-To-Do—by adopting approaches that work for you. Others make change by other methods. You tackle the tough stuff first, and get busy overcoming hurdles fast.

Now that you're feeling your Meant-To-Do, go at it full tilt, like a warrior, banishing everything in your way. You might encounter many things, but lack of commitment can't be one. Nor can laziness or timidity. No I'd-Rather-Be's can come slithering in. You know that *I'd Rather Be Fishing* sign that doesn't make any sense to me? If you'd rather be fishing, get up and go. If money's the issue stopping you, then figure out how to make fishing pay. I mean like, duh, sell fish, for one. Now, I'm a vegetarian. No fish-killing advocate am I. I'm just saying, do your Meant-To-Do regardless. Doesn't matter. Do it, because your Rather-Be-Doing is what you can do to change the world, and there's no sense acting like it's not.

Your thing isn't something you don't want to do. Your Meant-To-Do is what you love. But even though it's what you love, it may present a challenge. Accept it, believing nothing can stop you. Jump in the deep end. Swim with the sharks. Doggie paddle, if that's all you can do. Keep splashing until you make some waves and start to rock the boat. Because that's what change does, changes things. You're a Change Wizard. Do your stuff.

If anything tries to hang over your head, get rid of it and live your bliss.

You know what your bliss is. Lead with it.

I create. For you, it might the fishing. Or tech. Or the skincare or medical field. Or maybe it's an invention. Maybe it's robots you want to build. You'll know it because it feels like home. Anything keeping you from it feels like a millstone hung around your neck. Bliss surrounds your Meant-To-Do. You'll recognize the joy it brings. It's what you have to do. Avoid letting stuck-ness get to you, and keep you from your Meant-To-Do. You might feel stuck, but you never are. You just haven't dispatched the things that loom. Stuck is the opposite of change, so don't get stuck in changelessness. If you are, you're doing it to yourself.

Change Wizards refuse to get stuck. It's a rule. It's set down in the Change Wizard by-laws. Check it out. It's on page one. Not that I'm into rules at all, or into restrictions of any kind. But face it, there are boundaries to everything we do in life. I encourage you to set your own.

At the end of the day, you define yourself. Back taxes cannot define you. Nor can student loans, teen pregnancy, the bum knee you got while playing ball, or the geriatric hooptie you may be cruising in right now. Whatever looms over you, put it behind you. Take care of it. Don't let it waylay you. You. Are. On. A. Mission.

Define yourself by who you are, and who you know you're meant to be. Define what you do by what you *can* do, not by what you think you can't do because you're convinced something's blocking you, and certainly not by what others say. The manner in which you define yourself can be your motivation.

Motivation is why we do our thing even if we consider giving up when things don't seem to go our way. Giving up is not an alternative. Giving up is a cop-out we contemplate when too many things get in our way, or we sense what we're doing has no effect. But we're always having an effect—on someone, something, somewhere, somehow. That is unavoidable. When we yawn, our yawning catches on. People around us start to yawn, and the world starts seeming sleepy. When we laugh, a joke seems funnier to other people hearing it. When we're driving, there's someone in front and behind, and our driving affects their arrival time.

When you know you have something important to do, do it. Period. No excuses. Any looming obstacle is something you have to address, that's all. And though it's a thing you have to face, it is facing you as well. It's up against your Meant-To-Do, which is definitely going to happen. It's facing who you're meant to be, so it better look out, and that's for sure, because you are evolving constantly, growing at a rapacious pace. You are a force to be reckoned with. No stumbling block is bigger or more powerful than you. You are the only energy that can ever halt your progress, and you aren't standing in your way. Not now or in the future. You're moving forward from this point, and nothing's going to slow you down.

You are devoted, deploying your goodness to make the world a better place. No looming stress, societal ill, toxic personality, character flaw, deficiency, or taint of impossibility that others may plaster on your goal can stop your spaceship launch. No ego demolition team can torpedo your ascendancy. If something is looming, just unloom it. Attack it like a grizzly bear. Squash it. Get the beast out of the way. And guess what? It's a paper tiger, not the monster it appeared. Whatever appears to loom over you as a threat like the Sword of Damocles, once confronted, it's no sweat. Bullies are never as big or as bad as they seem or appear from a distance. So, do what you have to do, when you have to do it, to un-loom your fears, and get your sticky stuff un-stuck.

Get your dream implanted in your mind, envision what making it happen looks like, feel it deep in your heart and soul, determine what actions you have to take, what you want to do, when, where, how, why and with whom you're going to change the world!

THE SUN NEVER SETS ON YOUR DREAM

There is no limit to heights you can reach. Your horizons, like the Earth's, stretch way out into the unknown distance. You'll never know what you're capable of until you engage your prospects. Just as football players don't make goals unless they run into the end zone, you have a dream that requires goals, and your goals are arrived at through action, too. But ballers, unlike you, are in a game that can only last so long. The NFL has seen to that. But your dream isn't on the clock when it appeals for your help to be realized. It isn't going anywhere. It lasts as long as you do.

Your dream has no expiration date. It's not like a credit card, airline points, or expiring grocery coupons. It doesn't come in a medicine vial, or vitamin jar, or food packaging that tells you when to toss it out. It isn't perishable at all.

You're set upon the Earth as purposefully as stars in galaxies, galaxies grouped in clusters, and the billions of clusters of galaxies expanding the breadth of the universe. Your horizons are only as close, or as far away, as your vision perceives them to be. What you haven't achieved until this point remains a possibility that is never going to abandon you. It's waiting for your next attempt, your new idea, renewed commitment. It has never-ending hope. It's banking on you, your self-confidence and the plans you once had or are making now. It's as viable as it ever was, no matter your age, or what you've done, or what's happened in your life. Any dream you've ever had, are having, or will begin to conceive is as vital now as ever.

Your Meant-To-Do and Meant-To-Be are indelible, indestructible. They are embedded in your being. Believe this. Think it. Speak it. Act upon it. It is a sacred trust. What you are called upon to do are the challenges and experiences that will help you turn into the person you are meant to be, and that's your goal. Allow the universe to mold you. Actively transform yourself. Know, and believe in, your blessed journey, and you will reach your destination, which is your evolution. That cannot, and hasn't been, taken away by ill fortune or sands of time. You can be even more effective now than you have ever been.

At times, what we are called upon to do may seem outside our comfort zone, but rest assured it's not outside the realm of our abilities. We are not given tasks we cannot do. That wouldn't make any sense. We have everything we need to accomplish self-fulfillment.

In addition, when we need help these days, it is only a keystroke or click away.

According to *TIME* magazine, in a study conducted by the United Nations, more people in the world have cell phones than access to toilets. That means it's easier to make a phone call than to use a restroom. The Pew Research Center indicates that, in America alone, almost two-thirds—sixty-four percent—of adults own their own smartphone. These phones are major gateways to the exploding online community, accessible almost anywhere, and when you add apps of every kind, cell phones are changing lives.

That doesn't, by any means, imply that everyone has equal access, equal opportunity or even equal rights. This should be, but is not, the case. If we are honest with ourselves, we know that these aren't afforded in equal measure across demographic lines. There are racial, religious, gender, geographical, socio-economic and political maltreatments many of us have to face. But this cannot forestall our dreams, because, fortunately there is a limit to what is determined by these factors. Our nature as spiritual entities and unlimited power of the mind enable us in ways no foul condition can deter—else the many of us who have overcome odds would not have seen their dreams come true. Our goals are all but unstoppable, unless we, before we accomplish them, get discouraged and stop ourselves.

Change Wizards keep going, no matter what. There is always a way to do what we dream of doing. This is why we dream.

ASK FOR YOUR MEANT-TO-BE AND DO WHAT YOU'RE MEANT TO DO

Some of us seem born with our Meant-To-Be and Meant-To-Do in mind. Some of us have to search for it, and don't find it until our later years.

I always knew I wanted to write, and began at four, with a little book called *Cara Carrot and The Magic Garden*. It's probably boxed up somewhere now. The year before I wrote it, I got my library card at the local branch, and that got me going on writing and illustrating a book of my own. It had crayoned illustrations. Yes! It would hit the bestseller list.

Procuring my card was no small feat. In order that I might borrow books without having to use my Mom's or one of my two big sisters' cards, I needed a card of my very own. You see, borrowing on someone else's card meant I was confined to borrow only the number of books my family could check out for me after they borrowed theirs. This was an irksome impediment to my blossoming reading habits, not to mention an indignity.

    I loved to read. I was passionate. That glitch would have to go. I got that first library card at the age of three, because I was able to read and sign an application. I was determined to get that card, and thus the librarians, hearing my pleas, decided to put me to the test. I was placed on a chair at the reference desk, standing in patent leather shoes, hunching over it ready for action. I really racked my brain. But I did it. I secured the card. Once I had my own card, it was on. I rock a library. I've been cozying up to a library shelf ever since, wherever I go. I even brake for libraries, like bumper stickers say. I'm not a bumper sticker fan, but it's only fair I warn people. I'll swerve to a library parking lot on two wheels if I have to. I don't play. And don't get me started on bookstores. Don't come between me and a bookstore door. You're liable to regret it.

    My Mom was a librarian for the New York City school system, so she always had a stack of books beside her bed and blue chaise lounge. Reading was like breathing in our home, and a source of vicarious thrills for me, as well as a great escape. The small yellow suitcase I packed for running away from home (which I never did, but contemplated frequently) was mostly filled with children's books, among them my white Bible. Of course, there were other necessities, such as my tutu, leotards, ballet slippers, pads, crayons and pencils. These were all items Fern might need if she ran away in *Charlotte's Web*, stuff Heidi or Pippi Longstocking might take along if they took a powder. Or Aladdin in *1001 Arabian Nights*. He packed that magic oil lamp. He wanted to change his life around. He was poor, but he had a big dream to be rich, to "live in a palace, and never have any problems at all". I figured he would travel light.

    I wanted to write and be a performer. I'd sing, tell corny jokes, and dance for all my Daddy's customers when I accompanied him on sales rounds. He'd pick me up from day care, and we'd hang out all over the city, tooling around in the Plymouth, just the two of us, from the Bronx to Manhattan to Brooklyn and Queens, taking my one-toddler show on the road, seeing the sights and working the crowd. I'd rake in paper money too, not just coins like other kids. Adults would grin and pinch my cheeks, and fork over cash like I'd passed a hat. The feeling was delicious. I knew that's what I was meant to do—create, entertain and enlighten—and indeed that's what I've always done.

Some of us come to our Meant-To-Do later, and that's more special in many ways. It shows we can always do our Meant-To-Do. That is, unless we give up on life, which we need to avoid at any cost. As long as our hearts are beating, we can make our contribution any way that we see fit. As long as we set our beating hearts on accomplishing in our special way any task that is uniquely ours, the gifts we are given and work to develop don't ever go out of date. "It ain't over till it's over," said Yogi Berra, the baseball legend. It's never too late to do anything. Our timing is always perfect, because the universe places us in the right place at the right time when we are right for the job.

Take Laura Ingalls Wilder, for instance, who wrote *Little House On The Prairie*. She started writing at forty-four, and didn't get published until she was sixty-four. She didn't give up. And then there was Raymond Chandler, who lost his job as an oil executive at forty-four, began to write, and published his first detective mystery, the classic novel *The Big Sleep* when he was fifty-one years old. That isn't old, but comparatively, it isn't a child prodigy, though often people are. It doesn't matter what your age or background, you have a Meant-To-Do ripening. Don't let it die on the vine.

Some of us live out most of our lives doing what others want us to, or taking some job to try to survive, then finding our Meant-To-Do and Meant-To-Be long into our senior years, when our physical bodies start to fade. But each of us has a code implanted, opening up a space and time when we can move all the subatomic particles in the cosmos into a better configuration. Each of our codes is unique.

Those of us sensing these codes in ourselves are driven to do our Meant-To-Do such that we have perfect timing.

I think we can make how to key in the code a new normal perceived by everyone. Every molecular structure in humans could form around this new thought-itude, this growing collective phenomenon of consciousness of who we're meant to be and what we're meant to do, starting out at birth. We can be taught that thought creates, and we are creating with our thoughts. This could make us more responsible about how we conduct our lives. This could start in pre-school, early learning. We can be taught our Meant-To-Be and Meant-To-Do are why we live. Imagine that in the curriculum, how fewer dropouts we would have, how fewer discipline problems.

This could alter the way we function together, evolve, transform, and conduct ourselves, how we work through challenges, what we seek to learn. I know this may sound like pie in the sky, but that's how changes often seem to us when they're proposed. Knowing we have this great human technology, we ought to make the best of it. We have to know what to use it for. We have nothing to lose. As it is, we have violence taking lives that were meant to do fantastic things. We aren't controlling weapons, so let's get a grip on how we value life.

Start using your power the way we discussed. Ask for the life you want to live, and how to make it happen. Ask the universe for your Meant-To-Do, and for who you're meant to be.

Those who believe in a Higher Power can ask through prayer and meditation, believing you are always heard, and that your prayers are answered long before you kneel to pray. Go inside the stillness, listen to your inner voice. Silence eliminates white noise on the airwaves where the Universal Mind broadcasts your answers. Ask for help to reach your goal. Ask for angels to surround you. Ask for Ascended Masters to impart their wisdom, guide your choices.

It's the desires of your heart that, infused with your emotions, radiate outward, drawing the energy match to the dream you yearn to experience. Avoid emitting confusing signals, saying you want some wonderful thing and proceeding to think and act in ways that bring the opposite to you. No point in wanting relationships, and then sabotaging every chance to build, or to sustain, one. Saying you're an athlete while destroying your body with unhealthy habits will not, and cannot, court success. You have to ask for what you want by every means imaginable to seduce your wish to come to you in a form in which others can partake. You have to make a home for what you want, make space for change to fill, behave as if change has already occurred.

If you want a mate, make room for them. Carve out time for them in your schedule. Take care to become the person your ideal mate will be attracted to before you actually meet them. Be sure what you want in that mate, as well. If you want to invent the next iPad, innovate and fabricate the objects you're imagining. Study the market for your project. Draw it. Write down notes about it. Visualize it constantly. Save up, crowdsource, borrow funds. Hone your perfect pitch.

Believe the world is on your side, and ask for what you want with every single breath you take, knowing that nothing can hinder your Meant-To-Be as you do what you're meant to do.

Direct your questions to the source, and listen for the answers.

OBSTACLE COURSE

PERSEVERE PAST THE SEVERE

When we set out to take a long walk at the beach or a drive through the woods on a warm Spring day, we don't imagine that reaching our destination will require one step or only one turn of the steering wheel. We know there's a process we have to go through, and we're willing to go through it. We look forward to enjoying it. We don't consider a pothole a setback. We focus on where we're heading. Nor do we set out without any target in mind, even for a vacation. We plan a trip. We purchase maps. Even to go on a picnic, we take a myriad of supplies. And not only blankets, plates and food, but we have a spare tire in the trunk, maybe umbrellas in case it rains, a jacket, a pair of comfy shoes, a credit card for incidentals, even some places to stop along the route if we get sleepy. So should it be as we trek toward goals.

The first step only starts our journey. Thereafter, we have to persevere. The next step may be a mystery, but that's okay, we're geared for it. It may contain lucky pennies and rainbows, or land us in a pit of snakes. Even with all of our preparation, we do not know what our journey holds, how many mundane chores it takes, or what it will require of us. One phone call can easily turn into five on-holds as minutes tick away. An email can scuttle a business plan. Someone's out with a cold. Someone's in with an attitude. Plumbing bursts and springs a leak. The house sold faster than we thought, and we have to be out in thirty days. A new job offer wants us to move overseas.

When we set out on a journey, and commit to work to change the world, we can expect the unexpected. Not everything's going to fall in place exactly as predicted. We're liable to hit some bumps and take some lumps that slow us down. We're undertaking something huge, and we have to set out knowing this, believing we're where we are, and facing what we face, because it's best. Some keep going, others falter. Change Wizards see change as an odyssey, and they never abandon post. We never quit, or think of it. We're focused on the goal. We're glad to meet all the people we meet and touch all the lives we are privileged to touch, to go places we probably never would've gone if we lived for ourselves alone. We're excited by what we learn to do, the wells of strength we tap into, the achievements we never suspected we could attain when we began.

When we set a huge goal for a greater good, its process will surprise us. It may sputter and stall, then surge ahead. It often might seem like a charging bull that's bucking with us on its back. But a bull ride is exhilarating, though we know we may get bruised.

We may never see how we've affected change, for change may be invisible to us even though it's taken place. We may never know whom a change affects, or whom they might affect in turn. We may never know how our courage might have rubbed off on a timid soul, or who, seeing us, might recognize their Meant-To-Do and Meant-To-Be, and set off working for it. We may not know our full effect, or where, or with whom it has been felt. That isn't necessary. It's not an expectation we should have, nor should we doubt the ways in which our impact makes a change. It is only for us to persevere, and intend to be far-reaching.

We don't beef every drop of rain that falls. We carry an umbrella, wear a hood, don boots and splash through puddles, let rainwater wash our faces clean, and look up toward the sunshine beyond the clouds. For every door that gets slammed in our face, there's a "yes" from somebody opening one. Or we strap on Plan B, get loaded for bear, and climb in through a window.

Perseverance, more than most anything else, is liable to make things change.

#LETITBE

Not everything rests on us to solve, address, or be persuaded by. We don't have to take on everything, we take on what is right for us.

There are some things that are up to us, and yet sometimes we just have to let things be. We can just be, and that's enough. By just being, we approach the world of cause and effect with relaxation. We don't have to play games, manipulate, or engage in constant tit for tat.

Random horrors that happen don't spring from truth. Evil has no influence on who we are, what we do, or think, or say. Bad news about bad actors doing bad things in the world cannot warp our perspective. All it can do is encourage us to work harder for the good. We know there are so many good people trying to make things work for everyone, and we know there is so much more of this than any wrongdoer perpetrates. We're into good vibes. We value truth.

We don't get caught up in the lies about how the world is a terrible, awful place, and we might as well throw in the towel. How sin is our nature, and people are bad. How life is so awful, and then you die. That's ridiculous. Just look around. What you believe has made the mountains, sky and sea is in us all. It's the decisive reality. That's the real News at Eleven. Every shameful act is an outlier we don't have to pay attention to, except to put barriers in place so as to prevent a recurrence. We're meant for beauty, made for love. We function inside potential. We examine possibilities. Our mission is to make more good, not cower from what doesn't.

No one can make you believe what you know to be wrong is the natural order. Harmful things that hurt, or worse, destroy aren't meant to be. They exist within lower vibrations, and they may get all the press, but that doesn't mean that you or I must accept them as the norm. To the contrary, we need to fill our sphere with so much goodness, love and light that depravity can't touch anything or anybody anymore. Together, we can make this happen. We can drown out noise with music. We can foil hate with agape love. When we live on a higher plane, only things that vibrate at a higher level reach us. We are protected. That's just physics.

Consider when to get involved and pour your energy into things, and when to let it be.

If something resonates with you, consider it's something that you can affect. Know when a bone is yours to pick and when it's someone else's fight, because they'll likely win it.

Earth's highest layer of atmosphere is the exosphere. We can hang out there. Or at least, our spirits can hang out there, if only figuratively. From a height, we can choose to let things be. We should never get dragged into the mud. If we can't lift something up, we can't give it leeway to pull us down. We don't have to weep and gnash our teeth or grapple like crabs in a barrel. We know there isn't a gap between what's best for you, what's best for me or best for everybody.

Sometimes it's best to just let something be and apply all your energies elsewhere. You don't have to think about what others think about you, or eavesdrop on their thoughts. You don't have to feel it's up to you to make other people over. They're empowered, they can change themselves, and they're the only ones who can. Just be a great example. The person you want to mold is you, and you have no problem doing that.

Refrain from making demands on anybody. Let it be. You don't want to risk weighing others down. You don't want to ask anybody to change your world. You can change it around yourself. By changing yourself, you change the world. You don't need to control anybody else, you just need self-control. There's no need to push anyone else around. Let others be who they really are, without your criticism. You can listen, and not have to blurt your opinion.

You can give everything you can give and know you'll still have more. That doesn't mean to give everything you have, just all you have to give. There's a difference. You need to know what it is. You don't do anyone any favors by giving until you give out. Nobody benefits when you're completely depleted of your energies or drained of your resources. But you know giving circulates, so give generously, and let it be.

You believe everything's okay. If others don't, then let it be. Avoid letting others weigh you down in the sea of their complaint. Let the universe know you're aware it has your back. Avoid rubbing folks the wrong way just because you feel you must be right. Let it be.

Quit going against the grain in order to ruffle feathers, or swimming against the tide for the sake of being a contrarian.

Let nature's currents carry you, like the tides always follow the moon.

Arguing isn't the answer. You're a solution. Let it be. If you can't discuss it rationally, it's time to throttle back. Hot tempers blot out reasoning. The likelihood that you will change someone's mind by arguing with them is infinitesimal. Know when to assert your point and when not to waste your breath. You have no need for anger. Channel your energy into healing wounds, and heal yours from the inside out. From within, you can re-program. You can look at it through a compassionate lens. Feeling compassion makes answers plain, or you can let it be.

It's struggle that tends to cause us pain. Struggle brings on suffering, and suffering ensues from not letting go, from unwillingness to let it be. Those who feel pain cause pain, and that isn't who you're meant to be. Your presence alone can let it be. And it does. I feel it now.

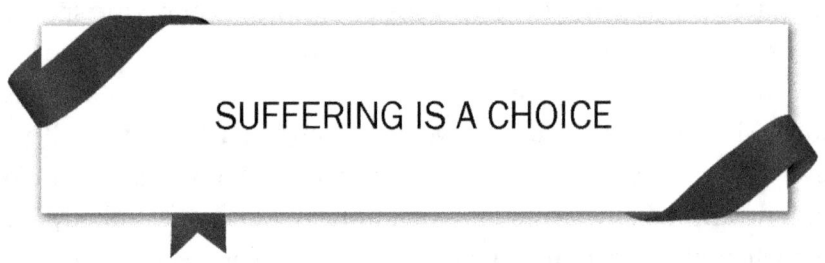

SUFFERING IS A CHOICE

This doesn't sound easy to swallow. Suffering is, what? Are you kidding, a choice? "I'm not suffering because I want to," you say, shaking your head, glaring down at this page. Yet it's true that suffering is a choice. Suffering derives from your choice to think you're suffering. What you think, you experience. Thus, suffering, like every emotion you feel, emanates from choice.

Even if you stub your toe, or decide you've been taken advantage of, you can take your mind off of it instantly. You get over these things eventually, right? Why not do so immediately.

You're not *into* pain, are you? Some might be, but let's just say you're likely not, because pain is, well . . . it's painful. And assuming you aren't a masochist, you most likely prefer to avoid it. You don't have to choose to feel mental pain. You can feel however you want to, and the proof is that you do. When you want to feel happy, boom! You're in. You think happy thoughts, you're a happy camper. Likewise, you have alternatives to suffering over some escapade that's probably totally over now—the one that might still have you steaming, or worse, suffering awful pain—pain that will tend to go unresolved, unless you're determined to make a change.

Whatever the root cause of your suffering was, you're empowered to move on. You could forgive and let it be. You either will, or won't. You could rationalize pain is the price you pay for having the causer of pain in your life. Or you could calmly speak to them, letting them know their behavior doesn't work for you, so from now on, you'll do you, and they'll do them, and never the twain shall meet again. In other words, you dump them. You're happy to let them do their thing—just not to do their thing *to you*.

You see, you have alternatives. Those are just a handful.

Only oftentimes, you think you don't. Have alternatives, that is. You just tend to default to suffering. Get in bed, pull the covers up over your head and cause suffering like a toothache. You might even phone a friend (one who presumably won't cause suffering), and burden them with your tale of woe. That way, they could choose to suffer, too. Or perhaps they might choose to hang up on you, or send you straight to voicemail. They may know they have alternatives. And you may have caused them to suffer before. They may choose not to go there again.

So, now you knock back some Appletinis (for those who drink, I don't). You might eat a whole pint of Häagen-Dazs, which, in the morning will cause you additional suffering when you hop onto the scale. You might cry until your eyes puff up, which, when you see them swollen, might give rise to further pain. You could endlessly wonder if you should call back and give that lousy creep what-for. You've thought of a zillion zingers you could've zapped them with, but didn't. You're suffering, so you grab your cell to give them a piece of our mind. But, at this point, you might not have much to spare.

And so now, it's another sleepless night. Due to the fact you chose suffering rather than other, more healthful alternatives. Frustration wells up in your stomach, causing ulcers and more pain. More pain that leads to more suffering.

It doesn't seem to make much sense. Yet people do it all the time. Give over their lives to suffering because of what other people do. And meanwhile, they're enjoying life, those others who caused the initial pain. They're out golfing, skiing, dating, getting mani-pedis, swimming laps. They're walking dogs, and streaming movies, munching popcorn, mowing lawns, driving along some scenic route, driving someone else insane. They aren't suffering one little bit. But you might be totally into it, pulling up a chair for suffering, inviting it to dinner. It's suffering's birthday at your place. It's now your BFF. It's invited heartbreak to your crib. Heartbreak is its Plus One. Heartbreak wants a pic of your broken heart to post on its Facebook page.

I thought my heart was broken once. Literally broken. I really did.

When my Daddy passed away, I had bronchitis and coughed so much that I actually busted ribs. They hurt so much, I considered that maybe I had a broken heart. This time, it wasn't betrayal, or disappointment, or an acting job for which they "went another way". I was coughing up blood, and my left side hurt as if I had been stabbed. It could really be a broken heart. I asked my doctor if it was. His diagnosis? No such thing. Yet many of us would be willing to swear we had one sometime in the past, or were suffering one right now. What other symptoms, you might ask? Listlessness? Poor appetite? Insomnia? Moodiness? Isolation? That was just for starters.

Now, I know it sounds ridiculous, and it might have been tied to the astronomical fever that was gripping me, or it could've just been my state of mind convincing me to think that way. A TV commercial would advertise: "See your doctor if Heartbreakalyfranistanosis could be what you're suffering from. Ask what Myfrickingpainintheyouknowhatalin can do for you, if its side effects don't take you out. Those are likely to make your head fall off, and your skin turn green, and the crack of your booty seal up for good, but hey, it's just what the doctor ordered, providing his pharmaceutical rep dropped by to slip him a sample just in time for your prescription. Heartbreak. Yup, you've got it, pal. And it might just be terminal. That is, unless you Change. Your. Mind. And realize suffering is a choice that you don't have to make."

I didn't take losing my father lying down. No way. I ran away. Finally. Not with my yellow suitcase. And not even by myself. I was smart, I took my Mom with me. Yes, I wanted my Mommy. Don't judge. I'm sure you've been there. My Mom and I hopped in the car right after the funeral, yelling, "Road trip!" We took off for eight states in eight days on a wild adventure we won't soon forget. More like, we'll always remember. We laugh about it all the time. That was our choice. We chose to live. We chose not to suffer. We chose to go on. We chose to embrace the moment, and in some small way, to change our stories and to change our lives. And in doing so, we changed other lives. We laughed with people we never would have laughed with if we were suffering at home, languishing, having a pity party. We had a real party. We had a blast. We celebrated Daddy's life. We chose to feel his presence. We chose to take him on our trip. We chose to share our memories. We inspired people, so they said, with our mother and daughter Thelma and Louise act—sans the robberies. We just had stolen moments.

I'm not sharing this to pat us on our backs or imply grieving isn't real. It is. I'm just grateful we made that choice. That we can look back on that time with a smile. A genuine smile. It empowers me when I miss my Dad like a stolen breath, like the sun got turned off in the sky. That trip helps me know, anytime I'm suffering, I do have a choice. I don't have to suffer. I can grow. I can live a new way. I can change my mind. I can change my life. I can plot my story as I wish, rewind the movie in my mind, click on a film I want to revisit, or press play on a new one. I can make my life a comedy just as easily as a horror flick. I can live out a fantasy, mystery or a thriller that's uniquely mine—with a little morality play tossed in.

I want to live a moral life. I want to change the world. But I can't change the world from a suffering place, a mentality racked by pain. I can only bring joy if I live in joy. I can only bring beauty from beauty, peace from my inner place of peace. I choose this over suffering.

This is not to suggest you repress your feelings. You have to stay in touch with them. You must be aware of them, know their intricacies, feel them fully, work them through. You have a right to your feelings. They connect you, help you to know you're alive. But your feelings are products of your thoughts, and you know you govern what you think. You know what you think materializes. When you change your thoughts, you change our feelings. That is a mighty proposition. Choose joy, or choose to feel miserable. People who feel good change the world.

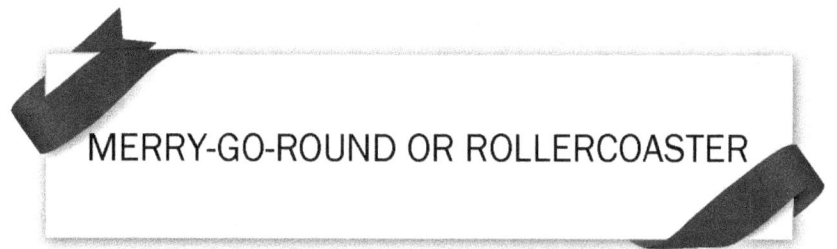

MERRY-GO-ROUND OR ROLLERCOASTER

Consider that whatever drama may haunt your reality comes from you, from the junk or the gem you've created of your mind with the thoughts that flow through it. Your life is a merry-go-round or a roller coaster ride running on thought. The thoughts you've been thinking moment to moment and day to day are playing out, and they won't change until you change.

The good news is, what you've created to this point is in the past. Now is all you have to go on. Now is what you're working with. You are creating your here and now. What are you creating? How are you feeling in this instant? Do you feel serenity, or do you feel frustration? Do you have feelings of love or resentment? Selfishness, generosity, detachment or connection? Are you open to all the good that is, or do you feel shut down? You can stop what you're doing right now, you know. You can turn the beat around. Or you can zip into turbo drive. You can go full speed ahead and blast off into the world you're dreaming of.

You can take a moment here and now to close your eyes, and go within, and change what you are feeling. You know simply by changing your thoughts, you can change your feelings, and thence change your life and change the lives of others.

Think of a time when the world was your oyster. Dip your emotional paintbrush into that colorful bucket of feeling great, and paint it on your future. Paint a rainbow through your sky. Feel your heartbeat. Hear your breathing. You're alive. You count for something. What you will count for is the question. You are meant for something

BIG. What you're thinking right now will add or detract. Believe it, or don't, it's going to happen. You believe what you believe, and it will reach out into space and return to you like a homing pigeon, assuming whatever you believe is what you want to undergo. It will retrieve what you believe. Take responsibility for it.

If what you believe is the sum of your fears, then every dread you see, you've wished, and the universal genie, having listened, plans to grant your wish. If you believe your shiniest, finest hour is ahead of you, and that, that is what you're destined for, it's unfolding straightaway. You're projecting whatever you have in your mind directly onto the screen before you. You're the developer of this game. You have the joystick in your hand. Decide to get on the rollercoaster or the merry-go-round of life. You'll either go for the ride of your life or get taken for a ride.

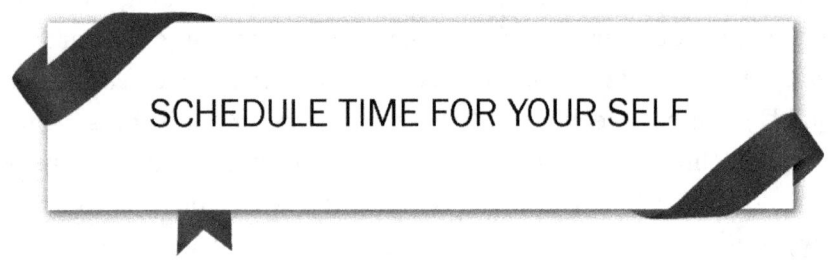

SCHEDULE TIME FOR YOUR SELF

Purposely schedule time for self. With everything from family, home and work to our hobbies or obligations, after all is said and done, our self is all we have to give to everything in our lives. If we don't keep ourselves in shape, we have nothing to give others. We have nothing with which to change the world if we can't even change ourselves.

If you don't take proper care of self, anything can pile on and throw your life off-balance. "The big picture," as my Dad called it, seems bigger than it ever was. And yet, even if you tackle one thing at a time, if you don't have health and energy, you can feel like you're trying to climb out of a hole before you climb out of bed. Small things can lead to overwhelm.

Now, it may sound rather obvious that, if we don't get our own stuff right, we have no business being Change Wizards working to change the world. That's why people in an airplane are advised to, in an emergency, put on their oxygen mask before they attempt to help anyone else. But too often, everything else comes first, and self-care can seem narcissistic. The needs of others loom so large, they cast a shadow over ours. We can think we're doing what we should even as we ignore our basic needs. But that isn't helping anyone. Ignoring what is good for us is more than self-abuse. It shortchanges everyone. Eventually, neglecting self will haunt not only us. We're not perfect, but we can be perfectly us—the us who fit perfectly into the whole. So, yes, we're needed, but happy, balanced, free and well is how we're needed most.

We need time to get our heads on straight. We need to walk, play sports or dance, work out, run, or take a hike. We need to just sit and do nothing sometimes. Get our hair cut. Take our vitamins. Make a protein smoothie. Read the mail. Have our nails done. Ride a bike. We need to get our teeth cleaned, go for a medical checkup, eye exam, get a new pair of shoes so our feet don't hurt. We need to drink juice and eat vegetables. We need to hang out with our girls or guys, and laugh, and pig out, and do crazy things. We need to get more sleep. We also need to commune with nature, write in a journal, take some pix. We need to garden, talk to plants, or take a day trip out of town. We need to replenish. We need downtime.

We can't give it all, or the well will run dry, and our health will begin to slide. We'll bark at our kids, or growl at the dog, or tell the boss some awful truth, or our mate a white lie we can't take back. We have to take care of ourselves without fail. If we don't, we stop functioning at our peak and want to tear our hair out.

We have to take care of our needs and desires, whatever they are, and all the time. This isn't selfish, this is real. We so often sympathize with strangers, only to begrudge ourselves the tiniest transgression. We have to wake up and be good to ourselves. We may be the only ones who will. How can we have people there when we need them if we're not here for Numero Uno.

We might not have yet met face to face, but I know you're reading this book right now, and the title *You Can Change The World* appealed to you for a reason. You got it because you deplore what you're seeing. You want to see everyone fulfilled. You want to do great things in life. You want to leave the world a better place for having lived. You want to take on the issues of the day, or maybe help clean the air, rescue pets or contribute things of beauty. You want to be extraordinary. You already are extraordinary. You deserve the best. You deserve to *be* your best.

I believe in you, and I cherish you. I want you to reach your potential, and I want you on your center. It hurts me to think you're exhausted, sad, frustrated or overwhelmed. I know what it is to feel those things, and it isn't the way we're meant to feel. We're built to be elated. So, I want to encourage you to do what you need to do for you. To evaluate where you are right now, to visualize where you want to be, and to learn how to do your Meant-To-Do. Because only that will do for you. Only your best will please you and will be the change you want to see.

By changing you, you change the world.

What you dream, you can only bring about with the healthiest mind and body. By feeding your spirit and soul, you concurrently nourish all your dreams. So take the time to heal yourself. Pay attention to your well-being.

A good place to start could be sizing up the different areas of our lives.

Grab hold of a pen and piece of paper. Let's see how you're doing and get some answers. Here are some questions to start you off. Your answers will transform your life. No judgment, stress or ridicule. The facts, ma'am, just the facts. To see how you're doing in various aspects of your life, let's check them out. Then we'll move on to specifics.

Here, as always, it's important that you be honest with yourself. Totally honest. You've nothing to lose. You can only gain some insight. No one's watching but you, your Higher Power and perhaps your pet. Even if your cat gives you the stink eye, plow on anyway. Answer the questions as fast as you can. The first thing that comes to your mind is probably most accurate, most informative, because it isn't censored. So, don't belabor anything. Feel free to expound on any answer, expressing all you want for each. If other questions arise, keep answering. You're discovering self. Self-discovery is fun. To transform, you need self-knowledge.

There are no right answers, there are only your thoughts. There's no "should", there's only what helps you grow and changes you for the better. Since your thoughts are creating, you must be aware of what they are, and if they work. It's not necessary to answer all questions at once, although that might be helpful. What you don't have immediate answers for could be what you need to answer most, so give those things more thought.

Remember any fear is out. Fear is paralyzing. Park any fear at the curb. You're safe here. You are secure in your mind and the world. Guilt, doubt and worry are out as well, as are concerns about penmanship, or what you may not have considered before. You can type your thoughts into your phone, use a notebook or an envelope, or jot in the margins of this book. You can scribble in your bathtub, kitchen, locker room after Pilates class, while you're out walking, or between bites on your lunch break. No one is grilling you. Relax. Just please don't text while driving. We're here to find what can support you in your change and metamorphosis, what will contribute to personal growth. You're searching for how you can best be you, and live in a state of peace and love. The questions below are in random order, to exercise your mind.

Here are the questions. We're off to the races, exploring your consciousness at your pace. See what you come up with. On your mark, get ready, set, and . . . go!

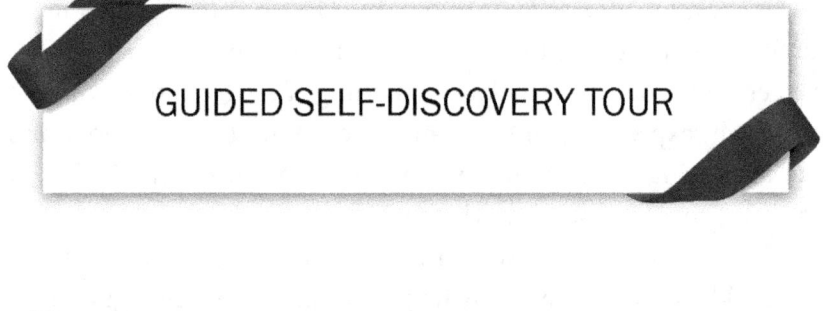

GUIDED SELF-DISCOVERY TOUR

☐ Am I happy? What makes me happy? How can I make myself happier?

☐ What do I want most in life?

☐ What has changed in my life recently, and how do I feel about it?

☐ What in my life do I want or need to change?

☐ Do I rely on myself for my happiness, or do I seek happiness elsewhere?

☐ If I seek happiness from an outside source, what source, and how is that working out?

- ☐ Do I feel free?
- ☐ If I don't feel free, what do I think is binding me or holding me back?
- ☐ If I do feel free, do I express my freedom? How do I express my freedom?
- ☐ What do I most want to accomplish?
- ☐ Am I usually tired or energetic?
- ☐ What is the best thing about my life?
- ☐ What are the things I'm grateful for?
- ☐ What do I wish was gone from my life? Why?
- ☐ If I could be anywhere right now (and I can), where would I be? Am I happy where I am?
- ☐ Do I have a support system, feel alone, or wish I had more solitude?
- ☐ Who are the people who support me?
- ☐ Does everyone in my support team know I trust and count on them?
- ☐ Do I thank those who support me? Do I support them as well?

- [ ] Who do I love? Have I told them so? Do my loved ones know I love them? How?
- [ ] Who loves me? How do I know they love me?
- [ ] What in my past is unresolved? Can I resolve it? How can I resolve it?
- [ ] What am I proud of?
- [ ] What is my most cherished possession?
- [ ] What do I need to purge from my environment?
- [ ] What is my greatest attribute?
- [ ] What do I believe? What do I believe in?
- [ ] Is there anything I am being told that I do *not* believe? Who or what is saying it?
- [ ] Am I a winner?
- [ ] What makes me a winner, or why do I think I'm not a winner?
- [ ] What was my most recent success?
- [ ] What was my most recent unsuccessful attempt? How can I succeed the next time I try?

- [ ] If I continue on the course I'm on now, what will my life be like a year from now?
- [ ] What would I like my life to be like a year from now? Does this answer match the prior answer?
- [ ] What do I wish to change in the world?
- [ ] What do I need to change about myself and about my life?
- [ ] Do I like where I'm living?
- [ ] Is there someplace I'd prefer to live? Where would I like to live? What must I do to live there?
- [ ] What is my Meant-To-Be? Who am I meant to be? Am I this person? How can I be more my true self?
- [ ] What is my Meant-To-Do?
- [ ] Does my job reflect my talents, abilities, Meant-To-Do and Meant-To-Be?
- [ ] Do I take enough time to care for myself?
- [ ] Do I use my Me-Time effectively?
- [ ] What do I do in my Me-Time?
- [ ] Am I spending my time the way I want? Why, or why not?

- [ ] Do I love what I'm doing most of the time? How can I do more of what I love?
- [ ] Am I punctual? Why, or why not?
- [ ] Is my social life active and fulfilling? If so, how? If not, why?
- [ ] Do I have a romantic life?
- [ ] Do I want a romantic life?
- [ ] Do I have the romantic life I want?
- [ ] What am I learning from my current romantic relationship?
- [ ] What did I learn from my last romantic relationship?
- [ ] What am I learning from my friends?
- [ ] Is there someone I'd like to get closer to?
- [ ] Is there someone I sense I need distance from?
- [ ] Am I handling my relationships well? Explain.
- [ ] What are the last words I said that I wish I could take back?
- [ ] What are the words I have not yet said that I need to say? To whom?

- [ ] Do I apologize if and when I'm wrong? Who do I need to apologize to now?
- [ ] Am I forgiving?
- [ ] Who do I need to forgive? For what?
- [ ] What do I need to forgive myself for?
- [ ] Who do I hope forgives me? For what?
- [ ] What are my bad habits?
- [ ] What are my good habits?
- [ ] How long has it been since I laughed?
- [ ] What last made me laugh? Who made me laugh? Who makes me laugh most?
- [ ] How long has it been since I made someone else laugh? Who was it?
- [ ] When did I last give money? How much did I give? Do I need to give more?
- [ ] What was the last thing I gave to a cause or individual? What will I give next?
- [ ] Am I thriving physically?

- [ ] Do I like the way I look?

- [ ] Is there some way I'd like to change my looks? Why?

- [ ] What are my best features?

- [ ] What about my body do I need to work on?

- [ ] How can I be healthier?

- [ ] Is my behavior, in general, what I would like? What behaviors do I need to change?

- [ ] How can I improve my behaviors toward myself and others? How *will* I improve them?

- [ ] What are my best personality traits? What are my worst personality traits?

- [ ] What are my talents?

- [ ] What skills do I have?

- [ ] When do I feel happiest? What am I doing? With whom? Where am I?

- [ ] What makes me feel most fulfilled?

- [ ] Have I lived up to my true potential?

- ☐ How can I live up to my highest potential?
- ☐ Is there something I feel I've been waiting for? If so, what is it?
- ☐ Am I ready to stop waiting and live full out? How will I do this?
- ☐ What has to change for my life to be the life I want to live?
- ☐ Do I compare myself to others? Who, and why? How does comparing make me feel?
- ☐ How am I striving to be my best self?
- ☐ What is my philosophy? Do I have one?
- ☐ Do I have a spiritual life? What does it include?
- ☐ How do I practice my beliefs? Am I behaving morally?
- ☐ Are my thoughts, words and deeds cohesive?
- ☐ Do I have a dream?
- ☐ What is my dream?
- ☐ Do I have goals? What are my goals?
- ☐ What is my number one goal?
- ☐ Do I have a plan to reach my goals?

- [ ] What is my plan?
- [ ] What are my long-term goals? Have they changed, and do they suit me?
- [ ] Do I want to change my long-term goals now?
- [ ] What are my short-term goals?
- [ ] Do I want to alter my short-term goals? How?
- [ ] What/who are my top ten (10) priorities? Are they currently in the right order?
- [ ] Who do I know that can help me achieve my goals?
- [ ] Do I have a mentor? Do I want one? How can I get one? How will I get one?
- [ ] Who can I help to achieve their goals? How can I help them?
- [ ] What can I change about myself right now, as I am writing this?
- [ ] In this moment, I commit to . . .
- [ ] I will fulfill my above commitment by this date_____.
- [ ] How will I fulfill my above commitment?

- [ ] Am I friendly? How can I be more friendly and outgoing?
- [ ] Am I kind? How can I be kinder, and to whom?
- [ ] Am I smart? How will I improve my knowledge and challenge my intellect?
- [ ] What is the last book I read, and what did I learn from it?
- [ ] What is the last film I saw, and what did I learn from it?
- [ ] What is the last TV show I saw, and what did I learn from it?
- [ ] In this instant, I let go of . . .
- [ ] What else do I need to let go of?
- [ ] What has changed about me in the past year?
- [ ] What do I plan to change about myself in the coming year?
- [ ] Am I changing for the better? If so, in what ways?
- [ ] Have I changed for the worse? If so, in what ways? How can I turn this around?
- [ ] Is my self-talk encouraging or debilitating? In what way?
- [ ] I will start today to tell myself . . .
- [ ] I will start today to stop telling myself . . .

- [ ] Are my eating habits healthy? How can I improve them?
- [ ] What is one word I would use to describe myself?
- [ ] What are five (5) more words I would use to describe myself?
- [ ] What are ten (10) more words I would use to describe myself?
- [ ] What is the one word others use to describe me most?
- [ ] How would I like others to describe me? Do I care?
- [ ] Does the face I wear for the world reflect who I feel I am inside?
- [ ] Am I shy or outgoing? Introverted or extraverted? Does this work for me?
- [ ] Am I brave or fearful?
- [ ] Is there anything I fear now? If so, what? Why?
- [ ] To let go of fear, I will . . .
- [ ] When is the last time I changed my hairstyle? Does it need changing now?
- [ ] Are my fingernails clean/manicured? Do I chew them or let them grow? Why?

- [ ] Am I physically pain-free, or am I living with some kind of pain?

- [ ] If I'm pained, where is the pain located? What causes it? How can I alleviate it?

- [ ] What do I need to do to eliminate or alleviate physical pain? Am I doing it?

- [ ] Am I doing what I need to do to eliminate or alleviate mental or emotional pain?

- [ ] When was my last doctor's appointment? What was it for?

- [ ] When was my last health check-up? Do I get regular yearly medical check-ups?

- [ ] Do I need to call for a doctor's appointment today? What for?

- [ ] Do I keep a To-Do list? Is it in writing or in my head?

- [ ] What is currently on my To-Do list? Does it reflect what I need to do most?

- [ ] What is the most important thing on my To-Do list? Why is it important?

- [ ] What has been on my To-Do list the longest? Why? I will get it done by_____.

- [ ] What long-term or short-term goals have I accomplished in the past year?

- [ ] How do those achievements make me feel?

- [ ] What long-term or short-term goals have I accomplished in the past month?

- [ ] What long-term or short-term goals have I accomplished in the past week?

- [ ] What did I accomplish yesterday?

- [ ] What will I accomplish today?

- [ ] What will I accomplish tomorrow?

- [ ] Are any of the above accomplishments in sync with what I most want to achieve?

- [ ] Does what I currently accomplish change the world in ways I desire to change it?

- [ ] What did I like more about myself three (3) years ago than I do now?

- [ ] What do I like more about myself now than I did three (3) years ago?
- [ ] What are my responsibilities?
- [ ] What do others consider to be my responsibilities?
- [ ] What are my obligations? Why do I feel obligated?
- [ ] What could I do with joy that I currently do out of obligation?
- [ ] How well am I handling what I consider to be my responsibilities?
- [ ] What is one thing I can change right now by changing my thoughts about it?
- [ ] How would the above change be life-changing and/or world-changing?
- [ ] What can I do today to improve someone else's quality of life?
- [ ] What questions do I now have that can be answered by giving greater LOVE?

Okay, so I'm not being nosy, I'm just interested in you.
Did you answer all the questions? Did you answer just a few? Will you give unanswered questions more thought? How do you feel? More self-aware? Ready to make some changes?

I have to admit, in formulating the questions I asked you, I discovered some things about myself. For one thing, I found that questions I asked are ones I already asked myself or needed to ask myself. I didn't have my own list composed for myself before I assembled yours, but it would have been a good idea. I queried myself to better understand my life, and wants and needs. I also confirmed my belief that, by merely thinking of making any change, a change is already happening. Every question I wrote made a change in me.

Every time you make a change, the universe is moving with you. You're coordinated with everything, because everything is changing. The cosmos changes constantly, exponentially expanding with more stars, more planets, more exoplanets, more galaxies and clusters. As if billions of galaxies aren't enough, the universe seeks to best itself, determined to be all it can be. We're meant to be expanding too, becoming super selves.

The world loves change, and change loves the world because it sees itself in it.

You either deliberately change for the better, or change for the not-as-great-as-you-could, because you choose to abdicate deliberately changing in favor of letting random energies change you in your absence. If you defer to outside forces, letting them program what you think, you might not recognize yourself. Not everyone has your values, so some energies you should not attract. Some thoughts aren't fit to think. Mind pollution fouls your air if you let thought garbage dump on you. Only self-change guarantees improvement. Letting changes around you cook up who you are and what you think is a recipe for disaster. That could be happening now if you fail to keep track of your inner world. Ask yourself the questions that will lead to self-discovery.

Change in your area of the world changes life for everyone. Unrest in you creates lack of peace around the globe. But for you, who live and breathe in peace, who commit to spreading love and joy, choice and change are interwoven. Either you figure out how to be your best and help others do the same, or change will occur without your say-so—even the changes in you. Insidious changes filter in that aren't who you want to be, if you don't resolve to know yourself.

You want change in you to come by choice, by changing yourself on purpose. You want change in the world to come from responsible people like you, who see the good in everyone and work to upgrade everything. You want change to come from love. From hearts like yours, and hearts like mine that want everyone to share abundance, everyone to live in joy. There's nothing the family of human can't do, if we grow and evolve together. Change has to start with you and me, and how we agree to change ourselves. Together, we're what the world is meant to be, and when we live as one, we do what the world is meant to do.

Every response you gave to the questions above is under your own control. You make change, and change makes you. Something's itching inside you, and now that you're scratching it, you feel changed. You adore the feeling. Change accelerates in you, and you accelerate with change. More changes happen as your changing thoughts draw energy matches into your world and into the world at large. You wanted to move from where you were, and now you're rolling, switching gears, turning on the afterburners. The engine of change is revving, vrooming, kicking up dust with new thought patterns, leaving behind what isn't working, heading toward solutions. You're swept up into a transformation whirlwind blowing winds of change. The ground beneath your feet is shaking.

Now that you've chosen to call out change, there is no turning back.

You want change, and change wants you.

YOUR SHIP IS COMING IN

Change is coming for the better, sooner rather than later. The change in you is fueling it. Feel the high vibration of it. The more you feel it, the faster it comes. You see self-improvement. You've begun to behave in the present as if you believe in the best of the future. Realize your ship is coming in. Gone are the days when nothing worked, if you ever had those days at all. Own the vision you are seeing. You cannot manifest lofty goals if you secretly believe you can't.

You have to work every day for change. You can't just sit back and complain about it, leave it to others, or close your eyes and wait to see what happens next. You have to dare to hope and dream. You have to be bona fide, authentic. It's living fully in the now that gives your dream its buoyancy. Your belief your ship is coming in is guiding it to port. Be the captain of your ship. Be a rising tide that lifts all boats. Dancing the night away on the Titanic, or playing shuffleboard below is fun, but if no one's on deck at the helm, you're going to hit the rocks. Navigate your ship to shore by doing whatever floats your boat, what you do best and love to do. And not to belabor the metaphor, but the quickest way to sink your ship is to fail to set a proper course, or worse, no course at all. You have to set sail to head somewhere, or you'll be going nowhere fast.

You have to believe you're the next big thing, and the next big thing is on its way to you because you're ready. You have a gigantic Power of One. You're Abraham Lincoln, Rosa Parks, John Kennedy, Gandhi, Nelson Mandela, Oprah and Einstein rolled into one. You're every soul who ever dreamed a dream that turned out to be big enough to beckon the angels and miracles it takes to change the world.

You're a Change Wizard extraordinaire. And you're just getting started.

MESSAGES COME IN MANY VOICES

When your Meant-To-Be and Meant-To-Do are clear to you, your clarity opens channels of communication, both in the natural world and in the supernatural. Your psyche sends out signals. Guidance comes in many ways, from unexpected sources. They queue up what you might do next, where you should go, who you're apt to meet, when the time is right to make a move, and whether the moves you've planned are going to yield your best result. Messages bolster your resolve, help you to find the strength you need, or get you to change whatever you must, so everything works out.

You have to be listening to hear them speak. They can be visual or auditory. Sometimes, they're epiphanies. Sometimes they appear as images, and sometimes as a knowing. Greet them with love, however they come. Through strangers you meet in a grocery store, or happen to pass by on the street, creatures that live around your home, numbers you see as you bike, or drive, or notice repeatedly on a clock. They're in the breeze, in emails you receive, on road signs, hidden in textbooks. They're in lyrics that resonate in songs, dialogue characters say in films, or in words we happen to hear people speak at a party or in a restaurant. You may overhear people say things at opportune times no matter where you are, or have butterflies land on your shoulders.

If your eyes, ears, heart and mind are open, you are in constant contact with the entity that thinks all thoughts. Be willing, even excited, to receive any wisdom that comes your way. Stay alert, listen, look, and feel. Be sensitive to your environment. Your surroundings hold keys to the mysteries you are trying to unravel in your mind. Listen with more than just your ears. See with more than just your eyes. Learn with every part of you. Let new notions, archetypes and revelations locate you and broaden your approach.

Deepen shallow relationships. Have meaningful conversations. Avoid letting interesting people you meet evaporate like vapor. Chit chat about weather and gadgets is fine, but it often adds little to your life. As does gossip, which is harmful. If you listen, you participate. Empty gab calories make your brain fat, blocking nutritional messages you could ingest from better vibes.

That's why complaining doesn't work, or listening to complaints. If you hang around in better headspace, you might predict the weather or access winning lotto numbers.

Keep lines open for incoming info that might add value to your life. When you're open to enlightenment, enlightening things will look for you. Send out a signal of love, and read all the love notes that come back to you. Even if you don't say a word, your energy can waft out over miles and converse with other beings—on this plane and elsewhere. Try it, you'll like it. It really works. How many times has someone been on your mind, and you got a call from them, an evite or unexpected gift? You can communicate many ways, and it's best to avail yourself of as many of them as you can.

Doers don't talk much about what they're doing. They're too busy doing it. You don't hear about it until it's done, unless you pay attention. Be a doer. Get things done.

Meaningful understandings come from meaningful relationships. If you're skimming the surface with everyone, you aren't seducing change. Change happens on a deeper level. You have to bring change, and bring it hard. And you have to know truth when you hear it. We exist to know the truth. Ultimate truth can elude us, but we ultimately rely on truth. Truth means different things to different people, but it will ring like a bell for those who seek enlightenment.

You can't shape truth to suit the occasion, or claim you alone possess the truth. You can only recognize the truth the instant it enters your realm of thought, because you're in the frame of mind to recognize a truth. Let your mental activity start and end in truth, and never deny it. You may want a truth to be what you want it to be instead of what it is, but "alternate truths" are not viable, nor is the twisting of facts. You are bombarded with lies that represent assaults upon the truth, but they must only strengthen your resolve to seek truth ardently.

Truth comes to you from a higher source. Seek its guidance fervently, in every way you can—in prayer and meditation, existential writings, science, history, anthropology, psychology, religion and mysticism. Ultimate truth is a precious gift, and it's within your grasp. Search for truth, commit to tell it, let it permeate your life and inform your behavior in the world.

Dictionary.com defines the word truth as:

1. the true or actual state of a matter: *He tried to find out the truth.*
2. conformity with fact or reality; verity: *the truth of a statement.*
3. a verified or indisputable fact, proposition, principle, or the like: *mathematical truths.*
4. the state or character of being true.
5. actuality or actual existence.

6. an obvious or accepted fact; truism; platitude.
7. honesty; integrity; truthfulness.

The Merriam-Webster Dictionary defines the word truth as:

a: archaic: fidelity, constancy

b: sincerity in action, character, and utterance

a (1): the state of being the case : fact *(2)* : the body of real things, events, and facts : actuality *(3) often capitalized* : a transcendent fundamental or spiritual reality

b: a judgment, proposition, or idea that is true or accepted as true <*truths of thermodynamics*>

c: the body of true statements and propositions

a: the property (as of a statement) of being in accord with fact or reality

b: chiefly British : true 2

c: fidelity to an original or to a standard

capitalized Christian Science : god

However you define your truth, it can't be something you concoct, but rather universal truth as you glean it.

Likewise, because some pernicious fact may strike you as true, you do not have to speak or promulgate it cursorily. Absolute truth exists, but it isn't casually conferred. Otherwise, truth is illusive. Your truth is your truth. My truth is my truth. And everyone else lays claim to theirs.

Truth is existential. We all have a set of experiences, the myriad biases they cause, and our ways of coping with the world that tinge what we perceive as truth. A personal "truth" is relative. What's true to you might not be true to the next guy or girl, and vice versa. Personal truths, being relative, are scarcely absolute. Personal truths are tied to perspective. Someone can tell a truth as they know it that's miles off-base from another's truth, or what others might see as reality, or even accept as fact. So, if something is grossly unkind or might be destructive, let it fizzle out. No one should wield truth like a sword or use it as a weapon.

The only truth that belongs to you is truth that comes straight from a higher source. Such truth belongs to everyone. It cannot be usurped.

You can easily spot universal truths. They're positive in nature.

On the other hand, if some personal truth that comes to you can lend support—elevate in even the tiniest way—speak it and make it evident. This kind of truth is constructive. You can relay it like a baton. Compliments and encouragement that issue from a truth you come to know are a brand of currency. When you impart truth with intent to uplift, you deposit it into the flow of change and positive transformation. You're just funneling it where it needs to go. You need not wonder how such truth will be received or handled, if maybe you're apt to be misunderstood or thought to overstep your bounds. Truth is a shield, not a weapon, then. You have to have faith it'll be received with the love with which you gave it.

The adage our grandmothers told us is true. If you don't have anything good to say, it's best to zip your lip. Positive change is relayed through positive words, so speak accordingly. Setting aside any hurtful words will make you a safe haven. The wheels of interaction, with such lubrication, turn more swiftly, bringing people close to you. Without fear of reproach or misunderstanding, even your most unique viewpoint is shared in a non-judgmental spirit. Your antenna is bringing in good signals, meaningful and purposeful. You enjoy others as they are, so they tend to open up. In this kind of encouraging atmosphere, mind melds happen easily. You're changing your environment in a kinder, gentler way, forging a bond that can do great things.

When there seems to be synchronicity—as acclaimed psychiatrist Carl Jung termed it, "meaningful coincidence"—it isn't mere coincidence. There is no coincidence. Everything is meant to be. Since everything works together for good, nothing happens randomly. When things coalesce around the same idea, it's the voice of the universe speaking, delivering helpful messages. It is the voice of your Higher Power. Call it instinct or a psychic gift, a sixth sense, a third eye, or intuition. It is the force showing you the path. It might be saying to exit here, or make a right, or go straight ahead at the fork in the road and never look back no matter what. Whether you believe in this constant companion or not, you will benefit when you listen for it and to it, and you value it, and you let it rule your actions.

FIFTEEN

STAR POWER

THE AGE OF CHANGE

We have entered into the Age of Change—metaphysical metamorphosis that's happening on a global scale. We no longer live the static lifestyle—same home and job for all our lives—that former generations lived. Reality is dynamic, even combustible at this point in time. The pace of our lives has accelerated to such a degree that we barely recall what we had for dinner yesterday, or whom we might have had it with.

Behind, is the Information Age. The Technological/Digital/Computer Age is giving way to usher in The Age of Change to advance life on the planet. Increasingly, we move into camps. To one extreme are those driven so overwhelmingly by greed, hate, acquisition, sex or usury that they're losing sight of every other measure by which we govern self—moral compass, sense of purpose, faith, generosity, compassion, who we love and who loves us. On the other hand, more hopeful is the movement toward a greater oneness, spiritual development and world peace that has taken shape, circling the globe. People who strive to uplift our species, work to respect and take care of the land, and leave the world better for their having lived. People whose mission is love and light in a world that works for everyone. Those steeped in higher consciousness, who think, speak and act in concert with their spiritual beliefs.

We're choosing who we want to be and how we truly see the world with every thought, word, action and reaction that we bring to it. New Media is cramming the Zeitgeist with a massive amount of information. This, we ingest and accept or reject in nanoseconds, processing it individually according to our consciousness and state of evolution. Social media consolidates and expands us into a technological outcrop of the Universal Mind from which all thoughts are drawn, and thus, all manner of emotion. For better or for worse, we make deposits into this thought bank day after day as a matter of habit. It is at once a clarifying trough from which we all draw sustenance and a polarizing culture clash, uniting and dividing us, crystalizing issues, setting the course we're on as spiritual beings living in that sexy form we call a human body.

When we like what we see in our politics, environment, economy, educational systems, financial institutions, mechanics of government, international peace and human rights, we continue upon the path we're on, until we reach a tipping point which may be born of a single event or cultivated over time. If we find these areas falling short of what we believe their potential to be—which seems to be the present case—we collectively make a better choice. Or not. Sometimes, we just choose change, though it may be change for the worse. We may do this individually, or as some form of community, city, state or nation, or the entire human race. We may band together or tear apart, dividing ourselves up racially, along socio-economic lines, or according to religion or the country of our origins. This doesn't make any sense at all, and when we do it anyway, if we're fortunate, some faction of society saves us from ourselves.

Here's where the Age of Change comes in, and the magic of Change Wizards.

When we choose to change ourselves as individuals, we take control. The extent to which we exercise this varies, but we have autonomy over every single choice we make. We cannot control situations and circumstances, but we do control the manner in which we respond to them. For instance, we can self-destruct, or we can embark on a corrective course requiring agility. We can adjust our entire paradigm, accepting change and incorporating changes at a rapid pace.

There are those who instead refuse to adjust, resisting change at every turn, and those who adjust begrudgingly, doing so in timeframes that can unnecessarily put change off or delay change for a period.

Some actually try to reverse a change that's so obviously irreversible that conflict arises with those who are craving a huge change for the better. This juxtaposition can be charged, and likely result in a violent struggle. No one enjoys any battle for change, but when tipping points come, they can make themselves known to even the most reluctant, making it clear that change is inevitable, no matter who stands to fight for it, or who's willing to die to roll it back or deny its positive results. There are even those intransigents who are willing to decimate everything and everyone to make a point. And they might not even know what the point is or have an agenda to make it advance.

Change is scary to some, goes completely unrecognized by others, is often opposed vociferously, and yet perpetually occurs.

Change is, was, and will always be, what helps us grow, transform, expand, and evolve into our highest selves, individually and collectively.

Change is the only thing that doesn't. Change, that is. Change rules the world. Things are always becoming different than they were, and unpredictably—whether anyone likes it or not. No creature or condition stays the same or ever could. Change is singularly immutable. Specific changes change, but the phenomenon of constant change is stronger than even time and space. Change is more real than either space or time, and older than both of them. If not, neither space nor time could change.

We want to be on the side of change, encouraging change and demanding it, because change is *supposed* to happen. It is the basis of all creation. Babies grow up and turn into adults. Caterpillars turn into butterflies. The universe itself is always changing, expanding at such a rapid clip that its vastness is unfathomable.

No one is able to hold back the dawn. The sun is going to rise and set, no matter who wants to remain in the dark of night. No matter what die hard perseveres, combats, or rebels, the heavens resolve to do their thing, and the tides will rise and ebb with the altering phases of the moon. Change is a reality, and as reality shifts with our perceptions, changes will occur. A change can occur in the blink of an eye or take eons to reveal itself. Change can be brutal, sharp or gradual. Change can be so subtle that we sometimes don't realize a change is occurring until it has taken place. A change can ensue with, without, or in spite of our input as individuals, but the changes we want on a grand scale that can form our world into our vision of good depend on cooperation. Together, we'll strive for an ideal world, or apart, court its destruction.

Though change can appear chaotic in its initial stages, change is good. This fact, we must ultimately accept. Change happens for a reason. We may not understand what the reason is, but we have to believe that all change will be for the better, if we make it so or simply let it be.

We're in massive change mode now, from all accounts and by almost every measure.

An Age of Change, such as we're currently in, might first show up with the ugly face of derision, fear and separateness, appearing to be a mushroom cloud. But change is what we make of it, just like everything else we encounter in life. If we process a change as the natural order of things, we surf it like a wave and are carried along with the ebb and flow. We are one with the rhythm of the universe, so change for the better is hastened by the speed of our positive input.

The Age of Change mandates that we pull together to integrate innovation, adopt new thoughts and new thought patterns, set equanimity as a goal, accept justice and equality as the norms of our social paradigm, and make the most of diversity to acculturate future generations to the aims of peace, light, love, respect and the joys of blended culture.

What anyone learns should be everyone's gift. The existence of Universal Laws allows us to access the innate power in each of us to lift us all. Our latent capabilities are accessed through these technologies, which have developed and contributed to the best use of human cumulative knowledge ever since the world began. We can harmonize with these laws in a comprehensive manner in the now by focusing all our minds in the one we share—universal consciousness. This is why more of us practice mind-expanding means to higher self. We sense we are in The Age of Change, and we realize that change must be for the better, else there is no point to change.

There is much more we can do.

For one, we can gather the stray bits of information wandering the Twitterverse, the Facebook-sphere and other social networks, and cross-pollinate them with a spiritual, scientific and sensate knowledge base to make the highest plane of thought available to everyone.

Information is useless absent wisdom. We should be able to use information for our most important goals, in cooperative, apolitical spaces. We can convert the sad energy drain of trolling—which uses the Internet to instigate negative interactions—into a hub of enlightenment where we interact as one. But we have to come out of the petty and inconsequential, start addressing issues. We have to stop obsessing with celebrities sleeping around, what watch they're wearing when they do, and whose purse cost more than the budget of many underdeveloped nations. It's a pity to tear others down when it's clear that the best way to rise is to lift others up. This should be our purpose statement rather than the current mantra "grab everybody's everything".

Human knowledge is meant to be cumulative. That's what separates us from ants. And yet, look at the way ants work together. Look at what they can accomplish. They're all for one, and one for all. If ants have ever invaded your kitchen, you know what I mean. Those suckers band together and jump it off, whatever their program is. Your sugar, crackers, paper bags. There's no gridlock in their game keeping them out of your Shredded Wheat. If ants and bees can do it, we can make our society work. We humans have change on speed-dial.

We follow trends in fashion, art, technology, entertainment, education, politics, sports and science. We're seemingly susceptible to any suggestion media makes. Well, what if we tap the collective vibrations that permeate the atmosphere in which we already share ideas, and focus them on a global purpose we can all agree on. And what if that purpose unites, instead of divides, us. What might come of that?

Mankind has advanced through many stages.

What if we consciously set our minds to evolving the present ethos?

What if, for example, we lay down our arms one day and join hands internationally? In chains that stretch from sea to sea. For a minute. Five minutes. An hour. A week. What if we try that once. What if even some of us—perhaps those most willing and eager for peace—decide to hug a stranger at noon on a date called Love Day sometime soon? What bridges might we build?

We fuse together in tragedy. When mass shootings happen, or leaders are lost, or natural disasters occur like earthquakes, fires, floods and hurricanes, we cast our differences aside, and act with one accord. We work to survive, rebuild, and triumph. Often, we wish these feelings and interactions lasted, yet they don't. We revert to distrust and alienation. The spirit of cooperation present in our times of need may fade as soon as the trauma passes, leaving us in a state of angst. This need not be our default position. This is a critical time of need, because it's an age of major change which must be for the better. Most of us are ready for it. Many of us are tired of war and the ravages of avarice. Of bankers taking everything from everyone, and all the time. Of battles raging everywhere. Of well-meaning people with hand-drawn signs living under the freeway instead of a roof. Of hungry children. Pestilence. Of girls all over the world being victimized by unspeakable violence. Of boys being shot in the street for merely existing in their skin. Of education being denied completely for some, diminished for others, and costing a mint for still other students doomed to spend a lifetime paying loans with salaries they can't earn.

The Age of Change is here to right the needless wrongs entangling us.

We are free spirits. We are alive. We are endlessly empowered.

YOU are empowered for sweeping change—change you and I can't envisage yet, change we have to brainstorm.

The Age of Change is designed to bring us together into a state of oneness unlike what we've seen before, unlike what we've been before. In the Age of Change, we think, speak, act, and create from enlightened consciousness. The gifts that make us unique inform our concept of who we're meant to be, and what it is we're meant to do.

We elevate solitary mind by focusing on the single mind that is the Universal Mind that elevates us all. Work crews do it. Sports teams do it. Huddle together. Sacrifice. They work toward the cause of excellence as a single body, a single mind. We can wake up as citizens of the world, unite for a greater good. We can create the ideal world, the world we can now only dream of. It exists. It's just waiting for us to evolve.

We have all we need. There's sufficiency. We don't have to fight over land, fuel, food or other abundant resources. There is plenty for all to live in peace, to prosper, happy, healthy, free, enjoying their best life. And there's something connecting all of us—the sanctity of love.

Love. The simplest path is LOVE. We can love everyone, love ourselves, and love the world we're living in. We only have to do it, friend. We have to decide to make it work. To let love win, and let peace will out. It's as easy as that, and as lightning fast. We don't have to one-up, or overwork, or bicker about what's best for us in every venue that we share. We don't have to have our political parties arguing into a stalemate. We as humans can use our minds to act as a conscious, creative collective, rather than wasting our energies in a divisive manner that brings us heartache, pain, the bad misuse of imagination, an array of detritus that clouds our judgment, and the illusion we must take sides.

It's time we stopped abusing the immutable Universal Laws—and misusing the gifts they provide to us—to descend to untenable world disorder.

We are meant to create unlimited avenues for the flow of unceasing good in a world of possibilities. We can do this through metaphysical laws that govern creativity, and by using them in our daily lives, upgrade and update our ability to act as one to change the world.

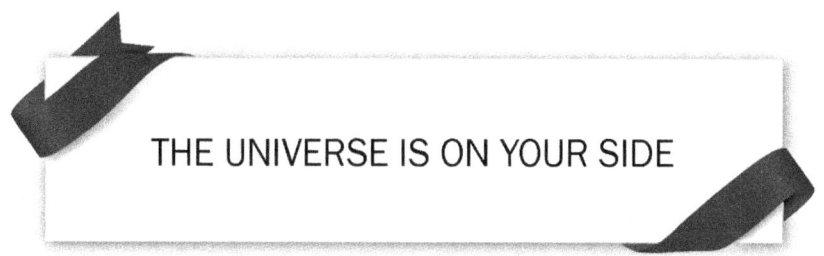

THE UNIVERSE IS ON YOUR SIDE

Begin with the premise—the absolute truth—that the universe is on your side. It supports you in everything you do. It makes your heart beat, gives you breath. You don't have to beg or entreat it to give you everything you want and need. It has promised to give you all you need. It has brought you into being. If you look for a moment at your life—where you are, what you're doing, the fact you're alive, the many gifts you're grateful for—your needs are taken care of. Your wants may not be things you need, or even be what you'll really want when all is said and done. But you can trust the universe to know what's conclusively best for you, and have faith that it's working for that now. You just have to stay out of its way.

I learned this lesson in first grade, and oh yeah, I learned it the hard way.

I came to want a certain doll. I wasn't even into dolls, but I wanted this doll more than anything. I wanted this doll because she could talk, and I loooved to talk, as I told my Mom. She asked if I ever got tired of talking, because I was babbling all the time, and that was my reply.

My favorite mode of talking was to ask a ton of questions. My Mom saw this as a sign of intelligence (she was my mother, after all). But other adults still wondered how she could stand it, having that chatterbox, that little girl who made up stories, and didn't seem to be interested in telling fact from fiction. But Mom just kept answering questions, vindicated by my IQ.

All those stories in my books had kind of blurred the line for me between fantasy and reality. My Mom had to ask me regularly, "Bev, is that real or make-believe?" And the first grade me would try to say, to the best of my abilities. I was young, and when you're a little creator, reality is nebulous. Even adult creative writers, actors and people that make stuff up for a living can cross those lines. Society is better for it. This is how we change the world.

So I loved to talk, and I still do. No coin-inky-dink I'm a voice over pro and have talked for a living for years.

But anyhoo, I was feeling this doll, this talking doll that was advertised. And I wasn't the only first grader who wanted the doll, I'll tell you that. The toy company had seen to it. Most first grade girls would've climbed Mount Everest if that doll was at the top. And climbed up there in party shoes, through all those mounds of snow. I wanted that doll with all my might. I thought we'd have long conversations like my older sisters had. My big sisters slept in a room together, able to chit chat all night long. My family moved to the house I grew up in shortly after I was born, so my room started out as a nursery. Now, I slept in it alone. Which was great. I'm certainly not beefing it. But naps and nights went by without a single conversation—except maybe when my paternal grandmother visited. She was a practical Island girl, and chewing the fat with a first grader wasn't her passion, granddaughter though I might be. I only conversed with imaginary friends, and the characters in my books—the ones I checked out of the library, and the books I made up for myself. Characters were so much fun. They still are, and the ones you create yourself are the closest friends you get sometimes. So this talking doll thing was a serious get for the first grade me, a had-to-have.

I figured my best bet was Santa Claus. I was a good girl, after all. I loved both of my parents dearly, and I wanted to always see them smile. I got fabulous grades—and okay, I was precocious, fearless, more than a little inquisitive and, yes, I had a mouth on me—but I basically tried to keep my behavior within the realm of reason. Santa would surely bring my doll. He'd set it beneath the tree for me on Christmas Day. He knew the deal. Knew I need companionship, that my friends' imaginations didn't roam to the places mine explored. Yep, Santa was a lock. Milk and cookies for Santa, my new best friend, and that talking doll was a shoo-in.

I'd bide my time. I'd wait it out.

I did. I held my water up until December 25th. Christmas Day came, and I knew she was there. I just knew she was wrapped up under the tree. If I didn't get anything else for Christmas—this one, or several ones to come, maybe until I was forty-six.

Please, Santa, bring me that doll, okay?

I didn't just want her, I needed her. Nobody seemed to understand me, but that doll would understand. She was a captive audience. I'd make her doll clothes, style her hair, read to her, and everything. All I had to do was wait until we opened gifts.

Well, I guess you know what happened. I had a rude awakening that fine day. But I was cool. I didn't cry. Not in front of my parents, anyway. Up in my room. For out of my Christmas box had come not the yearned-for doll, but a parting gift—a practical clock radio. And boy, was I disappointed. I could not believe my eyes. The radio talked, but it didn't matter. My best laid plans had gone awry. I was wrecked. I was thoroughly desolate.

I deduced they didn't love me, that my parents didn't understand or even want me anymore. I paced. I packed my yellow suitcase. Tutu. Bible. Ballet shoes. All the real necessities, the essentials of my misspent youth. I was crushed. I was gonna blow this pop stand. Nothing could talk me out of it. They wouldn't miss me, anyway. Oh, sure, they might miss their water once their well ran dry, but maybe not. Maybe they'd get some other kid. They already had two more. My sisters would be glad I left. Well, they might miss my piggy bank, but that'd be the extent of it. But where was I to go? I lived in New York City. It wouldn't be safe downtown. I could always join the circus. Everyone kind of stood out there. I wouldn't have to fit in.

I mulled over this conundrum while the turkey cooked, and the sweet potatoes and mac and cheese. I was really gonna miss that mac and cheese, but a girl had to take a stand sometime. As I debated destinations, I tried to think where I went wrong. I had to do something wrong to bring this catastrophe upon myself. If only I hadn't spilled pancake batter on the new rug in the living room. Or stapled my hand in class when I set up our dinosaur exhibit. Surely, one of these blunders was at the root of my failing to score my doll.

Remaining alone in my solitary orange chamber didn't help. My imagination ran away with me. I got lost in a darkened forest full of angry, furry creatures. I wondered if this was the start of—nay, the harbinger—of doom. Then, to make things worse, I found out one of my besties scored the doll, and that rubbed salt into my wound. The talking doll had come to her. And though I was happy as clams for her, it made me ponder all the more the cause of my doll debacle. Was I a good girl, after all? I mean, one never knew. And bad things could happen to good little girls. Look at poor Little Red Riding Hood.

I turned it over in my mind. It couldn't be. My life was charmed. Didn't the baker always give me free cookies at the bakery? I could pick them out all on my own. Everyone else was afraid of the baker. They thought he was mean. And it wasn't just kids with whom he had that fearful reputation. But he gave me cookies every time. And he called me Fearless, too. I guessed that's because I was. But this talking doll thing was gnawing at me all throughout the holiday. No talking doll. What could it mean? Would Santa do this every year? I wondered where I stood.

When Christmas vacation was over, and school resumed, I saw my friend with the talking doll. At least, I *thought* she had the doll. She told me the doll didn't talk anymore, that the doll broke down on Christmas Day. What a ripoff, she wailed, a shattered dream.

Well, I was feeling lucky now. My cute clock radio woke me up to music every morning, and sang me to sleep in the dark at night. I could hear anything I wanted. It was magic. Songs and stories. I took that baby to Stanford with me. It lasted all that time.

But way more than the value of that little piece of what was once primo technology was the lesson I learned from experience—that it's not always best to get what you want. It's better to get what's best for you. The universe provides what's best. And parents and Santa Claus, too.

What you need are priceless things, and you will be provided them.

The universe is on your side.

All I can say is to trust in that . . . and I wish you your clock radio.

ONE SCHLEP AT A TIME

Things tend to move faster and faster the more you attempt to achieve and contribute to the larger conversation. The energy building in your persona requires you to multitask. People seem to ask more of you, placing demands on your resources. Achievers tackle many things. The more you do, the more you can. Contemporary culture has an insatiable need for speed.

In short, if want to change the world, you have to keep it moving.

Keeping it moving takes some skill. One skill is staying in the present. Live in the now. Embrace the moment. Carpe diem. Seize the day. It might sound like an old refrain, but it is because it's true.

That's what makes a full, rich life. Being completely where you are, with whom, and receiving the present moment amps up life immeasurably. In live-in-the-now mode, we absorb experiences in Technicolor, Panavision and surround sound, fully immersed in our blessings. We are in total engagement mode. Our senses are bombarded. In the now, we feel our humanity and our mortality most keenly, for now is all we have and all we need, and now is beautiful. Whatever is in the now with us is truly all there is. Even pain can be born more easily when we aren't linking its challenges to prior pain, or fearful the pain might last forever into a future we can't see. In the now, we can live in our bliss, and own, and enjoy it totally.

As I'm writing, I'm now at the three-minute warning before heading out to perform a voice over. But, because I'm not there yet, I'm here inside this book with you. I am focused in total immersion mode on writing and sharing my truth. I've done this my whole career, switched from one discipline to the next. When I'm writing, I cannot be thinking about the audition I have for a TV show, or the voice over job I'm going to. When it's time for me to shift, I will. And I won't think of writing, driving, taking care of my family, or my home. I'll just be where I am.

When I shower, I'll bathe in the warmth of the water relaxing my muscles, washing my body, opening my pores. When I get in the car, I will concentrate on driving safely, watching traffic, loving my view of the mountains, drinking in sunshine, watching the beauty of the sky, and trees, and morning light. Maybe I'll listen to music, and let it soothe my soul and ease my mind. Maybe I'll turn on an audiobook, engage with the characters, peek in their world. I won't be at home, or at my show, or in the new world I am building for myself and others up the road. And I won't be reliving the death of the man I was married to for many years, or the jobs I worked, or didn't get. And I won't be walking at the beach, or thinking how nice it will be when I can. I will be there when I get there. I'll be in that moment like I'm in this one, letting it take me where it will. Now is the only place I can be. Here is the real, authentic place. And it will come and go like mist when the next *now* moment comes along.

Even the sentence you just read is in your past. You aren't there. You're in another now.

I'm living in the now not solely to live to the max, though I do cherish that. I'm doing it to be practical. I want to do the best I can, and if half of me is somewhere else, that isn't realistic. The idea I can be in all places and still operate with max effectiveness isn't practical at all. That being said, living in the now doesn't mean I don't have a choice of *how* I live my now. I do.

You have the power to focus your *now* on whatever you choose to focus on, and to choose the thoughts and emotions you experience in your now. When you're waiting on line at the grocery store, you can focus your thoughts and emotions on how the line is moving at a crawl, or you can consider how grateful you are to have groceries piled up in your cart, and the money you need to buy them. The latter choice will bring you joy. The other will not only raise discomfort, but it might thwart what could come next. If you focus in your now, you could chat with the person in line in front of you, and maybe make a brand-new friend. You could ogle the goodies at the checkstand. You could stretch your arms and legs, repeating helpful affirmations. You could peruse a magazine, check your lipstick, smooth your tie, or just look out the window.

You can draw from your now whatever you wish. Go for the choice that brings you joy, and you will replenish your joyfulness. You can make your life easy by taking it easy and making life easy for other folks. Press the Easy Button. Stay in the now, and focus on the best of it. Your life is good. Make choices one at a time. Sure, you can multitask sometime. I multitask like it's going out of style, as if it's some kind of Olympic event. Multitasking works best when you're fully absorbed by each task, and you do them each one at a time. It takes being present. Regardless of what else is in the hopper, you do one thing, then move on to the next.

Inspirational speaker Tony Robbins (*Unlimited Power*) put forth a theory that really works. I remember hearing him speak about it in person at an event. I'm going to paraphrase it here to the best of my memory rather than quoting, because what I managed to draw from his words, for me, was a revelation. It helped me understand why I'm a happy person, how I am, and why other people might not be. He basically said that—I'm paraphrasing—our memories define the quality of our emotions and direct our lives. According to him, we happy people tend to remember the good things large, up close, and in bright color. Conversely, we recall bad things far away, small, and in black in white. Whereas, unhappy people tend to remember bad things large, up close, and in color, and good things small, far away, and relegated to gray scale. So, his theory, his technology, was that we can manipulate our happiness and unhappiness by swapping these around. That, if folks who consider themselves unhappy recall good things up close, large and in color, and bad things distant, small, and gray, they can teach themselves to be happier.

Now, since I am a happy person type, I applied his theory with a twist. I tried it first at the dentist's office. Worked like a charm. I was really impressed. My memory of a root canal is dull, small, really far away, and almost totally painless. So, I used it in other trying times, to reshape painful memories and rework the way I processed them.

I encourage you to try it, too—the very next time an unpleasant memory burps up in your conscious mind. Make it smaller. Push it away from the camera recording the movie in your mind. Drain the color out of it, and make it pale and black-and-white. Fade it like an old-time movie. Crank the sound down. Soften the focus. Pause it. You can delete it, too. You don't want to repress your memories, but you have dominion over them. Keep those bad boys in the past, for now is where you can make change.

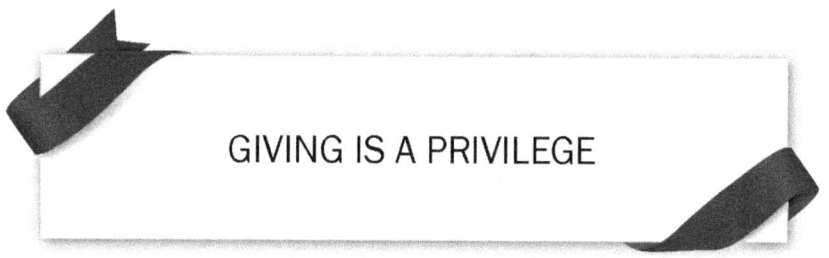

GIVING IS A PRIVILEGE

Our highest life emerges from giving, so it bears repeating at this point that giving is a gift. Givers make the world go around. When you give, you make a change—in yourself and in the receiver. Giving and receiving complete a cycle of abundance. The currency of change is the cycle of giving and receiving. You might not receive from a source you give to, but that isn't your concern. The universe provides for you from infinite supply. This allows you to give for the sake of others without expectation of return, to give for the sake of giving, nothing more and nothing less. When you fill your cup with gratitude, you give from a state of abundance. Your good is so great that it naturally overflows into the world. This is how changes keep rolling along.

You needn't ever be miserly. The universe doesn't run out of good. It can't, it *is* good, and ceaselessly. You can't out-give your Higher Power. You are its beneficiary, and its conduit as well. Regardless of how much you give to the world, it never makes you smaller. The reverse is true. The more you give, the more you signal the universal consciousness that you're a source of giving. The money you give is monetary energy you circulate. The information you pass on is energy building innovation, new technology, education, businesses systems and the like. The kindness you give is energy contributing to well-being. Clothes you give keep others warm. The time you give is a measurement of energy in a continuum. The love you give is the substance of the universal heart. When you give, you unleash your higher self. You tell the universe you're ready, willing and able to bring about change, and you are dispatched to help others evolve.

You have to give love to yourself as well. You give from what spills over. When you develop the habit of giving, you release the fear that giving diminishes or weakens you. You don't have to think about giving, you are circulating forms of matter, like breathing air in and out. You have to give something to make a change. You give what you can, and when you have more, you increase the amount of your giving. Employ your resources. Share your blessings.

When you give of yourself, you can change the world.

LOVE YOU, BABY

When we're doing something new because we want to obtain a different result than we might have obtained in the past, our new actions take us in new directions. We may not feel we have all it takes, but if and when we persevere, change is the likely result. Pump the brakes to slow your pace, or accelerate like an Indy car, when you love yourself and love your life, you persevere through any doubts or setbacks, rejections, refusals, missteps, misunderstandings and time constraints. The fog of war can accompany change, but not if you're clear-headed.

If you feel like quitting, love yourself and get right back in the game. If you feel like you're all alone in your quest, love yourself more and keep moving forward. LOVE YOU when no one else loves you. LOVE YOU, and keep on loving you. If you're tired or feeling put upon, take a load off your feet or take a nap. Your resolve will refill and renew itself. If you feel like you're hitting a wall, take a powder. Do something fun to refresh your mind. Your drive and energy will return, if only because you believe it will, and you paused to give it a chance. Love yourself in whatever form that takes. LOVE YOU in the way of the cosmos, not to the exclusion of anyone else. See to your needs, whatever they are.

You don't have to explain or excuse yourself, and you don't have to leave anybody flat. Arrange to get some breathing room. You can put yourself first whenever you want. Everyone benefits when you are whole and feeling at your best. Do what you must to uphold yourself. What anyone thinks is on them, not you. You're doing all you can to change.

If you're finding it hard to love yourself, it's crucial to learn the reason why. It may be buried in your past. Whatever it is, you need to know, because loving yourself is not only critical to your own health and development, but to everyone whose life you're touching now or will begin to touch. Your gift has been given to give away, and a lack of self-love is a block to that. Get it out of your way. You're invaluable. Your light is helping to light the world. Without you, the light goes out somewhere. But with you, dim corners can come alive. With you, and all that comes with you comes love, hope, creativity and an energy no one else can bring.

Love you, and others will love you, too. If you're waiting till someone else gives you permission to love yourself, then take your hand, and be that person loving you and being present for you. Like change, loving you is an inside job. Love and forgive you with no strings attached. See what happens. Watch love work. See how your self-love changes you, and changes the world you live in. The whole world is waiting to feel your love in the myriad ways it manifests with its awe-dropping possibilities, but it can't until you love yourself. Love yourself, and infect all the people around you with self-love of their own. Be missed when you're missing, because you're loved. And never be missing, because your love is special and ever-present. Take on the mantle of love and change, and give that gift to everyone, especially yourself.

You're loving. You deserve love, too.

Schedule ways to love yourself, like you schedule everything else. Put the time aside to do the things you have to do to help yourself. The feelings you're sending out into the world are the energies that will return to you, and the energies that are building the reality you want to see. If you feel that the world doesn't work for you, it won't, and you won't make the changes needed to change it so it will. As the universe hears your thoughts and feelings, and it sends their match to you, the way you love yourself relays a message you can't contravene. The universe won't sort messages for you, it will hear your thoughts and feelings as your wishes, and fulfill them.

Love yourself, and love the world, and the world will undoubtedly love you back.

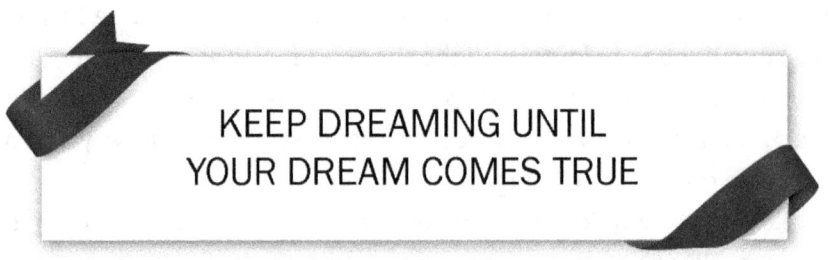

KEEP DREAMING UNTIL YOUR DREAM COMES TRUE

Tides follow moon phases, Earth orbits the sun, and the sun never, ever will set on your dream. Your dream is alive and energetic. It cannot fade or dissipate. It may recede from a mind that tires, but it is matter. It can't be destroyed. Your dreams and ideas are substantive. They are matter, and they matter. You may not be able to touch your dream, but it's real, and dreams come true. You can see your dream before it arrives, and the more you vest yourself in it, the more you can feel it coming true. This is what makes it manifest—your thoughts, beliefs and feelings. Dreams are formed in the mind of the eternal being. Yours is entrusted directly to you, so you can follow through on it. You have been chosen to dream your dream out of all of the souls in the universe, because you are uniquely qualified to make it manifest. This is why you must keep dreaming. Dream more dreams, and work to make them into experiences others feel.

You're not dreaming your dream by happenstance. You're not dreaming a thing that can't come true. Your dream is more than possible or probable. Your dream is truth. Your dream is a reality somewhere, counting on you to materialize. It's as attached to you as your hair or the tips of your fingernails. It's meant to be, and so are you. You're meant to be together. Your instincts are your dream's voice calling out to you, communicating, telling you who you're meant to be, so you can do what you're meant to do. That is why you dream your dream, and not somebody else. Your dream is yours to make come true. You just have to get out of the way of it, embrace it, and do what it asks of you without any lingering fear or doubt. Hold the hand of your dream like you would a mate, and love it into being. Your dream is not yours to give up on, walk away from, or be talked out of. Your dream is planted in your soul. It's your responsibility.

Your dream is how you'll change the world.

Many treat dreams like a luxury they have to relinquish when times get tough, give over to "reality", let go of in order to merely survive, or fit in, or at least avoid standing out. But you are made for standing out, and for standing up for a noble cause. The dream that lives inside of you is much more than a fantasy—it's your raison d'etre. It isn't a pipe dream unless it gets stuck in the pipeline between the source and the dreamer who failed to keep dreaming the dream until it was able to come true. That dreamer is your Meant-To-Be. Your dream is what you're meant to do. Your dream is depending on your belief, your thoughts, your words, your actions. You are its matching energy, willing to do whatever it takes to change yourself and change the world. So, dream your dream until it's touched, felt, heard, smelled, seen, and tasted.

All there is was once a dream.

Every single thing in the universe was an idea that grew in a being's head and heart with such an unflagging commitment that it reached existence. Your dream beams from your radiant light. Increase your wattage. Let it shine.

I can feel your dream right now. I know you want to change the world, and I'm invested in your dream. I'm writing to you to let you know I have confidence in your positive thoughts and ability to create a world that shines, and gleams, and sparkles.

I'm sending you love and gratitude for all you are and will become. I'm asking you to take my hand on our magical journey to change the world into that which we are thirsting for—the world that all of us dream about, a world inspired and built on LOVE. A world that embraces each of us, and lives and breathes the highest good.

Be your Meant-To-Be. Do your Meant-To-Do. Lift up your consciousness till it soars.

Fly, dear friend. And rest assured, I'll see you in the friendly skies.

BEVER-LEIGH BANFIELD is an award-winning writer, with an M.F.A. from the Yale University School of Drama and a B.A. from Stanford University. She has published numerous articles and celebrity interviews, and been gifted with psychic perception since childhood. As an actress, she has performed on television, in movies, and in Broadway theatre. Her professional voice overs are heard in TV and radio commercials, cartoons, animated films, planetarium star shows and the *You Can Change The World* audiobook.